Reader Reviews

'Laugh-out-loud funny, and at times heartbreakingly sad'

'This book had me howling, creasing, tearful and feeling nostalgic ... I didn't want it to end'

'Finally, a book that might make young Asians feel seen'

'Honest, humble and HILARIOUS'

'A must-read book'

'If there's one book I would suggest any British Asian Muslim to get it would be this. If there's any book I would suggest to others to understand a tiny part of the British Asian Muslim, this book would be it'

'It's the book you didn't realise you were missing'

'A fantastic read'

'I devoured it in a weekend'

'More than ever now it is important to see these stories represented. These stories need telling. 10/10 recommend'

The Secret Diary of a British Muslim Aged 13¾

TEZ ILYAS

SPHERE

SPHERE

First published in Great Britain in 2021 by Sphere
This paperback edition published by Sphere in 2022

3 5 7 9 10 8 6 4

A CIP catalogue record for this book
is available from the British Library.

ISBN 978-0-7515-8219-2

Typeset in Goudy by M Rules
Printed and bound in Great Britain by
Clays Ltd, Elcograf S.p.A.

Papers used by Sphere are from well-managed forests
and other responsible sources.

MIX
Paper from
responsible sources
FSC® C104740

Sphere
An imprint of
Little, Brown Book Group
Carmelite House
50 Victoria Embankment
London EC4Y 0DZ

An Hachette UK Company
www.hachette.co.uk

www.littlebrown.co.uk

For Tayyeba and Raees Ali
and Ibraheem and Aamina
and Qasim and Anisa
and Umaima.

I love you.

Contents

Foreword

In the name of Allah, the Most Gracious, the Most Merciful.

Thank you so much for choosing to read my book! It's very surreal that lil' old me even undertook the mammoth task of writing a book, let alone people being interested in reading it.

I'd love you to enjoy it, laugh at the funny bits, cry at the sad bits, nod attentively at the interesting bits. And really, I'd love you to develop a deeper understanding of what it was like for a young British Pakistani Muslim kid growing up in 90s northern England. I was the generation that was abandoned by Thatcher, that Enoch Powell wanted erased, that Tony Blair tried to embrace. It was truly a fascinating time. Also, who doesn't love a bit of cheeky 90s nostalgia? Bonbons, anyone?

Lots of people have asked me why I decided to write this book. I guess there isn't one clear answer. First and foremost, there were some things I needed to get off my chest.

I also wish there'd been a book like this for me growing up, about the generation of Asians who grew up in the 60s and 70s, and so I've written one for people who want to look back at what it was like in the 90s. And I wanted people to know about the struggles. That things aren't handed to people who come from where I come from and that while setbacks and drama are a part of life, they needn't define us.

And ... actually ... my life was kinda interesting and it seems like the best way to take you into that world is through a book.

I've always viewed my childhood through rose-tinted specs, so to properly rake through my memories and realise how much I went through was really eye-opening, and it's only with hindsight that I can truly appreciate how goddam annoying I must've been to my teachers.

It's been a real hoot and I had such a laugh reminiscing with my family and friends about the stupid things we got up to and got away with. I really hope it makes you laugh.

Some things to note:

The title aside, this is one person's experience – mine. Yes, there are some universal experiences, but this is my story, not the story of the entire British Muslim/Asian/Pakistani experience. While there will of course be some parallels, a black Muslim kid growing up in Birmingham or London will have had very different experiences to me, as will a middle-class Gujarati kid growing up in Canterbury. So please don't make any sweeping generalisations, positive or negative, based on my words. Ta.

Now, you might be thinking, wow Tez, I didn't realise you kept a diary when you were a kid! I didn't. The account here is based on memories and extensive conversations with my nearest and dearest. I also kept my Record of Achievement, my report cards and my certificates, which built a nice picture.

I did have a college diary, which was useful for some dates, but useless for actual real experiences, though I could tell you in which round Amelie Mauresmo was knocked out of Wimbledon in 2001,* because that's the sort of thing eighteen-year-old me thought

---

* Third round.

was useful to record 😶. Which is all to say, this is a genuine account of what went down. I've tried to be as honest as possible. Uncomfortably so. By accident, I have probably given teen me a little more foresight in some places than I might actually have had at the time – but then, as you'll notice, I was very intelligent and talented so there's a good chance I really would have predicted that our country would peak in 2012 as we hosted the world for the Olympics and then take a nosedive as we submitted ourselves to populism, making a series of bad decisions which will lead to the collapse of our economy and society in 2025. Lol.

Having stepped back into the mind of thirteen-year-old me, it felt only natural to write the diary from the perspective of my teenage self in the style in which I spoke at the time. So it's written in a colloquial way, which I personally prefer in books to long tricky words (you're welcome). I promise you'll understand it all … but just in case you think it's an error, yes, 'but' is supposed to fall at the end of sentences: we used it interchangeably with 'though'. And anything else you think is a typo is also purposeful.

In addition, I have a pretty large family and had a fair few friends (humblebrag), so I've included a character list at the front in case you forget who anyone is.

Oh, also … awkward … I know how my people are with rude bits. This is a teenager's diary. Sorry. There are three entries that could be considered a bit blue. They're clearly marked in the entry heading, so if you'd like to avoid that sort of thing, feel free to skip those.

Finally, for the non-Muslim and/or non-Punjabi speakers reading this, you'll likely come across words you don't recognise. Don't panic: there's a glossary. The first time you see a new word, it'll be asterisked to remind you of the glossary's existence. After that you should know the word, so you're on your own. There isn't a test at the end of the book, but remember, Allah is always watching.

Speaking of Whom . . . may Allah please forgive me for any errors in this book and for anything that I have written that upsets anybody or displeases Him.

Ameen.

Cast

Family

Ammi/Mum	
Rosey	older sister
Saeeda	younger half-sister
Zaheer	younger half-brother
Tanveer (Tany)	younger half-brother
Tauqeer	younger half-brother
Uneeb	brother-in-law,
Abu	stepdad
Dad	
Aunty	stepmum
Saira	younger half-sister
Yasmeen	younger half-sister
Suliman	younger half-brother

Wider Family, Friends, Acquaintances, Enemies

Abdulla	neighbourhood friend
Abid	Uneeb's cousin
Amina	school friend
Asghar	neighbourhood friend
Asma	cousin
Asma	school friend
Baaji	paternal grandad
Baeji Aisha	great-grandma
Big Poupoh	Dad's eldest sister
Big Riz	neighbourhood friend
Bilal	neighbourhood friend
Chacha Farooq	Uncle's younger brother
Christian	school friend
Chucky	school friend
Chyna	neighbourhood friend
Daley	neighbourhood friend
Deela	school friend
Deemy	neighbourhood friend
Ebrahim	school friend
Faisal	neighbourhood friend
Faiza	school friend
Farida	college friend
Farooq	neighbourhood friend
Fiona	school friend
Geery	school friend
Golly	school friend
Hadi	neighbourhood friend
Hafeezah	college friend
Haider	school friend
Halima	school friend
Harry	college frenemy

Harun	Mum's cousin
Hassim	school best friend
Hussain	college friend
Jack	school friend
Jaffer	cousin
Kafait	cousin
Karolia	school friend
Kelloggs	school friend
Kes	neighbourhood friend
Khala Fozia	Mum's sister
Khala Shaheen	Mum's sister
Khala Shakeela	Mum's sister
Laura	school friend
Maasi Rabia	Uneeb's mum
Mammu Abbas	maternal uncle
Mammu Habib	maternal uncle
Mammu Jamil	maternal uncle
Mammu Saeed	maternal uncle
Mammu Shama	maternal uncle
Mammu Toheed	Mum's cousin
Manny	neighbourhood friend
Mrs Fisher	RE teacher
Mrs Kirkpatrick	English teacher
Mrs Place	English teacher
Ms Williams	school tutor
Muj	cousin
Mushy	school friend
Naana Abu	maternal grandad
Naani Ammi	maternal grandma
Nads	cousin
Naeem	cousin
Nasir	neighbourhood friend
Nazir	neighbourhood friend

Neelam	college friend
Neelam	cousin
Neil	school friend
Nisar	neighbourhood friend
Noddi	school friend
Noreen	cousin
Pai Naseer	cousin
Pai Shehzad	family friend
Pats	neighbourhood friend
Peggy	neighbourhood friend
Poupoh Waliyat	Shehzad's mum
Poupoh	Dad's sister, Shibz's mum
Pua Said	Naana Abu's sister
Quiet Yasin	school friend
Rebecca	school friend
Rizzy	neighbourhood friend
Saddia	cousin
Safa	cousin
Saki	neighbourhood friend
Saleem	cousin
Sandra	college tutor
Seema	Uneeb's sister
Shabaz	Mum's cousin
Shaheen	cousin
Shahid	Mum's cousin
Shanaz	cousin
Shazad	neighbourhood friend
Shibz	cousin
Shiry	cousin
Shoaib	Faiza's brother
Siema	Mum's cousin
Sohail	Mum's cousin
Steve	New Bank Bulls

Steven	school friend
Taya	Dad's older brother, Was's dad
Tayi	Taya's wife, Was's mum
Tommy	school enemy
Trish	neighbourhood nemesis
Uncle Iqbal	Shehzad's dad
Uncle Zafar	Pua Said's husband
Uncle	Naani Ammi's brother, Shibz's dad
Usman	Shehzad's baby brother
Wadi Ammi	paternal grandma
Was	cousin
Yahya	neighbourhood friend
Yaqoob	college friend
Yasser	mosque friend
Yazid	school friend
Zakria	neighbourhood friend
Zameer	neighbourhood friend
Zara	cousin

1997

Wednesday 1st January

'For God's sake. You win. Again.'

You can throw your cards all you want, Baji* Rosey. Of course I won! I'm the best in our whole family at *Cluedo*. I ALWAYS win.

Saeeda smiled at me. 'You're well top at this game, Paijan*. You should become a police detective when you grow up.'

Thank you, Saeeda. That's more like it.

'Don't worry, when you grow up you'll be well top too,' I said. Saeeda's only eight. Baji's fifteen, so the chances of her having my *Cluedo* skills are probably gone.

Saeeda is wrong, but. I'm not gonna be a detective, I'm gonna be a doctor.

Baj took my win out on our little brothers. 'Take that Lego out of his mouth,' she said to Zaheer, who was in the corner of our front room, playing with Tany. No appreciation for my *Cluedo* skills from them two.

Ammi* was in the kitchen, I know that because the smell from her cooking was travelling past the living room into the front room. Special New Year's Day meal of salooneh chawal* and kofta* saalan*. Yum. Ammi jaan* had a good excuse for missing my victory.

So did Abu because he was at work. New Year's Day is one of

the busiest and best times for a taxi driver. But to be honest, my stepdad wouldn't even care how good I was at anything. Even if I won the Cricket World Cup in front of his face. I'm sure he'd ignore that too, like everything me and Baj do.

One of the best things about starting to keep a diary is that I can tell it things I can't tell my family and friends.

Secrets.

Like that I always win at *Cluedo* because I'm the one who always shuffles the cards and when I have to put the cards of the suspect, the room and the weapon into the special envelope, I always sneak a look (Professor Plum in the library with the rope today), and I never get caught!

Obviously, I would win anyway. That just makes sure that I do.

I hope Baj or Saeeda never read this.

Thursday 2nd January

Ninety per cent of things I do when I'm not at school or home is with my cousin brothers: football, cricket, cycling, swimming, messing about, buying and eating sweets or playing Mega Drive.

As usual, we were playing footy in the attic of Lancaster Place, me and Shiry v Muj and Shibz. Their attic is massive so there's loads of space to play. We use the back of a pool table with no legs for a goal on one side and a bed on the other side. I like going in goal in the attic because I can sit on my knees and proper dive about.

Muj always argues that his shots have gone in, like today: 'What you on about? That went in. Fuck off!'

'I saved it on to the post, man.' I tried my best to make Muj think he'd missed. But to be honest, I'm not sure.

Shiry backed me up anyway. He usually does. 'Yeah, Terry saved it. No goal.'

Muj looked at Shibz. Even though Muj is the eldest brother,

Shibz has always been the more responsible one. He flicked back his curtains from his sweaty forehead. 'Doesn't matter, we're winning anyway. No goal.'

Me and Shiry were still in it!

Typical Muj: 'FUCK SAKE, MAN.'

Which made Baji Shanaz shout, 'Is everything all right upstairs?'

Shiry let her know that it was just Muj being Muj. He always shouts, but never does anything. It's just his way to get rid of his frustrations.

Baji Shanaz is so sweet. She's twenty, the oldest in their family. Shibz is in the same year and tutor group as me, Shiry is a year younger (Year 8) and Muj is two years older (Year 11, same as Baji Rosey). There's also another sister, Saddia, who's in between Muj and Shibz, and a little brother, Jaffer, who's the same age as Saeeda (eight).

I love going to Lancaster Place. It's the biggest house in our family. A front garden, three big rooms downstairs plus a kitchen, three bedrooms upstairs and then the massive (football pitch) attic.

I used to stay over quite a bit a few years back, whenever my family were visiting Pakistan without me. All four of us slept in the same room. Me on the top bunk bed, Shiry on the bottom, and Shibz and Muj in two single beds next to each other. That was havoc because we would always just carry on playing and then we'd hear footsteps on the stairs and Muj would run and switch the lights off and jump in bed and we'd all lie really still. Is the loudest I've heard my heartbeat. Then Poupoh* would come in and shout that she knows we're messing about and that we have to sleep, and I would try my best not to laugh.

Shibz lot's mum and dad, Poupoh and Uncle, are like my second parents. Poupoh is my dad's sister and Uncle is Ammi's mum's (Naani Ammi's*) brother, so I'm related to them two ways!

*

After the match, we were sat in the middle room drinking Vimto, and me and Shibz and Shiry were talking about what we wanna do when we grow up. Shibz wants to be a lawyer and he goes, 'I'm gonna be more like you and do every homework on time this year.'

I warned him to get ready for everyone calling him a SWOT.

And then he said summat really nice: 'Yeah, but who be's laughing when the exam results come out?'

'Our mum said we should be more like you and study more,' Shiry goes.

That's funny. I wish I was more like them. Strong and tough and fast. I didn't say that, though. I actually hate it when mums compare us against each other. Ammi always goes, *Bandeyah dee rees nee karee dee*: Don't copy other people. But then she also says, be more like so and so. You can't sometimes say don't be like them and then other times say be like them. It's confusing.

Anyway, I just said, 'Really, we're all as clever as each other, just my mum forces me to do reading and writing all the time.'

Sunday 5th January

Dad picked me and Baji Rosey up today like he does every Sunday. I love Dad. Everyone loves Dad. He's well famous in Blackburn because he plays football and he's got loads of trophies.

As usual he dropped us off at Randal Street, where our grandparents and cousins live.

'Go see your grandma and grandad before you go play,' he told us. Baj asked where he was going to be.

'I've got a game in half an hour; I'll be back later.'

'Can I come?' I asked.

He looked at me. 'No. Sorry. It's chuckin' it, you'll freeze to death standing on the side.'

He must've known I got sad, because he reached into his pocket and gave us £1 each. He ruffled my hair, I smiled and then he left.

The front door is never locked during the day, so I went straight in. Wadi Ammi, my grandma, is definitely the best cook in our whole family: as soon as I opened the door I could smell a sweet and sour mixture of buttery saag* paratah* and filthy hookah*. She was sat on her settee, wearing her trademark white dupatta over her mehndi-dyed red and white hair, smoking her pipe. No one else in our family smokes a pipe, but Wadi Ammi is the strongest personality in our family. She does what she wants!

She breathed out the smoke, looking like a smiling dragon, gave me salaam* and called me over for a hug.

Baaji was in his chair opposite her. He smiled, so I went over to him and let him put his hand over my head, the way old people always greet young people. Oh, we call Baaji, Baaji and not Daada Abu, because when my eldest cousins Baji Shanaz and Nads were small, they couldn't pronounce Babaji, which is what you can also call your grandad. Instead they said Baaji, and that name stuck, so that's what all his grandkids call him now.

He is looking really old these days. He barely said anything. I mean, I actually miss the scary Baaji that would chase us out of the house. Maybe my imagination is rubbish, but I can't imagine how he was in the army in World War II.

As always, Wadi Ammi tried to feed me, but I pretended I'd already eaten because I wanted to use my £1 to buy some samosas. Before I left she took her purse out and said, 'Eh leh. Cheezie leh lavee': Here. Buy yourself something.

'Thank you, Wadi Ammi!' Now I had £2!

Then I went next door to Was's. Literally.

Their door is always open too. I used to be a bit jealous that Was (my cousin who's my age and in the same tutor group as me and Shibz in school) lived next door to my dad. But Dad's moved two streets away, to Inkerman Street, now, so I don't need to be.

I said hi to everyone: Tayi, my aunt; dodged a slap from Taya, my uncle (Dad's older brother. He actually caught my shoulder: OW!); Noreen, Shaheen and Asma – Was's sisters – who were chilling in the kitchen and told me 'Was is out back.'

The best thing about Randal Street: they have a park right behind their house! Swings, slides and monkey bars. Even in this freezing weather and rain, Was was on the top of the monkey bars. If he falls?! He never does.

Basically, if we went on TV, Was would be on *Gladiators*. I would be on *They Think It's All Over*, Shibz would be on *Crystal Maze*, Muj would be on *A Question of Sport* and Shiry would be on *Krypton Factor*.

I called him and Was jumped off like it was the height of a bed and not a hundred times bigger than us.

We went to Manchester Sweet Centre and got two samosas each, then drowned them in the famous Sweet Centre onion chutney and ate them back in the park, sat on the swings. Was gave one of his samosas to his little brothers, Naeem and Saleem, to share, so I gave him half of one of mine, so we had one and a half each.

I asked him about Baaji.

'Yeah man, Wadi Ammi's worried about him. He's proper slowed down.'

We swung quietly. Eating our samosas. When we finished, he goes, 'Oh, I need to show you something . . . ' I followed him across the park to Kendal Street. He gave me his rubbish: 'Hold this.'

And then he kicked the door of No. 16 with all his force and legged it. I just stood and stared at him as he ran off. He turned around . . .

'RUN!'

I dropped the rubbish and started running. He never gives me a warning, man! He knows I'm slower than him. If he wasn't so cool and funny, I'd be mad.

At 5ish I went over to Dad's, said hi to Aunty (my stepmum) and Saira and Yasmeen, my little stepsisters.* I watched a bit of *Aladdin* with them and then Dad took me and Baj back home.

I love Sundays.

Tuesday 7th January

Is first school day of 1997. I wrote 1996 in three different classes.

'It's my turn to sit next to Was today,' remembered Shibz as we walked into Ms Williams's tutor group.

Was is probably the coolest and most popular guy in our year. Shibz got to sit next to him in tutor group because I sat next to him on the last day before Christmas holidays. So I sat next to Hassim. It doesn't really matter anyway, because we just turn our chairs around so we can all talk to each other.

But if it doesn't matter, then why do me and Shibz take turns sitting next to Was? So it must matter, then. I wonder if Was thinks it's weird. Like he's Eric Cantona or summat.

Hassim said, 'You'll never believe what I got for Christmas.'

Hassim is always getting presents. He always has more money than us and wears better clothes. But even still he's my best friend at school. I met him on induction day, when we were in Year 6. We randomly sat next to each other and we must have looked at each other and thought, *yeah, let's be best friends in school.* And we have been ever since. Like a lot of my friends, he's clever, but he doesn't try as hard, which is why I always beat him in exams.

The rest of us call him Boojo*, because he looks a bit like a monkey. But he's also still quite handsome, with curtains and hazel eyes. It's weird.

'A banana,' I guessed. Shibz and Was laughed. We are always taking the piss out of each other and laughing.

---

* I mean half-sisters, but we all thought the term was stepsister when I was that age.

'Very funny. No.'

He got a PlayStation!

'But you already have a Mega Drive and a SNES.' I didn't mean it to sound like a complaint, but I think it did.

'Hassim, Tehzeeb, turn around and be quiet.'

I hate Ms Williams, our form tutor. She's proper strict and always tells me off for talking, especially when I'm talking.

Danyal and Yazid are talking too. It's not my fault our Pakistani voices are louder than Indian voices. And actually, Fiona and her friends are talking as well. Not that I'd want my future wife to get into trouble. I'm just saying it's not fair.

Also, why's she called Ms and not Miss or Mrs?

Wednesday 8th January

Today I am 13¾ years old. I can do fractions and two press-ups!

I sat next to Was in tutor group today.

Thursday 9th January

In school everyone was talking about first roza* tomorrow, the start of Ramazan*.

'I'm gonna keep 'em all* again this year. A hundred per cent,' I said, with my mouth full of chips.

'Obviously. It's not even hard.' Shibz is right. It actually isn't.

'The real challenge is tarawee*,' Was goes. 'Who's gonna do that every day?'

Ufft. That'll actually be rock hard, because they take a long time. The molbi* saab* reads the full Qur'an in tarawee prayers, so like a spaara* a day. Takes around about an hour.

'At my mosque tarawee only takes thirty minutes,' Hassim said.

---

* The fasts. To keep a fast means you fasted.

'That's because your mosque has got a Division Two molbi who doesn't pray the full Qur'an because he doesn't know it by heart.' Was delivering a fatality there.

'*Baist*!*' I grabbed Hassim's last fish finger.

That's the rule, if you get baist, you have to lose something to the person who calls baist. Unlucky for Hassim, he was eating.

'Boojo, you got done, bro. Lucky he didn't take your jam roly-poly hot custard,' Shibz told him as he tried to complain. I high-fived Shibz. Hassim is lucky he's my best friend, so I can't be that tight on him to take his last dessert before Ramazan.

Update: What an anti-climax. I was proper excited, but the mosque people said that it wasn't the new moon today so our first roza is on Saturday. I bet the Indians start tomorrow.

Friday 10th January

The Indians* started rozay today. I knew it!

It's definitely first roza tomorrow. I went to the first tarawee at Lancaster Place mosque. Uffft. It took SO SO long, man. I think Qari* saab* read two spaareh today instead of one. It's gonna be a long month, I think.

Thursday 16th January

Me, Shibz and Shiry got shouted at in tarawee. We got there early so we could pray near the front but Uncle Bhatti goes, '*Na, picheh javo*': No, go to the back.

One thing I've noticed about mosque (and it doesn't matter

---

* Blackburn is split between its white population and Asians. The Asians are Pakistani, Indian or Bangladeshi. The Indians are mostly Gujarati Muslim; there is a handful of Hindu families. I don't remember being around any Sikhs growing up. I only knew two black kids.

which mosque I've been to, I bet it's the same in any mosque in the world), there's always three types of uncles and buddeh* that be there:

The grumpy one, that hates it that anyone under fifty-three is at the mosque, like as if namaaz* isn't farz* for all of us. At Lancaster Place, that's Uncle Bhatti. He literally lives across the road from the mosque, what's he got to be annoyed about?

Then there's a kind one, who loves kids in the community having an interest in praying and being in the mosque. At Lancaster Place, that's definitely Uncle Jerry.

And then the rest of the uncles and buddeh, who don't mind you being there as long as you don't make any noise, and don't take up their space, which is basically anywhere except the back row! But if you put all the kids together ... we're gonna mess about. That's a scientific fact.

That's why me, Shibz and Shiry tried to pray near the front, so we wouldn't mess about, so it's not our fault that we did.

Monday 10th February

Eid Mubarak!

Oh man, can't believe it's been nearly a month since I last wrote in you. Don't worry, you haven't missed much. All I've been doing is fasting, scoffing, praying and annoying Ms Williams.

Eid being on a Monday is usually the best day it could be on because it means two extra days off school! Plus, including Saturday and Sunday, it would mean a little holiday. But this week is half term, what a waste!

In the evening, me, Shibz, Shiry and Was sat in Wadi Ammi's front room and talked about how Eid's been proper boring this year. Usually we'll go out and play footy and just mess about, but it was raining all day and it's so cold. Now I know how the girls must feel on Eid. Just being stuck inside all day. Was said we should do something more exciting for next Eid. Top idea.

Shiry asked me how much Eidi* I got. I did a quick calculation in my head ... £5 each from Ammi, Uncle, Dad, Taya, Wadi Ammi and Mammu* Saeed: 'Thirty pounds.'

'Yeah, we got the same,' Shibz said.

Phew. I mean, it's not a competition, but at the same time you don't wanna have less than anyone.

Was said, 'Don't forget your Eid clothes. They cost money as well.' A sensible comment from Was. Must be a blue moon outside.

I was wearing brand-new green trousers and a green and white stripy top. Ammi said I looked really smart when I came downstairs this morning. She was right. I did.

'Plus all the food we ate,' Shiry said with a mouthful of Wadi Ammi's gajrela*.

Does food count as a gift? If it does, then man I was spoilt this year. I ate at home, went to Shibz's house and ate there. Then I ate at Was's house and now I've just eaten again at Wadi Ammi's. More roast, kebabs, samosas, chaat*, chawal, gajrela and ras malai* than I know what to do with.

Well, I do know what I did with it ... It was a long visit to the toilet when I got home!

Tuesday 11th February

Oh my God.

I just nearly died. I'm in shock. On Eid as well. That would have been a proper tragedy for my family!

I went to Uncle Sardar's* shop at the bottom of our street to

---

* Despite the name, he is a Muslim guy, and also the owner and founder of Lancaster Place mosque.

buy some crisps and chocolate. I got some for Baj, Saeeda, Zaheer and Tanveer too (my treat from my Eidi). If I'm going shop to buy sweets and chocolate, I always try and get stuff for my brothers and sisters if I have enough money. I remember one time when we were small, Abu came home with chocolate for Saeeda and Zaheer, but not me. I went to the front room because I got upset and I didn't wanna show him. Ammi got proper upset as well and I could hear her shouting at him from the living room. After that he always buys me what he buys them. Sometimes I feel like not taking it. But I do take it, because I love sweets more than pride, which is gunnah*.

Anyway, I walked out of the shop with a carrier bag full of treats for everyone and my other hand full of my stuff. The road was really busy, but I sneaked between two cars that were on my side and then went to run across the road . . .

BANG!

I got hit by a car!

I went flying, my Time Out went flying, my Skips went flying, the plastic bag went flying.

I got up straight away. This random uncle came to ask me 'Are you all right?' but I didn't answer. I needed to find my goodies. I found the bag and my Time Out next to it. I couldn't find the Skips. Where are my Skips? I started panicking.

'WHERE ARE MY SKIPS?!'

The uncle saw them underneath a car and he got them for me. I didn't even say thank you, I just snatched them and ran full whack all the way up Edmundson Street. It's proper steep.

I ran into the house and went straight upstairs. I checked my clothes, they were fine. I washed my face and went downstairs and gave everyone their treats.

I haven't told Ammi. I don't dare. I'll be in deep trouble. You can't get hit by a car and not be in trouble. No, I'll keep it to myself.

Best thing about it, though? I got hit by a car and I'm not even hurt. Not even a little bit. Maybe I'm a superhero.

The worst thing? My Skips were all crushed.

Wednesday 12th February

Usually, we (us kids) go mosque every day.* After school, 5–7 p.m., so we never get to watch *Blue Peter* or *Neighbours* or anything like that. But they gave us holiday for Christmas time. Obviously not especially for Christmas, but because we weren't at school. And then Ramazan started a week after Christmas holiday and we get holiday for all of Ramazan too, so they thought there was no point going back just for one week. So, basically, we've been off for like seven weeks!

Today was our first class since before Christmas holidays. I followed Shibz and Shiry into Lancaster Place mosque through the double wooden doors. Shibz stood staring at the wooden shoe rack in the corner of the entrance hall.

'What you looking at?' I know curiosity killed the cat, but it's just a shoe rack.

'Just everyone's new trainers they got for Eid.' Ah. That makes sense. Shibz definitely has the best style out of all our friends at school and mosque, so he was looking at all the latest trainers that the other boys are wearing.

I left him to it and followed Shiry into the jamaat khana*. Unlike other mosques, we only have one big prayer room in Lancaster Place. It has a green carpet that is split in rows and along each row is a rectangle, decorated with an arch and flowers, that means one space for someone to pray in.

---

* Virtually every Muslim kid in Britain goes to after-school madrassa (Arabic for school) in a mosque or someone's house to learn how to read the Qur'an in its native Arabic, to learn how to pray salah (the daily prayers) and the basics of Islam.

The small kids sit together at the bottom of the room: they have their own molbi saab. Me and Shiry walked to where the older kids were sat at the top of the classroom: the boys on the right and the girls on the left. I went and sat next to Yasser and Shiry sat next to Pats, his best friend – as Shiry's a year younger than the rest of us cousin brothers, he has a lot of other close friends too.

I sat down, took my rail out, put it down and put my Qur'an on top of it and started reading out loud.

Sometimes I wondered what a gora* would think if they walked into mosque and basically saw about fifty Pakistani kids wearing topis* or hijabs rocking back and forth praying out loud in Arabic.

After I read my sabak* five times, I turned to Yasser.

'So what did you do for Eid—'

THWACK!

OUCH.

I fell forward. I just about caught my Qur'an as it slid off the rail.

Hafiz* saab had just kicked me in the back for talking. I turned to look at him. He didn't say anything, just gave me a stern look.

Yup. Got it. Don't talk. Story of my life.

Hafiz saab was the main Imam of Lancaster Place till Qari saab came from Pakistan. Ninety per cent of the time he's really nice and friendly, and he's got this big white beard and nice kind smile. He also does the most creative swearing I've ever heard in my life. Because you're not allowed to actually swear in the mosque, when someone doesn't know their sabak, he'll call them *suti maa da puttar*, which means 'a sleeping mother's son'. Which is, I mean, what is that? Or sometimes he'll call one of us *moosi phaid*, which means 'mouldy sheep'! I have never heard anyone else say those insults ever.

We pay a pound a week for this: 20p today, to find out that I'm not in fact a superhero.

Friday 14th February

I saw the news today. They were talking about Stephen Lawrence. It was really sad, man. He was this black boy and he got stabbed to death in London a few years ago. It proper reminded me of Pai Shehzad. ~~But it was a little diff~~ Actually ... I ... I'm not ready to write about that yet.

The news said that they did an investigation and that Stephen was killed in a racist attack by five goreh* boys. WHAT THE HELL, MAN? There bes racism in Blackburn, like when we had the Johnson Street riots, but I can't imagine that a gang of boys will just kill you. I feel proper sorry for his family. It's well scary.

Monday 24th February [CONTAINS RUDE BITS]

Okay ... So, it was PE today. And for this term it's our class's turn to be in the school gym, doing weight training.

I don't know what normal gyms be like, but our school's one is proper weird. It's at the back of the stage of our assembly hall in North Building.

Witton Park has two buildings, North and South. Years 7–9 have tutor groups in North Building and Years 10 and 11 have tutor group in South Building. But lessons be in both buildings, depending on the subject, so sometimes we have to run between them to get to a lesson on time. North to South is easy because it's downhill, but South to North is a mission. They should just make us do that in PE.

The equipment in the gym looks proper old. My dad probably used it when he went to school here.

My favourite machine is the leg press because I'm really good at it. I can push the whole rack! It says 150 kg! That's strong, I think. I have to cheat a bit to do it but, by sitting up a bit to get a better angle.

Anyway ... I did a circuit of the gym and then it was my turn on the dips bar. I can't do any dips (I'm up to five press-ups, but!) – my legs are like tree trunks, but my arms are like twigs, so I use the dips bar to do stomach crunches instead, because my tummy's like jelly.

I was doing loads of them ... and then ... I don't know how to write this ... I started getting a funny feeling. Downstairs. I carried on and I think I was getting more and more excited. I clenched my teeth and closed my eyes, my brain started thinking about Fiona. I ... I carried on and then just as I was about to give up because my arms were tired ... I ... there was this sort of explosion in my hips.

It was proper weird and nice. I stopped after that and got down, lucky no one was looking at me. I wonder if it was just a fluke?

I thought about telling Hassim and Shibz, but I thought, What if they laugh at me and it's baist? So I didn't tell anyone. I didn't wanna risk losing my cornflake tart.

Tuesday 25th February

Ms Williams went round class and handed an envelope to each student today.

'Remember to get your slips signed by your parents, to show that they've read your Records of Achievement,' she said.

Yeah. Yeah. Just give me mine, please.

I can't tell if mine is good or bad. This is what I got, and compared to my first two years (out of 5: 1 is excellent, 5 is shit):

SUBJECT	YEAR 9	YEAR 8	YEAR 7
Art	2	3	2
English	3/4	2/3	2
Geography	2/3	2	1

SUBJECT	YEAR 9	YEAR 8	YEAR 7
German	1	1	1
History	2	3	2
IT	1	1	1
Maths	2	3	2
Music	No music teacher	2	1
PE	1	2/3	2
RE	2	2	2
Science	2	2	1
Technology	1	1	2

I mean, that English score is well bad. I shouldn't be getting less than 2 in anything – look at Year 7!

I turned to Hassim. 'What did you get in English?'

'2. But I got a 3 in maths.'

'2! Why did Mrs Place give me a 3/4?'

'Read quietly, please.' Ms Williams sounding exactly like Mrs Place there.

'You know what's a piss-take?' I whispered to Was, Shibz and Hassim. 'This is an effort score, but it's what's on top of our report. It's not about how clever we are, or how well we did in exams. It's about how much effort the teacher *thinks* we making.'

'So, basically, if they don't like you, they give you a shit score, innit.'

'Exactly.' Was gets it.

I carried on. I was on a roll: 'Last year, I got a hundred per cent in my history exam. A hundred per cent! But Mrs Watson gave me a 3!'

'Yeah, but remember that time Mrs Watson told you not to push your luck and then you wrote luck on your hand and started pushing it with your other hand and she caught you?'

Shibz has got a good memory.

I started replying but Ms Williams piped up: 'Tehzeeb, will you shut up, or do I have to move you?'

I sat quietly. I took Was's and had a look at what he got. I quickly gave it back to him.

'They must really hate me,' he laughed. Actually, maybe my scores aren't too bad!

In the summary part, Ms Williams said that I talk too much, which was the exact same in Year 8 and Year 7. Ammi wasn't happy.

Monday 10th March

Big news in school today. All the teachers were really excited. Excited or nervous? I think they were nervous actually, but pretending to be excited.

Basically, there's something called an Ofsted inspection next week. That's where these government inspectors come and look around the school and then tell the school if they're a good school or not.

In every single lesson the teachers banged on about it.

All right, we get it. We'll be good. It can't be that hard.

Tuesday 11th March

It finally happened.

We got caught. Big time.

For the last three years, nearly every dinnertime, the gang* I'm in go sneaking into the woods.

I love doing this. At dinnertime, loads of us – me, Was, Shibz, Boojo, Haider, Kelloggs, Chucky, Immy, Mushy, Golly, Geery,

---

* In this context 'gang' means group of boys who hang around with each other.

Kalpesh, Zameer and Master – head down to the pavilion by the athletics track, grab some horrible £1 chips (sometimes they're soft, sometimes they're hard, make your mind up, man) and then go off exploring.

It's proper beautiful. We climb trees, do roly-polys down hills, skim stones in ponds, jump across streams. The boys that smoke, smoke, which I hate. It feels proper like I'm in the Famous Five or Secret Seven. I never told anyone else that – they already think I'm a proper 'speccy four-eyed swot' as it is.

Every day we see how far and deep into the woods we can go, before we have to turn around and get back to school by bell time.

Today we went too far.

Okay, what I'm gonna write next sounds worse than it actually was in real life.

We came to a big clearing and saw some sheep. And ... and we started chasing them. Just for a laugh. We weren't gonna shag 'em or anything!

BANG!

We all froze. The sheeps legged it. Birds flew out of trees.

'What the hell was that?' My ears were ringing but I could just about hear Hassim's voice.

'DON'T MOVE!' a voice boomed in the valley.

We looked up, and at the top of the hill there was a big truck, like the ones they have in American films. Pick-up trucks, I think they call them: the ones that have a big, long, empty boot at the back. There were two dogs either side of the truck. Someone was obviously driving the truck, it wasn't Knight Rider, but I couldn't see who. In the back of the truck was a farmer stood up with a shotgun. The shotgun was pointed at us!

'RUN!'

I don't know who shouted it. But I was absolutely frozen to the spot. The dogs and the pick-up truck started motoring down the hill towards me.

I felt a tug on the back of my coat, Shibz pulled me in front of him and I started running. We heard a shout . . .

'OI! THIS WAY!' I looked up, and Was and Hassim were heading towards some trees, so me and Shibz snaked our way up and into the trees too. Clever. The car can't chase us in the actual woods. We ran and we ran and ran. I have never run so fast in my entire life. My heart was pounding.

'Don't stop, Terry,' Shibz kept saying, staying behind me. He has long legs and is much faster than me, but he made sure to stay behind me so I wouldn't get left behind.

We'd never been that way before, but we kept heading in the general direction of what we thought was the school.

Eventually, we came out near North Building, right by the playing fields. We looked at each other, we were all very muddy! We dusted each other off as best we could and went around to the front of North. Hassim tried to make us feel good: 'Listen, we're fine, as long as—'

'LOOK!' It was like Punch and Judy: Hassim, it's behind you!

THE PICK-UP TRUCK WAS ON ITS WAY. Up the hill to North. Not only that, there were some Asian boys in the truck with the farmer. He'd caught some of us!

Shit.

We had a strict no grassing up rule in the gang, but the teachers aren't daft. They know who's friends with who. Plus, that rule never said what to do if a farmer pointed a shotgun in your face.

We ran inside North Building, through the canteen and split up.

I went through the hall, through the corridor, past the boys' changing rooms and sports hall and came out the other side. I spotted the Indian boys from my year playing football on one of the yards. I stood on the sidelines watching them, pretending I'd been there all dinnertime.

The bell went. No one had come for me. Phew.

I blended in with the other students as we went back into the building. I went into Ms Williams's class and sat down. No Was, no Shibz, no Hassim.

Shit.

Ms Williams asked me where they were. I said I didn't know. Which was true. She asked me why I was so muddy. I said I fell playing football. Which was not true.

Right at the end of tutor group, they came in. Hassim gave Ms Williams a piece of paper, she looked at it and told them to sit down. She looked at me. It was weird. I knew she knew and I'm sure she knew that I knew that she knew, but she didn't say anything. Did she just cover for me?

On the way to next lesson, I asked Shibz and Hassim what happened (Was's lesson was somewhere else).

Hassim started: 'Basically, Mr Cameron, yeah, he went around gripping anyone he thought would be hanging around with Kelloggs and Kalpesh because them daft bastards got caught, innit.' Shit, Mr Cameron's our deputy head and a proper serious guy, you don't wanna mess with him. He was a teacher when Dad was here, and Dad said he was strict then as well.

Shibz added, 'Yeah, so he gripped us, and then the painchod* farmer said he recognised us. How could he have recognised us from so far away?' Shibz sounded annoyed that the farmer had guessed that they were there. Even though they were there.

'Well, your clothes are muddy.' I didn't know if that helped, but they couldn't really deny it.

I'm just grateful they didn't grass on me. Everyone who got caught has got detention for two weeks.

I think the teachers were so angry because just yesterday they were telling us about the Ofsted inspection and how we had to behave ourselves. And today we did this. I think if Ofsted weren't coming, they would've got suspended.

Lucky.

Wednesday 12th March

Dinnertime was proper boring today. Halfway through I went to the detention room and just sat with Shibz, Was and Hassim lot.

Now I'm in voluntary detention for two weeks too, but unlike them, at least it's not on my record.

Monday 17th March

The Ofsted inspections started today. The school looks really nice. All last week they had people coming in painting and cleaning. I was thinking is a shame they don't make the school look this nice for us anyway, not just when inspectors come.

The teachers are definitely nervous because they are overreacting to everything. Mr Taylor screamed at Tommy for having muddy shoes. But also, I was happy Tommy got shouted at. He's this boy that I hate in my year. Actually, probably who I hate the most in the whole school. He's this strawberry-blond shit and he's only the same size as me – what's he got to be cocky about? Plus, I definitely think he's racist. Just by the way he talks about apne*.

'I don't wanna sit next to Junaid, sir, he smells funny.'

Sometimes people don't actually have to say summat racist, you can just tell by the way they be.

Mr Cameron made a deal with the detention kids, and he said there would be no detentions this week, as long as everyone behaves themselves.

If they behave, the teachers will halve the original detention, but if they mess about, they'll double what's left. That's the difference between having only two days left next week or an extra seven days on top of the seven days left. Pressure.

At least we can have our dinnertimes again this week.

Friday 21st March

That was a proper stressful week. Every lesson, the teachers were acting strange. Speaking in this nice soft almost sing-song voice. Even Mr Hutchinson was being nice. That was well weird.

In some lessons an inspector would be there, sat in a corner just watching us and taking some notes, like Mr Claw in *Inspector Gadget*.

I don't know about other classes, but everyone in ours was on their best behaviour every lesson. We put our hands up before we spoke and only spoke when the teacher said our name.

Even I shut up, and I queued for dinners instead of pushing in. I could tell that it meant a lot to the teachers, I didn't want to let them down.

I think it went well, to be honest. It's a good school, the inspectors must have seen that.

Tuesday 25th March

Last day of voluntary detention today. I hope my friends appreciate my sacrifice.

My sacrifice of not wanting to hang out with anyone else/ having no other friends.

Sunday 30th March

My little brother Zaheer turned four years old yesterday. He's still cute but he's got so big so fast. He's definitely not a baby any more.

What's exciting today is there's gonna be a brand-new channel on TV, Channel 5. It's called that because it's the fifth channel.

It starts at 6 p.m. It's nearly time, I'm gonna grab Baj, Saeeda and Zaheer and we're gonna watch it together. I'll write what I think about it in a bit.

Update: Er ... okay. So, I watched Channel 5 for two hours. At the beginning it was exciting, the Spice Girls sang a song and then there were loads of highlights of the shows that are gonna come on. We'd already lost Zaheer by this point.

The first proper show that came on was *Family Affairs* and it was like *Coronation Street*, proper boring. Saeeda left half-way through.

Then the next programme was boring as well. Baj looked at me like it was my fault. As if it's my dad's channel. I mean, if it was, it'd be her fault too.

I don't know what we were expecting, but better than that crap.

Tuesday 8th April

I'm fourteen today!

I actually love my birthday. Even if it's only a small celebration like today.

Ammi brought the cake into the living room, Saeeda switched the lights off and they and Baj and Zaheer started singing 'Happy birthday to you ...'

It felt really nice. I could feel my cheeks going red. Poor Tany was just staring at us. He doesn't know the words yet.

Ammi put the cake in front of me, it was a football! There was one candle on it, and I made a wish (Rovers to win the league again!) and I blew it out.

Ammi gave me a big hug and kiss.

'Do you want to cut the first piece, puttar*?'

Er ... Yes! I can tell I'm growing up now, because usually Ammi holds the knife with me when I cut a cake, but this time she let me cut it by myself. It was Victoria sponge, my favourite.

Baj gave me my present, she said it was from everyone. I opened the bag ... *Mortal Kombat II* for my Mega Drive.

'YES!!! Thank you!'

I hugged my brothers and sisters one by one. When I hugged Tany and Zaheer, I joked that they must've paid the most for my present.

Good job Abu wasn't there, that would've been awkward. He probably would've made a face if I tried to hug him.

Ammi gave me my birthday card. I opened it and £5 fell out.

'From now on you get £5 pocket money every week.'

What the hell?!

'Thank you, Ammi.' This time I gave her a hug.

'I love you.' Ammi squeezed super tight.

I was thrashing Saeeda in *Mortal Kombat II* with Kitana and I looked round the front room, Baj playing with her glasses while reading a book, Tany and Zaheer playing Lego, Saeeda bashing the buttons of the joypad and I thought, kasam*, I'm proper lucky, you know.

Monday 14th April

Eid Mubarak!

As you will remember, diary, last Eid me and my cousin brothers said we gonna do something more fun for Eid. Was has it figured out, but he hasn't told us what it is yet. I can't wait.

So far it's been normal. I went to pray Eid namaaz in the morning and then I came home, hugged Ammi and got changed into my new Eid clothes: jeans and a cream jumper, and Hi-Tec trainers. I put some thail* in my hand and rubbed it in my hair, and then combed it into a side parting. I looked well fit. Ammi and Baj said cute. Which is not the same thing.

Ammi made us some roast, kebabs, chawal, lamb saalan, doodh

sawiya* (I warmed mine up, I don't like it cold) and I washed it all down with two glasses of Coke.

Every Eid I eat in the morning and think, *how am I gonna eat any more?* But I always manage to squeeze it in.

Ammi gave me £10(!) Eidi. Woah!

I can't wait for the rest of the day. I'm just about to leave to go to Shibz's.

Update: Er. Wow.

So, the early afternoon was normal. Went Shibz and Shiry's house, ate some more food, got some more Eidi.

Then we went to Was's house.

'What's the plan then?' I asked him straight away.

He quickly looked around him nervously and goes, 'Sshhh. I'll tell you.'

After saying Eid Mubarak to Dad, Wadi Ammi, Baaji, Aunty, Saira, Yasmeen and Taya and Tayi, and having some food, me, Shiry, Shibz and Was left Randal Street about 2 p.m. We walked all through Blackburn town centre: past Tesco, Boots and WH Smith, past the cathedral and Midland Bank and Morrisons. We kept asking Was where we were going but he wouldn't tell us . . . until we got to the train station.

'We going Preston.'

'Sick.' Shiry was excited. I had a question:

'Why?'

Shibz nudged me. 'Yaraa*, just buy your ticket, we'll find out when we get there.' Fair enough, Shibz.

The return ticket (I today learnt 'return ticket' means there and back. It's cheaper than buying a single ticket there and a single ticket back. And I was definitely planning to come back) cost £3.50. Normally I would think that's a lot of money, but it was Eid, so I had £35 in my pocket. We got on the train, which was small and old and smelt funny.

'How shit is this train?' I'm glad Shibz said it!

Was said, 'Imagine we stayed on and just went all the way to Blackpool?'

I glared at him. 'No way, Was, that's too far!' I wasn't ready to go to Blackpool.

They all laughed at me. 'He's joking, man,' Shiry goes.

At Preston train station, which is like ten times bigger than Blackburn train station, we got in a black cab and Was told him where to go. I didn't recognise the name (so far, I'd spent £5 and we'd just had a train and taxi ride).

When we got there, Was got out first.

'Ta-da!'

Now I was smiling. We were stood outside this massive arcade. It looked well fun. We spent all afternoon playing games and ten-pin bowling. On this one turn, I threw my ball in such a daft way that it landed in the lane NEXT to ours and rolled and knocked all their pins over. STRIKE!

'ALLAH!' Was shouted. It was too funny; we pissed ourselves.

Shibz shushed us, though. We couldn't make too much noise because the people playing next to us didn't even realise what happened. When they turned around, we pretended we were talking about our own game. They looked so confused about where their pins had gone.

'Ay ay ay you flukey guy. Kasam,' Shiry grinned. Except it didn't count because it wasn't our lane! You're welcome, whosever turn it was, because I just got you a strike! Ha ha.

We had a McDonald's after all that excitement. Filet-O-Fish, obviously. I had large, but *Allah di kasam**, I could've had another one. It was proper tasty, but. It's only the second time I've had McDonald's. The first time was on my tenth birthday, when Ammi took me and after we went to Argos and I got *Street Fighter II* for my Mega Drive. That was one of my most favourite days ever! This was four years later, so I guess next time I'll have McDonald's will be when I'm eighteen, then.

After that we went cinema and watched *Space Jam*. What a sick film. I love going to the cinema!

The first film I ever watched in cinema was *Jurassic Park*. Four years ago – Dad took me, Was, Shibz, Shiry and Muj to Blackburn cinema as a wicked surprise. We got popcorn and a drink each. The popcorn was so big, I couldn't even finish it all. What a day.

Abu's never taken me anywhere.

When the film finished, Was realised that it was getting a bit late and home lot might be worried as they didn't know where we were, so we had to leg it all the way back to the train station. If we missed the 8.05 p.m. train, we wouldn't get home till after 9.30 p.m. and that is TOO late.

We ran and ran and ran. I was SO tired. But luckily, we got there and I was the last one on just as it was about to set off. Phew.

We all collapsed on some seats and laughed.

'Top day, kasam,' Shibz said. I agree, Shibz.

That is, until we got back. I would've sacrificed Rovers' next three wins to have just gone straight home. Instead, we went back to Was's house, because that's where we had set off from.

When we got there, Was's sister Asma met us in the park behind their house.

She said, 'They know.' By 'they', she meant the grown-ups.

As we walked back into the house, Was was really panicking: 'Shit, shit, man. What we gonna say?'

'I'm sure it'll be all right, man,' I said. I couldn't see the big deal.

Shiry said, 'We're back in one piece,' which was a good point. No harm done. Oh boy, were we wrong.

When we walked into Was's house we were met by a committee.

Dad, Wadi Ammi, Taya, Tayi, Poupoh and Uncle were all sat inside, looking really angry and upset. Bajis Noreen, Shaheen, Shanaz, Rosey and Asma were there too.

'Sit down.' That wasn't a request from Taya, it was an instruction. I could tell by the way he said it he was angry. Or disappointed. Or both.

I looked around the cramped living room; there wasn't anywhere to sit. I almost laughed at that (when I'm nervous I laugh so easily) but luckily I spotted a space in the corner near Baji Rosey and just looked down. The other boys had found space on other parts of the floor. It's not a big room and there were fifteen of us in there.

And then they started. Ay ay ay. One by one. All of 'em letting us have it.

'WHOSE IDEA WAS IT?'

'WHAT IF SOMETHING HAPPENED TO YOU?'

'ARE YOU STUPID?'

'IS THIS HOW WE BROUGHT YOU UP?'

'DO YOU NOT CARE ABOUT US?'

It was the biggest bollocking I've ever had in my life. And I was at St Barnabas when the school got burnt down and they thought one of the students had done it.

'IF SOMETHING HAPPENED TO ONE OF YOU AND YOUR WADI AMMI HAD A HEART ATTACK, WHAT THEN?'

What?

One by one, all the grown-ups took turns to give us a lecture. Baji Shanaz and Noreen tried to intervene one or two times: 'Chalo*, I'm sure they learned their lesson, they won't do it again, will you, boys?'

If I'm honest, I don't understand the big deal.

I wanted to say, 'Taya, was it any more dangerous than the time you put twelve of us cousins in the back of your van, with no windows or seats, and drove us to Southport for the day?' Like we were being smuggled from Pakistan to Europe.

I never said that. Obviously. Because I like being alive.

When I came home, I didn't tell Ammi, and Baji Rosey didn't either. Thank God. The last thing I needed was another lecture.

I wonder what happened to Was after we left, and Shibz and Shiry when they went home. I hope they didn't get in more trouble.

I'm gonna write it now but . . . I don't regret it. I'm glad we went. I had a top day with my favourite cousins.

Tuesday 15th April

I can't stop thinking about yesterday.

There are SOOO many rules in life I have to follow, man.

i.	Make sure there's no food left on your plate
ii.	Come home straight from school
iii.	Be home before dark
iv.	Only go out with this and this person
v.	Only eat halal* food
vi.	Check the ingredients on the back for gelatine or E471
vii.	Eat with your right hand
viii.	Write with your right hand
ix.	In fact, do everything with your right hand . . . except picking your nose and washing your bum
x.	No smoking
xi.	Pray namaaz five times a day
xii.	Don't talk back
xiii.	Don't talk when you're eating
xiv.	Don't talk

xv.   Wash your hands before you eat

xvi.   Go to bed at 10 p.m.

xvii.   Don't wake up too early

xviii.   Don't wake up too late

xix.   Don't be late

xx.   Why are you early?

xxi.   Do your homework

xxii.   Do your writing

xxiii.   Do your reading

xxiv.   Read your sabak

xxv.   Don't open the new cereal box to get the
           toy out until the cereal box already open is
           finished

xxvi.   Don't hit your little brothers and sisters

xxvii.   Don't eat sweets or chocolates or crisps in front of
           your little brothers and sisters

xxviii.   Don't rock back and forth when you're reading in
           class, it's distracting

xxix.   Rock back and forth when you're reading in
           mosque, it helps with concentration

xxx.   Don't talk to girls

xxxi.   Skip the rude parts on TV

xxxii.   Don't listen to music loud

xxxiii.   Don't get mud on your trousers

xxxiv.   Don't push in the dinner queue

xxxv.   Learn this surah* off by heart

xxxvi.   Hang out with Asians not goreh

xxxvii.   You're only allowed to marry a gujjar*

xxxviii.   Don't accept anything when you go to someone
           else's house

xxxix.   Don't touch dogs

xl.   Don't go to Preston on Eid

I know most of these are for my own good and some of it's about haram* and halal, but sometimes I think about the boys that don't follow the rules. What's going on in their heads?

Do they feel how I feel when I open a cereal box before I'm supposed to?

Proper naughty?

Monday 21st April

Skinny Speccy Sweet Sixteen, Baji Rosey! I'm so glad she's back from Pakistan and here with us.

Wednesday 23rd April

We started training again today!

Basically, last year, Dad started a football team for me and my cousins and our friends called Whalley Range Tigers. I say me, I'm the shittest player in the team, but still. Me, Was, Shibz, Shiry and Hassim all play.

Last year, in the first game of the season, I started up front. I felt like Kevin Gallacher!

In the first five minutes the ball bounced off my thigh and Was ran onto it and smashed it into the top corner from outside the box. Had already got an assist. And then five minutes later, Was returned the favour: he put me through on goal, I took a touch, the goalkeeper came off his line to close me down and out of the corner of my left eye I could see a defender running in; I took one more touch and then with my right foot (my WRONG foot) I placed it past the keeper and it went in! I SCORED! I ran all the way along the touchline and jumped into Dad's arms. Was, Shibz, Shiry and Hassim came running over to me as well.

Is funny that we hug each other when we score goals, but not normally in everyday situations.

That day was one of the best days of my life. We won that game 3–1.

After that, I didn't start a single game or score another goal all season. I peaked way too soon.

I'm not sure what's gonna happen this season. But today was hell. On our fifth lap of St Mary's, I looked at Hassim and his pale face had turned red, puffing away. I could tell he was thinking bad things about Dad.

The entire team were dead halfway through the session. Was goes, 'Chach, can we just play some footy now?'

'You'll play when I tell you to play. And I'm not Chach here, I'm your coach. Drop down and give me ten.'

Was just looked at him. He couldn't believe it. Neither could I. Dad is proper chilled out. It's why everyone loves him. Plus Was is his favourite nephew. You can tell. I sometimes think Dad wishes Was was his son instead of me. So when he snapped at him, it was a bit like, woah, Dad's proper serious this season.

'Now.'

Was slowly went down and started doing ten press-ups. Then Shibz dropped down to his knees and did ten press-ups. Then Shiry followed, then Hassim . . .

FUCK SAKE.

Because Was is our captain and best player, the rest of the team thought we should follow our leader. I was SO tired and I'm so unfit, for a second I thought about not joining them. But I couldn't do that to the team or Was. So we all did ten press-ups too.

Dad's face looked like he'd just won the lottery. 'We're gonna win the league this year.'

Monday 28th April

Nearly every lesson we mess about. Yet what happened today has never happened in my life before.

We all like Mr Lawrence, but it's a bit of a doss. He's a nice teacher, but not strict like Mr Hutchinson. So as usual, me and Hassim were chatting, everyone was chatting. Suddenly, Mr Lawrence shouted at the top of his voice and told us to 'SHUT UP!'

Jack goes 'Ooooooooooh.' And we all laughed. But then went quiet when we saw that he was serious.

While everyone was working I quietly made a paper plane, and when Mr Lawrence wasn't looking, I threw it. And kasam, it was a really good paper plane, it proper floated for a long time. Everyone started laughing loads.

And then . . .

Mr Lawrence went to his desk, sat down in his chair and started sobbing.

Dead silence. We were all shocked. We made a teacher cry. Oh my God.

He goes, 'What's the point? Why doesn't anyone listen to me?'

Fiona went up to him and put her arm around his shoulder, which was a nice thing to do. We started saying 'sorry Mr Lawrence'. He went a bit quiet. We all felt well bad. Fiona sat back down. The rest of the lesson we were all proper quiet.

When the bell went, everyone got up quietly and one by one we all said 'sorry Mr Lawrence' on our way out.

I think the worst thing about the whole thing was that we're set 1. The GOOD kids. I bet that's never happened anywhere before. I think we might have broken a world record.

Friday 2nd May

Conservatives are not gonna be the government any more! Yay! Ammi said they're the baddies and the reason I stopped getting milk at infant school. Ammi voted for the goodies: Labour.

That means we've got a new Prime Minister, Tony Blair. He looks well good and young compared to John Major.

I like Labour because their logo is a red rose, the same as Rovers.

Plus, my next-door neighbour, Mr Khan, he's a MP* for Labour – in Blackburn but, not in London. I think he makes sure they do a good job in our town. So we have to support Labour, otherwise we'd be traitors to our neighbours.

Thursday 8th May

I'm not bloody happy, man.

Today we found out what papers we gonna be sitting for our SATS. English and maths is fine, they gonna put me in for the higher paper, level 6–8, but in science . . .

I looked at the slip Mr Watts gave me: lower-middle paper, level 4–6. I put my hand up.

'Yes, Tehzeeb.'

'Sir, why am I in the lower-middle paper? The highest I can get is only level 6.'

'That's the level the department feels comfortable putting you in. Now—'

'Sir, can I go in the level 5–7 paper at least?'

'No, you cannot. The decision is final. Now . . . '

Your dad's ass is final. They know I wanna be a doctor, so I have to get high marks in science. Proper piss-take.

---

* Obviously I meant councillor.

To make it worse, I was in geography, yeah, and Deela, this nice girl in our year, asked to borrow a pencil, so I gave her one and then Hassim goes really loudly,

'Ooooh, Terry fancies Deela! Oooooooooh.'

It was SO embarrassing.

'NO I DON'T!'

I went red, Deela went red. The whole class laughed. I was well pissed off at Hassim.

'Shut up, you boojo bastard. I don't fancy her.' I fancy Halima and Fiona. I didn't say that part.

And then he goes, 'Terry, man, she's the female you. You should go out with her.'

Everyone laughed again.

I looked at Deela. She was just looking down, bechari*. But for a second I hated her, even though it wasn't her fault. She looks nothing like me! Yes, she's short. Yes, she wears glasses. Yes, she's clever. Yes, she's quite cute. But why would I fancy someone who looks like me? I might as well shag a mirror then, innit? Proper daft guy, man.

Wednesday 14th May

This new kid started in our school today and they put him in our tutor group. His name is Christopher and he's German. I don't mean his parents are from Germany. He's not German like how I'm Pakistani. He was born in Germany.

Ms Williams said he has to sit with us lot, because me, Shibz and Hassim do German. He seemed quiet and shy, so I thought I'd say something first.

'*Wie heißt du?*'

'Christopher,' he said quietly. We could barely hear him.

'*Woher kommen Sie?*' Hassim goes.

'*Deutschland.*'

That's what Germans call Germany. I think it's weird that they call it that but we don't. Surely we should just call it what they call it? They call England England, not Shermany or something completely different.

We already knew he was from Germany, and under pressure we couldn't think of the German word for town or city or village, so we started discussing it. Was does French, so he was no help at all – and then I said to Hassim, 'I bet it's a shit town.'

And Christopher goes, IN ENGLISH, 'I'm from Frankfurt.'

'Eintracht Frankfurt!' Was shouted, so excited that he recognised a word.

I wouldn't have said '*I bet it's a shit town*' if I knew Christopher could speak English.

Afterwards I said to Hassim, 'Why the hell did Ms Williams sit him next to us and not Christian Frankland? They have very similar first names.'

And Hassim pointed out, 'Christian's surname is very nearly the same as where Christopher is from. Frankland . . . Frankfurt.'

She's so dumb. They would've had loads to talk about!

I wonder if there's Pakistanis in Germany, or if we're the first brown people Christopher's ever seen and spoken to in his life. I don't know how to ask that in German.

Thursday 29th May

Today was really emotional. Pai Shehzad would've been twenty today. It was his second birthday that he's not been here for.

Like last year, his mum, Poupoh Waliyat, invited us all to their house for a big khatam*.

I was looking at his handsome face on a picture on the wall in the front room and I still find it so hard to believe that anyone would kill him.

Taubah*.

It's still so painful, I can't even imagine 1 per cent of what Poupoh Waliyat and Uncle Iqbal must feel every day.

Friday 6th June

I fully messed up today. I feel well bad.

It's Christopher's last day with us in our school. We were talking to him in tutor group and we were asking loads of questions. Shibz asked him what his parents do, and without hesitating Christopher said, 'Meine Mutter und Vater ist kaputt.'

And ... And I burst out laughing.

Kasam, I couldn't stop. Not because I thought it was funny that his mum and dad were dead. It's just ... kaputt is a really funny word.

Luckily, just as he said it, I must've realised it looked well bad, and I put my head in my arms on the desk, but my shoulders and body were moving up and down. Shibz tried to cover for me and said, 'Oh, he's crying because he's sad.'

But Christopher knew and he goes, 'No, he's hehe hehehe.'

Which made me laugh even more!

To try and change the subject Was brought up how to say 'science' in German. Basically, because I do German and Was does French, I say German is better and easier and he says French is better and easier. To figure it out, a while ago we did a test to compare different words. After a few words, it was a draw and then he got me when we compared how to say science.

In German, it's Naturwissenschaft. He found that really funny. He keeps saying it wrong on purpose: every time he shouts 'NATIONAL BISSEN SHAFT' and then starts laughing.

When I asked him, 'Well how do you say it in French, then?', he goes, 'Science.' But in a weird accent. Anyway, it's easier in French.

So, to change the subject Was asked Christopher how to say science in German and of course I immediately started laughing more because all I could think about was Was saying 'NATIONAL BISSEN SHAFT'. I think he asked him on purpose because he knew it would make me laugh even more and make me look like even more of a kameenah*.

Christopher said, '*Wissenschaft*.' Heh?

At that point I stopped laughing and lifted my head from my arms. I had tears rolling down my cheeks, which hopefully made him think I was crying, and I said, 'Isn't it *Naturwissenschaft*?'

And he said, 'No, that's natural science. Just science is *Wissenschaft*.'

'In your face, Was!' Then Was rightly pointed out, '*Wissenschaft* is still harder to say than *science*!' Fair enough.

Was, Shibz and Hassim gave me full baist for that. Me getting baist cheered Christopher up and he'd obviously learnt the rules of baist, because he took my pen from the table and put it in his pocket.

I don't think Christopher and me are gonna be pen pals.

Which reminds me, I haven't replied to my pen pal for nearly a year. Ah, I'm sure he's fine.

Sunday 8th June

Exams start tomorrow. I've been revising really hard. InshAllah* I get good scores on everything! Especially science. I really wanna prove them teachers wrong!

I'm not gonna write in my diary during school days for the next two weeks. I think that's fair because my exams are more important.

Saturday 14th June

It's been a really strange week.

My three exams, English, maths and science, have been really good.

But . . .

On Monday, on the way home from school, me and Was were walking up Buncer Lane. We were just about to turn the corner on to Livingstone Road when a police car drove past and Was shouted out 'PIGS!' I honestly can't believe him sometimes.

The police car screeched in the road and it started turning around, I'm staring at it like this isn't a life-ruining situation for me, Was grabs me and we start running, we turn the corner onto Livingstone Road and run. Was was ahead of me and turned right on to the steps that lead down to French Road. Just as I'm about to get there, the police car pulls up and a policeman shouts 'STOP!'

And like an idiot I stop. Shit.

The policeman calls me over and asks me why I shouted 'pigs'. I say, 'I didn't.'

He goes, 'Where's your friend?'

'He's . . . he's gone.' I'm not gonna be a grass.

'Right. Let me ask you: if you or a member of your family got hurt, who would you call?'

'A . . . an ambulance.' I wasn't even trying to be cheeky, it's just what came out.

'All right. If you got burgled, then?' He said proper annoyed.

I said the police. He said, 'You should show more respect to the police, then.' I said okay, then he let me go.

I caught up with Was a bit further down the road. He couldn't believe I didn't get in more trouble. Neither could I.

On Wednesday, the news said that the government is gonna ban all handguns in the UK. It's because of that crazy guy who killed all those kids in that school in a town called Dunblane in Scotland. That's proper crazy. Scary and mental. I can't imagine how scary that must have been for everyone in that school that day. *Taubah*. May Allah grant all them kids Jannat* and give those kids' families patience.

On Friday . . . the court . . . I don't understand. The court dropped the case against Pai Shehzad's killers. I don't get it. The *Lancashire Telegraph* said summat about the solicitor of the guy who murdered Pai Shehzad doing a really bad job and so that means he's been cleared of the murder. THAT DOESN'T MAKE ANY SENSE. What the hell, man!

PIGS.

Friday 20th June

Kasameh*, when I turned the page and realised I'd finished the last question I breathed out big time. I turned around and looked at Hassim; he was still writing. He looked up at me and I turned my head to let him know I was done. He smiled and nodded and then turned back and carried on scribbling away.

'TIME!'

I pushed my chair back and gave Hassim a high-five.

As I left the hall I heard Was's voice somewhere ahead of me: 'FREEDOM!'

I laughed because no one else had watched *Braveheart* at Wadi Ammi's last Sunday. (Was is sleeping next door at Wadi Ammi's at the moment. Baaji's in hospital, so he's staying there to make sure she's not alone at night.)

Sunday 29th June

My first game of the season today for Whalley Range Cubs. That's right, I'm a stupid Cub now. Not a Tiger.

Basically, because everyone wanted to play for Dad, he ended up having thirty boys at training, so he decided to make two teams, Whalley Range Tigers (A team) and Whalley Range Cubs (B team).

Even more baisti, I started on the bench. I came on with twenty minutes to go and did nothing. We lost. I was pissed off. I thought Dad started this team so me and my cousins could play together.

I know I'm a bit angry today, but I obviously wasn't as angry as Mike Tyson. Bloody hell. In his fight last night, he bit the other guy's ear off! HIS EAR! HE BIT IT OFF! What a mad guy. I get that if you're losing a fight, is a bit of baisti, but you can't bite someone's ear off, man!

Tuesday 1st July

On the news today it said that we handed Hong Kong back to China in a big ceremony. I was saying to Hassim that I don't really understand why we had Hong Kong in the first place. On the map they showed it's basically next to China. He said it didn't make sense either. Innit? Is like if China owned the Isle of Man. Why?

Anyway, Hong Kong is independent now, or back to China. I didn't understand properly.

Saturday 5th July

I'm in love. Forget Fiona or Halima or Madhuri Dixit.

Martina Hingis.

Ay ay ay ay ay.

She's sixteen, so only two years older than me, and she won

Wimbledon! Against proper grown-ups. What a hero. Her legs, man. Her face. I love her, kasam.

Sunday 6th July

In honour of my new future wife Martina Hingis, I'm gonna play well good in footy today. I mean, she's sporty, so she'll want a husband who's a bit sporty as well, innit. I'm going to the match now, I just wanted to write this before for good luck.

Update: Maybe Martina Hingis will want someone a bit different to her. She's sporty, so she probably wants a husband who's clever and has a good job, like a doctor.

Tuesday 8th July

The last two weeks of school are the best. Is a proper doss. Today we went on a school trip to Camelot! Miss gave us maps before we got on the coach, so by the time we got there I had the whole day planned for us. When I say us, it was just me, Boojo and Was. Shibz is scared of rides so he didn't come, which I think is crazy because he's so tough.

What a top time man. *Kasam.* I LOVE theme parks and going on all the big rides. Me, Was and Hassim went on the Beast, Dragon Flyer, Sorcerer, the Log Flume, Pirate Ship, Dungeons of Doom, the Rack and Excalibur. But the best was Tower of Terror. Ufft. In the queue, Hassim dared us, 'If you can do the whole ride no-handed I'll buy you a candyfloss.'

That was a challenge. Was and I looked at each other, then looked at the big loop-the-loop and said, 'Go on then.'

'But if you don't do it, you have to buy me one.'

Was said, 'Cheeky boojo bastard,' but I know how to make a deal:

'Only if you do it no-handed too.' Fair's fair, I thought.

We eventually got on (we had to wait longer, because we wanted to sit at the front). And ... well ... we each bought our own candyfloss. Even Was couldn't do the whole ride no-handed. After setting the challenge, Hassim was actually the first to put his hands down, then me when we went down the big slope and then Was on the loop-the-loop. Chicken shits, all three of us!

Miss said that we had to be back on the coach at 5 p.m. Exact.

At 4.50 p.m. we could see that everyone was headed to the exit, so we looked at each other and it's like we read each other's minds.

Was goes, 'If everyone's going out, that means there's no queues!'

We ran to the closest ride, the Log Flume, where there was only a small queue, so we got to go on it again! We got fully soaked!

After the ride we legged it well hard all the way to the coach. Lucky for us, Dawn was desperate for the toilet and she came back at just the same time we did. I think Miss knew what we did because our clothes were wet, but we couldn't have left any quicker, because of Dawn, so we got away with it.

Yes! We're like the A-Team. I love it when a plan comes together.

Tuesday 15th July

Today was my last-ever drama class. I don't know how to feel about it. Because I like drama a lot. It's really fun. We get to do games like wink murder and boppity-bop-bop-bop and energy ball.

Plus, I think I'm quite good at it. Today, there was a thing we were doing in class where everyone is sat on a train, the train sets off and then ten seconds later it crashes, and everyone has to act like the train crashed, basically throw themselves about. All the chairs were lined up in a row like train seats and everyone in the class sat in the seats, waiting for the train to leave. I didn't take a seat. I stood at the back of the drama room, pacing up and down pretending that I was looking for the train. When the teacher goes, *The train has set off*, I 'ran' after the train but realised I missed it and looked really gutted, but then the train crashed and I fell to the floor and looked up in horror at the 'train crash' and then looked up towards the sky and thanked God that I missed the train. The teacher said that what I did was something called 'imp rov', and that it was wicked.

But that was my last drama class, because basically, for GCSEs everyone has to study English, maths, science, IT, German (or French) and RE. And then in our subject choices for GCSE, we have to choose:

- one technology subject: graphics, woodwork, electronics, food or textiles;
- geography or history; and
- one from art, business studies, PE or drama.

I chose graphics for my technology; me, Shibz and Hassim decided to choose history because we always get better marks than in geography. And then for the last one, I hate art and PE, so that's easy. It was between drama and business studies. I do love drama, but what's the point in that? I'm never ever gonna use drama when I grow up. I'm not gonna be an actor[*] or summat.

Hassim said maybe one day I'll want to open up my own GP surgery, so actually business studies might be more useful. That's a good point. Hassim is more business-minded, so we're doing business studies. Basically, the lesson there is, don't do the thing you love, do the thing that is most sensible for when you grow up.

We still have to do PE, but it won't be for a GCSE, it'll just be for the pervert teachers.[†]

---

[*] Lol.

[†] Note from lawyer: they were not perverts. As far as I know.

Wednesday 16th July

Ms Williams gave us our results, same as usual. An envelope with our name on it. I couldn't wait to open mine.

Was said we should all open each other's. He has some proper crap ideas, but before I knew it, Hassim had snatched my envelope: 'Top idea.' So I ended up with Shibz's, Shibz had Hassim's, Hassim had Was's and Hassim gave Was mine.

'Okay, go!'

We opened the envelopes.

'Aw shit, Terry.' I tried to snatch mine back, but Was held it out of reach and said we all had to 'read it one by one'.

It was so painful.

'Okay, Shibz, you got 6 6 6. Shaitan would be very happy with those results,' I said.

'Shut up, man. Don't say that.' Shibz took his paper back and told Hassim what he got: 'Boojo, you clever basket, you got 7 6 6.'

'Wicked.' Hassim didn't even bother to check. I wish I could be as relaxed as him. 'Was, you got 6 6 5.' Was didn't even react to his.

'Terry, you got 6—'

No. I wanted more than that.

'5 5.'

Full baist. Kasam. That's shit.

Shibz and Hassim were quiet. They must've looked at my face. I was about to cry.

'I'm JOKING, yaraa,' Was said. 'Don't cry.' He gave me my paper back.

I looked down. '7 7 6!'

'Well done, you speccy four-eyed swot.' Was smiled.

I got level 7s in English and maths and level 6 in science. I was really happy with that, but actually still a bit pissed off.

'See, if they let me sit the higher, or even the upper intermediate paper in science I would've got three 7s, man. It's not fair.'

I looked up and they were looking at me like I was daft.

'Yaraa, it says here the average for science in our whole year was 4,' Shibz told me, looking at his paper.

'That's well shit!' I said a bit harshly.

'Exactly. You did good. Chill out. The doctor dream's still on.' Thanks, Shibz.

'Yeah, you'll still be a brain surgeon, man.' Hassim always says that, even though I've never said I want to be a brain surgeon. Just a surgeon.

The average in our year was 5 for English, 4 in maths and 4 in science. At least we all did better than that.

Ammi hugged me and said 'Shaabash*, puttar!' when I showed her. I love getting hugs from Ammi and her telling me well done.

'Just make sure you keep working hard for your GCSEs too.'

'I will, Ammi.'

'Promise?'

'Jee, Ammi.'

I can have a nice six weeks' holidays now. Get in.

Thursday 17th July

I think I spoke too soon.

'Oi, chill out,' I shouted to Hassim from my side of the pitch. We were playing footy in the bottom fields, just near the boundary of the pavilion.

I noticed that Shibz and Hassim were playing a bit rough with each other, in how they were tackling. It's a dinnertime game between friends, not the Merseyside derby. It must have been the fourth time they had come together in a tackle.

'What the fuck's your problem, dickhead?' shouted Shibz as he pushed Hassim.

'Come on then,' Hassim shouted back.

And before anyone could get over to them, they started wrestling each other.

I was well shocked. Friends shouldn't fight friends.

They fell to the ground and they were throwing mukkay* at each other's faces.

Was was closest to them and he pulled Shibz off Hassim and let him go. We thought that was the end of it but then, as Hassim was getting up off the ground, Shibz booted him in the back of the head.

I heard the crack.

Was grabbed Shibz again.

Hassim went down clutching the back of his head with both hands. It sounded really bad. I ran over to him, but he pushed me away. 'Fuck off.'

What the hell did I do?

It sounded worse than it was, I think, because he slowly got up and walked off, and there was no blood, thank God. He was clearly crying, but.

'Boojo, are you all right?' I shouted after him, but he didn't even look back.

'Why did you kick him, man?' Was asked Shibz, and then he ran after Hassim.

'Where are you going?' Shibz asked him.

'To make sure he doesn't bloody grass on you.'

Clever.

'And to make sure he's all right,' he added.

That was the end of the game. I asked Shibz if he was all right, but he didn't wanna talk about it. I think he felt bad.

At tutor group, Hassim sat on his own.

Was told me and Shibz that he's upset but he's not gonna grass on Shibz. Good. Good.

Even though Hassim is my best friend in school, I'm glad Shibz won the fight because he's my cousin and you always have to support your family first. But I do wish they hadn't fought. I felt proper tight on Hassim.

I caught his eye and smiled at him, which probably wasn't the right response, looking back at it.

I wonder what it'll be like tomorrow. It's the last day of term.

Friday 18th July

When Was, Shibz and me came into the tutor group in the morning Hassim was already there, sat on his own. I went and sat next to him as usual, and Shibz and Was sat behind us. But he ignored me. He ignored us all. So I just turned around and started talking to Shibz and Was.

In our first lesson, German it was, I sat next to Hassim and knew we would have to talk to each other, because you always have to practise your phrases with the person next to you.

I stuck my hand out to shake his hand. He didn't take it.

'In Islam you can't be cross with your Muslim brother for more than three days,' I said.

'It hasn't been three days.'

Shit, that's true.

'Yeah, but it's the last day of term today, so if you leave without being my friend today, I won't see you for six weeks!'

He thought about it for a second and then he shook my hand. Thank God.

I asked him if he was okay. He said he was.

I'm glad.

Shibz made friends with him again as well in afternoon tutor group. They both said sorry to each other.

Hopefully everything will go back to normal after the holidays.

Wednesday 23rd July

Oh my God.

I scored one of the best goals I've ever scored in my life today. The only problem was, it was an own goal.

We were in training and it was a practice game, Tigers v Cubs. I was playing as a defender and my team had a corner, the Tigers cleared it, basically Hassim booted it out way over my head into my half, so I'm now running after the ball facing my goal, I'm the last man and I could feel the Tigers' striker (Nasser) catching up to me. Whatever happens, I can't let him get the ball, so what I tried to do was boot the ball out for a corner. What I ended up doing was booting it into the top corner from thirty yards out.

I mean, it was a Tony Yeboah.

I felt like celebrating. It was such a good goal. Shiry dived for it full stretch and couldn't get near it.

Everyone started laughing. I started laughing.

But the best bit was Dad said I can start up front on Sunday in the cup final.

Sunday 27th July

True to his word, Dad started me up front today. In the final of the cup. Tigers v Cubs. The Dad derby. I didn't even have one chance, let alone score a thirty-yard screamer into the top corner.

Speccy asked Dad who he was supporting. He goes, 'I don't care, I can't lose today.'

I could, but. And I did. Tigers won 3–1.

Was scored a bicycle kick. It was crazy. I was behind the goal, after I got subbed off, so had the best view. It'll be proper sad if Was doesn't get to be a professional football player. But Dad says that the scouts for the teams don't come to watch Asians play football. That's not fair. How are Asians meant to be foot-ballers then?

There's so many players who play in our league that could be pros, I think: Was, Shibz, Sunnoo, Zamal, Shaky.

I wish someone from Rovers or United or Liverpool, or even Accrington Stanley (Who are they? Exactly) would come and watch them play.

Wednesday 6th August

I hate this town sometimes.

Hadi is my neighbour. I practise footy with him across the road from our houses nearly every week. Hadi always goes in nets which is good, because it's let me get really good at shooting. He's two years younger than me. He was born in Pakistan, but came to England when he was small, I think under someone else's passport or his uncle adopted him, I'm not really sure about the full story.

Anyway, we thought we'd play somewhere else today, the little park behind Abid's shop on Devonport Road. It's only five minutes from where we live.

We were just minding our own business when this group of goreh kids, about seven or eight of 'em, came into the park and ran over to us. I could see what was about to happen, so I told Hadi to leg it. They surrounded me and started pushing me. I fell on the floor and they started kicking and punching me.

'Fuckin' smelly Paki!'

It didn't really hurt me that much because I curled into a ball and covered myself up properly with my hands, but I started to cry, because I was upset. Sometimes I cry more when I get upset than when I'm physically hurt. I used to be a proper cry-baby when I was small, but I'm a bit better now. But at least crying was sort of useful today because one of the goreh saw I was upset and he stopped his friends from hitting me.

'That's enough.' He picked me up and told me to go home.

I walked away feeling sad, shame and sore. Just as I was about to turn the corner, I really wanted to shout FUCK OFF YOU FUCKING BASTARDS! But I was too scared so I never.

Hadi asked me if I was all right. I nodded my head, but I was still too upset and ashamed to speak. I'm not upset at him. I'm glad he ran. There was no point both of us getting twatted. Plus he's smaller than me, so I had to protect him.

Thursday 21st August

Baji Rosey got her GCSE results today. She got mainly Bs and Cs. Her results are all right, but they're not that good. I feel sorry for her. I think if Ammi didn't leave her in Pakistan for three years when she was twelve, she could've got well good grades because she's really clever. But she basically missed all of high school so she could go to a madrassa* in Pakistan. But she came back last year, so she didn't complete her Islamic education there and she didn't get a full education here. What a waste of time.

I proper missed her when she wasn't here. Even though we used to fight a lot when we were small, she's my big sister and we used to tell each other everything and watch all the same cartoons together and stuff. I love Saeeda and Zaheer, but they're well smaller than me, so it's not the same.

Sometimes I think our parents don't make the best decisions.

I feel sorry for Baji Rosey, and Saeeda and Saira and Yasmeen actually. And for Baji Shanaz and Saddia, and Baji Noreen, Shaheen and Asma, and Baji Siema too. We boys, we can go and play outside, go and mess around with our friends whenever we want. We can wear whatever we want as well. Shorts, T-shirts, whatever. But the girls in my family, it's proper strict for them.

They can't go out unless it's for school or college or work. They can't just meet up with their friends and go to town or cinema or the park. They all wear shalwar kameezes* at home and the only time they wear Western clothes is for school or work. They do all, or at least most, of the housework. They basically have no freedom to make their own choices or mistakes or do what they want. That's tight.

I know the older people go on about izzat* and all that, but actually in Islam if a boy makes a mistake or a girl makes a mistake, is the exact same gunnah. It's not more for girls or less for boys. It's the same. Because Allah created us equal. So, this izzat stuff is just in our thinking and we can change that.

Some families don't even let their girls go college or work. So at least we're not that bad.

Sometimes I think, I should help out with housework … but then no one asks me, and housework is boring. So that means I must prefer to be lazy than I prefer to have a fairer world.

That's well bad.

Saturday 23rd August

I love Waves, they've got a water slide that loops out of the building and then back in again and a wave machine that comes on every half an hour. It's such a top place.

I actually love going swimming and that's all thanks to Shibz's dad. I love Uncle. He was like my dad growing up. Because he's Naani Ammi's brother, he would take me everywhere he took Shibz, Shiry and Muj and he'd watch out for me, always making sure I was okay.

He made sure I learnt how to swim. Every weekend, he would take us all swimming at Belpers, which is nowhere near as fun as Waves. Except when they have the inflatable obstacle course on. Then it is.

I remember when I went swimming for the first time in junior school, and in the very first lesson I got my width and length certificates. All the other Asian kids looked at me like I was a traitor! Haha. I was the only Asian kid who could swim, and because I'm so shit at every sport it was proper confusing for everyone.

Uncle Ashfaq taught me how to eat roti properly as well. 'You've got to make a pipe. Make a pipe, scoop up the lavan and get it down your throat. That's it, Terrence.'

I like it when he calls me Terrence. He's the only person in the whole world who calls me that.

Uncle wasn't with us today, which meant we could mess about. Did we? Is the molbi saab a Muslim?

Today, me, Shiry, Shibz, Jaffer and Muj broke the rules. AT THE SAME TIME!

We were queuing up for the water slide. The lifeguards are really strict and you're only allowed to go in one at a time, with a twenty-second gap between each person.

But we made a plan on the way up the stairs. Shibz was the director: 'Muj, you go first, budge up a bit, then you Shiry, then Jaffer, then you Terry and then I'll jump in last.'

I mean, it sounded fun, but it was a very bad idea.

It was pandemonium. Arms and legs flying everywhere as we went round and round, eventually falling on top of each other into the pool in the bottom. OUCH.

Muj got it the worst, because he was at the front.

As we got out, the lifeguard shouted at us. He looked at Jaffer, who's only nine, and then shouted at us even more and we got told to leave straight away.

Worth it, but!

Sunday 24th August

It was the last game of the season today. We were playing the bottom team, and we thrashed them! 8–0.

And I scored! It was a tap in, but still. I'm really happy. That means I scored in the first game of last season and the last game of this season.

I might not be good at football, but damn I'm good at winding people up and distracting them. Tigers were playing Audley and I was on the sidelines. Some of our friends from school play for Audley, like Ebrahim. I kept shouting from the side: 'IBBY!! IBBY!! IBBY!!' Then, when he would look over at me, I'd shout: 'CONCENTRATE ON THE GAME, IBBY!!' It was well funny.

Tigers won the league! They deserved it. I'm really happy for Was, Shibz and Hassim and the rest of the team, and Dad of course. Dad made me join in the celebrations, which I was happy about. We train together after all.

Thursday 28th August

I'm heartbroken. My bike got stolen today.

I lent it to Shiry to help with his paper round and he left it outside the newsagents to go inside and get the newspapers, and when he came outside it was gone.

We phoned the police and gave them a description, but they said is very unlikely that they'll be able to find it.

I loved that bike!

Dad got it for me for my tenth birthday. It's the best present I've ever got.

So many days I used to cycle to school with Was and sometimes other people like Hassim, or Shibz and Shiry who would join us at the bottom of Bromley Street. I remember we used to go through the gate at the top of north fields, riding through the last bit of woods, then cycling down the field and jumping over the little edge onto the bottom field, then locking our bikes up in the staff car park and saying hi to the teachers.

I used to ride it to football practice as well. It used to be all the way uphill, so on the way there it was well hard! But on the way back it was all downhill! And I used to be able to go from the top of the East Park Road entrance of Corpy Park all the way to the pond with no hands, leaning my body left or right to do the turns, like those guys who race the motorbikes really fast. Was taught me how to do it.

I remember when I went on that big twenty-kilometre bike ride with my cousins. It took us ages, but it was so much fun, riding along the canals laughing and joking about what if one of us fell in and if there were crocodiles in there.

I'm gonna miss her.

Sunday 31st August

Taubah.

Princess Diana died today. I'm really sad. She was so nice.

It was a really bad car accident in Paris. Her boyfriend Dodi died as well.

Ammi's really upset. She proper loves Diana. Obviously, everyone does – like Tony Blair said today, she's the People's Princess – but Ammi especially loves her. I think because Diana got married to Prince Charles one year after Ammi came to England, and they're round about the same age, so she was part of Ammi's life in England from the beginning.

It's so sad cos she's got two small sons, William (only one year older than me) and Harry (only one year younger than me). I don't know what I'd do if Ammi died. It makes me cry to just even think about it.

RIP Princess Diana.

Monday 1st September

I was well nervous before I told him.

'*Hafiz saab. Aaj mera akhri dyara veh masjid vich*': Hafiz saab, it's my last day at madrassa today.

School starts again tomorrow and it's the start of my GCSEs. I have to concentrate on them to get top marks. Also, I've basically learnt everything now: I know how to read the Qur'an; I know all my kalimeh*; I know how to read namaaz; I know twelve surahs and Ayatul Kursi* off by heart.

I didn't tell Hafiz saab that. I did what everyone my age does:

'*Ammi neh akyeh vi huun kaar rehne*': Mum said I have to stay home. I blamed my parents.

To be honest, I'm glad I don't have to go mosque class any more; gives me more free time. But part of me is gonna miss it. I remember the first time I ever went to mosque. I was six and I had no idea what was going on. Towards the end of the class, the molbi saab did a quiz and he asked a few questions, one of which was: 'Which people have to read namaaz?'

And I shouted '*Waday bandeh!*': big people (adults). Oh, how everyone laughed. I mean the correct answer is Muslims, but also, I wasn't exactly wrong.

Ten minutes later I fell into a squat toilet. I've been scared of them ever since.

Tuesday 2nd September

First day of school. First day of Year 10. First year of upper school! Good news and bad news.

Two good newses:

1. It was such a nice sunny day. I've noticed that it's always sunny the first week of the new school year. Like Allah saying, *I know you have to go back to school but have a nice time on your first day at least.*
2. I'm gonna be with Hassim for the next two years. That means we'll have been in the same tutor group every year of school. That's why he's my best friend. I've missed him.

But also, two bad newses:

1. Was and Shibz have moved to Mrs Watson's tutor group. At least they're together, which is good.
2. Me and Hassim have stayed with Ms Williams. Instead of getting a new tutor, she's moved with us to South Building. It would've been nice to have a fun tutor. Like Mrs Blake or Miss Rose. No, actually, Miss Rose would be too distracting – she's too fit.

In English today, Mrs Place told us that the school is doing an experiment. For the first time ever, and only for top-set English, boys and girls are gonna be split up. So there's gonna be a top-set English boys' class and a top-set English girls' class.

Mrs Place told us that to get the best grades we 'all need to read more'.

'What should I read, miss?' I asked her.

'Newspapers.'

'What, the *Sun*?' Jack said for a joke. We all laughed, because we knew that he was talking about page 3, where there bes a naked model girl there every day. Proper rude, that, because anyone can just pick it up. It's really weird.

'Obviously not the *Sun*. Broadsheets – the big newspapers on the bottom shelf of the newsagents, with the small writing and long words,' she said.

She gave us some examples and then told us that *The Times* is only 10p on Mondays. So every Monday now I'm gonna buy *The Times* and read it.

She also said to me that I need to take greater care in my writing and use a wider vocabulary, explaining that I ought to make use of a thesaurus to assist me. Thus I shall endeavour to record my diary less carelessly, ensuring it showcases the breadth of my lexicon,^ as well as being more grammatically sound.

If I can be asked.

^ I thought it was quite ironic that I had to look in my thesaurus for a different word for vocabulary.

Saturday 6th September

It was Lady Princess Diana's funeral today.

It looked like the whole world was there. It's so sad, man.

It was proper heart-breaking to see William and Harry walking behind their mum's coffin. Especially with Prince Charles and their racist grandad, Prince Philip.

EVERYONE knows that Prince Philip and the Queen made MI5 kill Diana because she was going to marry a Muslim, and there's no way that when Prince William becomes king his mum can be Muslim and he might have little Muslim brothers and sisters. NO WAY.

Also, in my opinion, there is no way that Prince Charles didn't know what his mum and dad were up to. Even if he didn't agree with it, he should have stopped them. So when I saw them all walking with Prince William and Prince Harry, pretending to be sad, it made me proper angry.*

It was a nice funeral, though, so many famous people from all over the world were there: Tom Cruise from *Mission: Impossible*, that famous opera singer Pavarotti and Tom Hanks from *Turner & Hooch*.

Then this guy sang a song, which was all right. Something about a candle in the wind, which is weird because I would expect a candle to not be lit in the wind. Maybe I didn't understand it, but I was a bit distracted because the whole time I was thinking, *why is this guy singing, when Pavarotti is right there?* Which is like playing Darren Huckerby when Alan Shearer is sat on the bench.

Obviously, we don't have singing at Muslim funerals, but if there was, I would want Michael Jackson to sing at my funeral. Or Baloo the Bear.

Mum's still really sad about it. She gave me a big hug when they showed Prince Harry crying. And I squeezed her hard because I know how much Princess Diana meant to her. She was truly the People's Princess.

Monday 8th September

I bought *The Times* newspaper today for 10p. Obviously a lot of it was about Diana and how much the funeral cost and stuff like that.

There was nothing in there about how the Queen and Prince Philip killed her, which I thought was strange, because there were a lot of words, but none of them were used for that.

---

* Obviously, this was my opinion as a child and there is no evidence that the royal family were involved in Diana's death. Nor do I believe this now as a grown-up 👀.

It's weird being in upper school. The Year 7s look SO tiny. It's weird that that was me three years ago, and now in three months I'm gonna be a prefect and they're all going to look up to me. I can't wait.

Sunday 5th October

I feel like my whole life has changed.

So, on Tuesday, Hassim brought a cassette to school.

'Here, listen to this.'

I don't have a portable cassette player, so this was very exciting. I put the headphones on and Hassim pressed play.

I'd never heard anything like this before:

My ambitionz as a ridah!

'What is it?'

'Rap music. From America.'

'They're swearing, man!'

'Innit. It's well top.'

It was ... Oh my God.

He let me listen to the cassette all dinnertime. He called it a mixtape. I didn't know what that is.

'Is when there's all different songs from different people on one cassette. On this you've got Tupac, Dr. Dre, Snoop Doggy Dogg, Ice Cube and Biggie.'

That's what I love about Hassim: he knows a lot about real-life stuff, but he never makes me feel stupid when I don't know. He just explains it nicely. Also, he's really generous. He knows he has more money than me, but he never rubs it in or anything.

'Borrow me this cassette, innit, Boojo? Kasam I'll bring it back tomorrow.' I thought I could copy it overnight on the tape player.

Hassim laughed.

'Terry, this one's yours. I copied it for you.'

That's why he's my best friend!

I have to be a bit careful when I'm listening to it at home because I don't own headphones and there's so much 'fuck this' and 'bitch', and a lot of times they say the N-word as well. Mum wouldn't like it at all.

This is my favourite music now. I love how angry and real it is. Sometimes I feel like that, but I don't know how to say it, so I just end up swearing at the person or situation I'm angry with in my head.

> *Listen, Ms Williams, you can't tell me what to do.*
> *If you do, then you'll have to deal with a big poo.*

Is that rap? Did I just do rapping?

Wednesday 8th October

This evening, Shahid, Sohail and Shabaz came around to play.

Their mum (Pua Said, Ammi's aunty) and dad (Uncle Zafar) were sat with Ammi and Abu in the living room, and we were in the front room playing on my Mega Drive.

Even though they're technically Mum's cousins, it feels like they're my cousins because they're more my age, not old like her.

I don't see them as much as I see Shibz and Shiry, or Was, but I like them a lot. Especially Shahid. He's always so nice. He's the eldest, about twenty, I think.

I don't know if this is weird, but one of the reasons I like their whole family is because they look different to the rest of us. Pua Said has the same skin colour as us lot, but Uncle Zafar has darker skin. Three of the brothers, Shahid, Shabaz and Harun, have darker skin, and Siema, Halima and Sohail have lighter skin, but they're all one family. I don't know why, but I like that. I think it's because it doesn't matter if you look different, if you have lighter skin or darker skin, it doesn't mean you can't be family with each other.

Anyway, we had loads of fun. We took turns playing *Mortal Kombat II*, winner stays on. I was the best, but that's because they have a Nintendo and I have a Mega Drive, so I'm more used to the joypad.

At one point, I thought I heard shouting coming from the living room, but before I could figure it out Shahid started asking me loads of questions about *Mortal Kombat* and who my favourite character is. Johnny Cage, obviously.

Now that I think about it, maybe Shahid and his brothers only came around to make sure I was distracted from the grown-ups arguing.

I'm being *cynical*. I just looked it up in my thesaurus.

Actually, if that is what happened, then that's very nice of them. Especially Shahid. Because he's older, he could've just stayed at home, instead of spending his evening with a fourteen-and-a-half-year-old.

Monday 20th October

There was a big argument in German today.

It was group work and me and Hassim were on a table with Noddi and Christian.

Noddi asked me who my favourite singer is.

'Tupac, man.'

'Rappers don't count. It's not singing.'

'I think it counts. It's still saying words over music, innit?'

'Okay. But I mean actual singers. Fine, Tupac's the best rapper, if you want.'

Hassim said, 'Michael Jackson, then. Easy.'

'Yeah. I agree with Hassim. Michael Jackson,' I said.

'What do you think of Freddie Mercury? He's mine.'

I looked at Hassim and he looked as blank as I did.

'We don't know who that is, Christian.'

'Oh my God!' Christian said. 'No Way. Come on, lead singer of Queen?'

'Bro, I have no idea.' I said that because I had no idea, and what sort of name is Queen?

'You'll 100 per cent know their songs. "We Will Rock You", "We are the Champions"?' You've definitely heard of them!'

Me and Hassim started singing 'We are the champions of the world!'

'Plus he's Asian, you know.'

I feel like Christian should've started with that information, to make me and Hassim interested.

'Is he fuck,' Noddi said.

'He is, Nodds. His parents are Indian.'

'No fuckin' way.' Noddi wasn't having it.

'Yeah man, his real name's Farooq.'

I said, 'Ha! I go to mosque with a guy called Farooq!' I do.

'He's still not better than Michael Jackson.' Hassim wasn't budging.

Noddi said, 'Michael Jackson fucks kids, though.'

'WOAH!'

That's when the argument broke out. Because first of all there's no proof that he did, and even if he did, that didn't make him any less good at singing, did it?

Then Faiza, who's my favourite girl in the school, I think because she's the only other Asian I know with divorced parents, goes, 'Well Freddie Mercury died of Aids.'

I didn't really know what that had to do with anything, to be honest, and Hassim looked confused too, but Noddi goes, 'Okay, fair enough.'

'Who's your favourite singer then, Noddi?' I wanted to know now.

'The best ever. The one and only King of Rock 'n' Roll, Elvis Presley.'

Who? 'Who?'

Everyone laughed. But I was serious.

Faiza explained that he's one of the most famous singers ever, but he died a long time ago. Hassim knew who he was and so did Christian. Noddi was flabbergasted: 'Come on, man. Flares, big shiny hair, "Jailhouse Rock".' It didn't help. I have NO idea who this man is, or what any of those words mean.

Later I asked Shibz and Was, and they both knew who he was. Who the hell is this guy I've never heard of?

When I went home, I asked Ammi who Elvis Presley is, and she didn't know him either, which made me feel better. He can't be THAT famous, then.

I asked her who she thinks the best singer ever is and she said, 'Ustad Nusrat Fateh Ali Khan,' and I thought, fair enough. He actually probably is.

Who the fuck is Elvis Presley, though?

Wednesday 29th October

It's Saeeda's birthday. She grew up faster today than I would've liked.

I took her to library after school so she could get some books. She asked me what I think she should read, so I picked out my favourite Asterix and Obelix book for her, *Asterix the Gladiator*.

On the way home, we walked past Waves and I teased her that when the waves come out there bes sharks.

'No way.'

'Kasam. They haven't got teeth, but. They live underneath the swimming pool.'

'Woah.'

Kids are so daft! I love 'em.

We walked past Blackburn College, taking a shortcut through the college garden, and then we crossed the car park to get to Montague Street.

'Paijan, if the sharks don't have teeth, then how do they chew their food?'

'They ... they er—'

I was a bit distracted. On the other side of the car park, I could see these goreh, about six of them.

'They drink from a blender using a straw. Listen. Let's see who the faster walker is. Go! No slowing down.'

I just had a bad feeling.

'That's it. Go on. Faster if you can.'

She's only small, so she can't walk that fast.

'Oi!'

'Don't look up, Saeeda.'

'Oi! Listen, I wanna talk to youse.'

They had caught us up.

'What you got there, mate?'

We were surrounded. The main guy who was talking was taller than me. He had short brown hair and he looked really mean, like he hated me.

'I said, what you got there?'

'It's just library books. For my little sister.'

'Let us take a look, then?'

I didn't do anything. Suddenly, from behind, one of the other goreh grabbed the bag off my shoulder and tipped our books all out in the middle of the car park.

I desperately looked around, but there was nobody to help us. Saeeda started crying. I was so angry. And scared. The leader guy pushed me.

'Jump up and down, lad. I wanna hear how much money you've got in your pockets.'

'I haven't got any money.'

'I said fuckin' jump.'

I jumped up and down and he and his friends all started laughing. I didn't have any money for them to steal. He pretended he was gonna punch me, I flinched and then they all left while laughing some more.

I was well embarrassed. If they had done something worse I wouldn't have been able to protect Saeeda.

I picked the books up and put them back in the bag which she was now holding. I wiped her tears and told her, 'They're just bullies, okay? Don't tell Ammi. She'll just get upset and next time she won't let us come library. Okay?'

'Okay, paijan.'

'Good girl.' I patted her on the head and we carried on walking home.

'Those bullies were like sharks, paijan.'

'Yeah.'

Great white sharks. The most dangerous kind.

'But like the sharks at Waves, they were toothless.' She laughed.

She turned nine years old today and I'm so, so, so angry and upset that she had to see that.

Bitch motherfucking cunts.

Wednesday 5th November

Tonight was bonfire night and Ammi let me go to Randal Street to play with Was. They always have a massive bonfire in the park behind his house, and there bes loads of fireworks too.

I took some sparklers and a packet of rockets. The rockets didn't last long, but it was fun lighting them and then running for cover!

The bonfire was really big, and actually it's really hot even if you don't stand that close to it. It made me think of films where there bes a fire in a building and people run around the house tryna find their cat. No way. We were outside and the heat was too much. I can't imagine what that would feel like inside.

It was fun finding stuff to throw in the fire with Was. Loads of people dump stuff in the back alleys so we got it and put it on the bonfire. Some older boys were carrying a sofa and dumped it on the fire; it let off loads of sparks and everyone screamed. It was proper exciting.

At about ten we had to all leg it because at the top of the park (the park's on a slope, split over three levels) a guy had lit a 32-time repeater and the crazy guy was shooting at people like it was a gun.

Everyone went flying everywhere. Most people ran inside. I hid behind the railings at the bottom of the park but Was stayed so the guy could try and shoot him. I could see the back of his curly-haired head as the fireworks man aimed for him. Of course he dodged them all like he was in *Mission: Impossible*.

Was's explanation was that he was a distraction so everyone else could escape while the guy tried to get him. Okay, Tom Cruise.

Tuesday 18th November

I'm not even sure what happened, but I was leaving South Building with Haider, one of our main gang guys, to go North and we start taking the mick out of each other. For a joke, I called his graphics project shit, and before I knew it he pushed me to the floor really hard.

I got well angry. I stood up and went 'Come on then!' But, lucky for me, he started laughing and walked away.

I'm glad we didn't actually get into a fight because he would've twatted me, but I was surprised that I was brave enough to want to have a fight.

That's not like me.

I think it was because in that moment I got immediately angry like the Ultimate Warrior, but as soon as that feeling went I calmed down and didn't want to fight, like the Ultimate Worrier.

Sunday 23rd November

Today was the second anniversary of Pai Shehzad's death. It's still too painful to think about.

We had a big khatam at Uncle Iqbal and Poupoh Waliyat's house. We played a bit with Usman, Shehzad's little brother, who's three months older than Tanveer. He's proper massive now and Shibz said he thinks he's gonna be a big lad, mashAllah*.

They're not our cousins, but really close family friends. So they feel like family.

I still don't fully understand what happened the day Pai Shehzad died. He was in a car with his friends on the way home from college, and on Preston New Road, just in front of Corporation Park, they saw another friend of theirs involved in a fight with people they didn't recognise. They parked the car around the corner on West Park Road and jumped out to help. Then the guys they didn't recognise took a knife out. Everyone legged it. But when the boys got back to their car, they realised that Shehzad wasn't with them, they ran back straight away in a panic and ... and ... Shehzad was on the floor in a pool of his own blood.

He'd been stabbed.

The guys with the knife had run off, I think. I don't know the full details properly.

His friends carried him back to the car and drove him to hospital. Whoever was driving was obviously not driving properly because they were panicking about Shehzad and they got pulled over by the police, who then saw what was happening and took over.

They couldn't save him ... and ...

He died.

I think what makes the whole thing even more painful is that Pai Shehzad was just in the wrong place at the wrong time. He wasn't involved. He was just trying to help.

But when it's your turn to go, logic goes out the window. The circumstances don't matter. It doesn't have to make sense.

It's just time to go.

I remember this night two years ago. Me, Shibz, Shiry and Muj had just finished mosque and we were standing outside their house. Freezing, because no one was home. That in itself was weird, their door is *never* locked.

About twenty minutes later Dad and Baji Shanaz [I'm crying as I write this now] came. Baji Shanaz was really upset. I'd never seen her like that in my life. She was crying her eyes out.

We went inside and Baji Shanaz was saying, 'Don't tell them, don't tell them.'

We all started crying and panicking, 'What's happened? What's happened? Please tell us. Please . . .'

Then Dad told us. That Pai Shehzad had passed away.

I didn't know what to do. I just hugged Dad really tightly and put my head down and started crying even more. When you hear news you're just not expecting, it doesn't make any sense.

Then he told us he was killed. Murdered. And things made even less sense. The whole world didn't make sense.

Who? Why? Why would anyone hurt Pai Shehzad? Let alone kill him.

Eventually we all sat down on the settees. Crying our eyes out.

Muj asked Dad what happened, but Dad didn't know himself.

Another half an hour must have passed. We were all sobbing, sat there quietly, so numb. No one knowing what to say or how to act. This was the first tragedy me and my cousins had ever faced in our lives and there was no preparation for it. No hand-holding. Just out of the blue. Confusion, sadness and anger.

I remember when I went home later that night and saw Ammi, her eyes all red and puffy. I asked her if it was true. I just needed someone to say it wasn't and there'd just been wrong information and stupid rumours. Sadly, she didn't say that.

A few days later it was Pai Shehzad's funeral. Three thousand people from all over the country came. That's how popular he was. Everyone loved him. He was handsome, kind, and was always smiling. He was a top cricketer as well. I never saw him play myself, but he had lots of cricket trophies at home.

The funeral was so haunting. I can even now remember the melody of the prayer as people took their turns to see his face in his coffin.

'BOLO: LA ILLAHA ILLALAH HOO LA ILLAHA ILLALAH HOO LA ILLAHA ILLALAH ...'

He looked so peaceful, which makes sense because he's in a better place now.

RIP Pai Shehzad Iqbal.

May Allah grant you the very highest station of Paradise.

Gone but never forgotten.

Thursday 27th November

Ay ay ay.

This morning, everyone was just doing their work and an argument broke out between Tommy and Rebecca, I'm not really sure what about.

Rebecca told Tommy to shut up, then Tommy turns around and goes, 'You shut up, you dirty Paki-shagger!'

What the HELL?

The whole class was stunned into silence. Mrs Brand didn't know what to do. After a moment of silence, she goes, 'That's enough,' but didn't address what was said and just carried on with the class.

Maybe she didn't want to deal with what she would have to do if she actually took action. Because that was serious.

I was a bit confused. I'd never heard that term before. Is that what they call a gori* who goes out with Asian boys? Is that how low they think of us?

I know Rebecca went out with Mushy for like two weeks, but they never shagged or anything like that.

It was so weird, because everyone heard it, but everyone was too shocked, or maybe upset, to do anything about it.

Someone needs to twat Tommy.

Wednesday 10th December

Over the last few weeks, Kelloggs has been going back and forth with a few goreh lads. In particular Tommy, the little motherfucker.

But this week they went too far.

Sadly, Kelloggs's dad died recently and these painchods were taking the mick out of him for it. Saying horrible things like 'we'll dig him out from his grave'. Taubah tauhbah. And obviously we hadn't forgotten the Paki-shagger comment from a couple weeks ago either. This prick just doesn't learn.

So, yesterday Kelloggs went for Tommy, innit. He proper twatted him at morning break in the maths corridor of North Building. I wish I'd been there!

But then at afternoon break, around the side of South Building, a few of Tommy's mates jumped Kelloggs. It was literally outside some classrooms, but not a single teacher went outside to break it up.

One of the classes was a Year 9 class and Kelloggs's cousin, Mehrban, was in that class with Shiry, so they and couple of others legged it outside to help him, and an even bigger fight broke out.

Today, there was an assembly for the whole school, in which Mr

Gosling told everyone to calm down and leave it to the teachers to sort out any beef between students. He didn't say beef.

'But why did the teachers just watch Kelloggs get twatted then?' Haider wasn't having it.

The whole assembly started shouting over each other. Eventually Mr Gosling calmed everyone down. He promised to look into it and then we were dismissed.

So, assembly finishes, we start going outside and I'm not sure what or who started it exactly, because I was a bit away from the action, but it kicked off. There was a mass brawl between apne and goreh. Year 9s, 10s and 11s.

Girls were screaming. It was crazy.

Hassim was next to me. He tried to run and join in, but I grabbed him and shook my head. 'Boojo, no, man. Stay here.' Thankfully, he stayed put.

It took about twenty minutes for everything to calm down. Basically, we had a race riot.

Now, I know I'm biased, but it was fully the goreh lot's fault, because it started with what Tommy was saying to Kelloggs. There's always a bit of aggro between us, jokes that go too far, threats that never turn into anything. But what happened today has been coming for a long time. I think almost the entire time I've been at Witton. Everyone in Years 9, 10 and 11 got sent home. Asians first. They kept the goreh behind.

We all walked each other home.

Like two hundred kids walking to town for each other's protection.

I've never seen anything like it.

Crazy.

Thursday 11th December

No fights today. It seems like everyone got it out of their system yesterday. Plus, a couple of unofficial suspensions and phone calls home did the trick, I think.

In other news, I started my first-ever job today. I'm the new paper boy for the *Citizen* for the Hope Street area. The *Citizen* is the free weekly newspaper of Blackburn, so it's a big responsibility.

I got a map of the area I have to deliver in and two big piles of newspapers, plus two big yellow newspaper delivery bags. Ufft.

I loaded up both bags and slowly walked over to Hope Street like a cross between Santa and the Lollipop Man, delivering glad tidings about what had happened in Blackburn that week.

I was a bit worried because there was no way I could deliver the newspapers carrying both bags, they're too big and heavy. Luckily, there's a corner shop at the bottom of Hope Street and I asked the shop owner if I could put one of the bags in his shop while I delivered the other. He looked at me and went, 'What's in it for me, kiddo?'

I thought about it for a second and said, 'I can give you one of the papers for free.' He laughed. I think he felt sorry for me and he liked my joke, so he said I could. Thank God!

It took well over an hour and a half to go around all the houses and flats, up and down stairs. Plus, some of the houses on the map were boarded up and others were empty shops (in these ones I put like twenty papers through, to lighten my load).

I eventually finished and went home and had a lie down.

Working life is hard.

Tuesday 16th December

Oh man. Can this year end already?

Please.

It's been snowing for a few days and today me, Shibz, Was and Hassim were having snowball fights just before the end of dinner-time. Then these boys from Year 11 came to the top of the bank of grass, above where we were, on the concrete netball court, where the Indians usually play footy. They started throwing snowballs at us, so we started throwing 'em back. They had the advantage because they were on higher ground, but it was still fun.

Then everything just happened in slow motion. One of the Year 11 guys threw a snowball at Hassim, it hit him in the face and he spun in the air and fell flat on the floor. It was like something from *Street Fighter*. He proper spun in the air like M. Bison.

Everyone started laughing, except me. It just didn't look right. I ran over to Hassim and then I stopped dead. He was lying still and there was blood coming from his face, covering the white snow around it.

'YOU KILLED HIM, YOU FUCKING BASTARDS!' I screamed.

The Year 11 boys legged it.

'Go get a teacher, man,' Was told Shibz.

Shibz ran. Was and I went over to Hassim and turned him over. His face was a proper mess. I put my ear next to his nostrils.

Please, Allah. Please.

'He's breathing!' THANK GOD.

We weren't really sure what to do. But we'd seen enough episodes of 999 that we knew we should do something. Was took his coat off and we put it under Hassim's head so he had something to lie on.

Thankfully Mr Garrison came running over with Shibz and took over. He checked Hassim's neck and then he must've thought it was okay because he picked him up and carried him back to school and told us to go to our tutor groups.

I looked back and there was a giant pool of blood where Hassim fell.

Bloody hell.

When Ms Williams asked where Hassim was I couldn't even answer her. I could feel the tears coming from my eyes, so I just shrugged my shoulders.

When everyone left the class, I told her. She looked really worried too. She promised she'd find out from Mr Garrison what happened.

I fully couldn't concentrate the rest of the day.

After school, instead of going straight home I went to the staff room to ask about Hassim, and Ms Williams said that he'd been taken to hospital. Basically, those boys threw an iceball, not a snowball, and it stabbed him and went through his cheek. He's getting stitches but will otherwise be okay.

Obviously, I'm glad that Hassim is okay. But I'm so angry.

Someone has to twat those boys.

Thursday 18th December

Hassim came back to school today. He's got a bandage on his face, but otherwise he's okay. He can't talk a lot, which I'm not gonna lie, I found funny.

In every class, whenever the teacher asked us a question, I go, 'Miss, Hassim knows.'

And then the teacher would look at Hassim, realise that he couldn't answer, then look at me, then I would look proper innocent and the teacher would shake their head and carry on. It got funnier every time I did it. Hassim couldn't even tell me to stop. Hahaha.

It's the last day of term tomorrow and my last day wearing this tie, because at the beginning of next term, in the first week, they're going to tell the Year 10s who the new prefects are. Obviously, I'll be one because I'm one of the cleverest in my year and then I'll have to get a new red tie, because that's what prefects wear. I can't wait. I can put that in my application form when I apply to study medicine at uni.

I got my first-ever wages today, for last week's work! For delivering 250 newspapers, I got £4.57. I'm on my way to my first million! Haha.

Friday 19th December

Well, it's nice to actually learn something on the last day of term.

On the way to school today I saw one of the boys who threw the iceball at Hassim that nearly killed him. I tried to square up to him to start a fight. I didn't really think it through, but I did know that Was was with me. I had back-up.

The guy pulled a move I wasn't expecting. He goes, 'Listen, if you want a fight I'll give you one at dinnertime, but right now I don't have time, I have to get to school because I have remedial class before first lesson and I can't be late,' and then he just walked off.

I didn't know what to do, so I just shouted at him:

'Yeah, I'll twat you at dinnertime, then.'

Then Was said, 'You know that if the fight is in school, it has to be a fair fight?'

I hadn't thought of that. Shit.

In tutor group, I saw Hassim and told him that I was gonna fight one of the guys who threw the iceball at him.

'Why?' he said. I wasn't expecting that.

'Because you're my friend and he hurt you, man.'

'Nah, it's all right, my bro took care of it.'

What? When? Surely that's the sort of thing friends should tell each other?

Suddenly all my confidence left me. I worried about it all morning. I couldn't concentrate on anything. I started fantasising in my head about how the fight could go. He's about the same size as me. But can he fight? I know I can't fight. It's fifty-fifty. Heads or tails.

Luckily, I saw him on the way to my lesson just before lunch and I casually went up to him and went, 'I don't want a fight, actually.'

And he just goes, 'Okay.'

And that was it. I didn't have to fight.

Thank God.

I'm such a proper soft guy. Kasam.

There's been too much fighting this year. My friends fighting each other. Fighting other people, getting hurt. I hope it stops.

Myself, I need to concentrate on things I'm good at and not worry about fighting. I especially have to learn to control those first ten seconds when I just wanna fight.

The Prophet Muhammad (Peace Be Upon Him) once said that the toughest and strongest person is the one who controls himself when he is angry.

I have to try and remember that.

I know: next time I get in that situation I'll just challenge the guy to a spelling or maths contest. Can you imagine? In a big circle surrounded by the school boys and girls shouting 'FIGHT! FIGHT! FIGHT! FIGHT!' and I turn around and go, 'Okay, so what's the square root of 256?' Hahaha.

Thursday 25th December

It's Christmas Day!

Which doesn't mean anything in my house.

No tree. No decorations. No presents. No mistletoe. No turkey.

But lots of top TV. I watched *Honey, I Shrunk the Kids*, *The Muppet Christmas Carol* and *The Mask*. Plus, I recorded *The Flintstones* and *Willy Wonka and the Chocolate Factory*.

I always record films in the Christmas holidays. What I do is,

I record them on long play: that way, a three-hour tape becomes six hours, so I can fit three films on it instead of just one and a cartoon.

Also, Ammi made a really nice meal as well. Roast chicken legs and cholay chawal* and custard cake. Yum yum, in my tum. Mum is like a superhero, because she did all that and still spent a lot of the day making samosas with Baj to freeze for Ramazan, which is coming up. They had put all the stuff out on the wooden table in the living room. Pastry, egg mixture which acts as the glue, and the masala to put in the samosas. They folded the pastry, scooped some masala in, put the egg mixture on the edges and then folded it closed. I asked to do one. I messed it up so bad! The masala was coming out of the bottom. They make it look so easy and they must've made about three hundred. Because Ammi will fry like ten a day for thirty days straight. SubhanAllah*!

In the evening, me, Baji Rosey, Saeeda and Zaheer played *Honey, I Shrunk the Kids*. That was really fun. Obviously you had to use your imagination, especially when we pretended that Tanveer was a giant baby like from *Honey, I Blew Up the Kid* ... Aaaaaaaaaaargh!

1998

Thursday 1st January

HAPPY NEW YEAR!

AND ...

RAMAZAN MUBARAK!

Not only is it the first day of the new year, it's also the first day of Ramazan and so the first day of rozay.

Now, if you are reading this diary in the future and I'm dead and Muslims haven't conquered the world yet, so you don't know everything about Islam and us, then let me explain, because you might be confused that in my 1997 diary I started fasting on 11 January, but in my 1998 diary I started fasting on 1 January.

Okay, so you know how the earth goes around the sun and takes 365.25 days (which gets rounded off every four years into a leap year)? That's the solar (sun) calendar. However, Islam follows the lunar (moon) calendar and the lunar calendar is about ten days shorter than the solar calendar. So, in the solar calendar, the Muslim calendar goes back about ten days every year and that's why Ramazan (the ninth month of the Muslim calendar) started ten days earlier than last year.

You're welcome for that lesson, diary.

*

I reckon I should think about and write some new year's resolutions, but I need to open a new cassette tape, peel the stickers off, put them on the cassette, write *Forrest Gump* on them, put the cassette in the video and then press record when it comes on. So I'll do that instead.

Saturday 3rd January

It proper snowed these last two days, so me, Baj, Saeeda and Zaheer built a snowman in the back garden. Tany wasn't allowed out because he's too little, so he lifted the jaali* up and watched us from the living room.

Our snowman came to about the height of my shoulder. We put a hat on it, one of Mum's scarfs. We put an orange for its nose, because we didn't have a carrot, and Saeeda asked Ammi for some empty bottles, so it had a Coke bottle for one arm and a green 7-Up bottle for the other. Then we got Zaheer to use some of his Lego for the eyes, smile and buttons on its belly.

We stepped back to admire it.

'I think we did a good job everyone, well done.' Baji was happy with our team effort.

'Is not as good as the snowman from the cartoon, but.' Saeeda was obviously harder to please.

'Yeah, but that boy had a massive garden and a whole field to roll big bits of snow in,' Baj reminded her. I mean, our garden is eight steps long and four steps wide, it was never gonna be as good as that.

'What's his name?' Zaheer wanted to know.

Er . . . Good question. We thought about it.

'Snowman Man.' I laughed so hard at how rubbish Saeeda's suggestion was. Then it came to me.

'I know: Nouman. Nouman because it rhymes with Snowman.'

'Nouman the Snowman.' Zaheer laughed as he said it. Yes.

You know what the best bit about playing in the snow is? When you're freezing cold and you can't make all your fingers touch each other, but then you go inside and turn the radiator and heaters on full blast and put your hands or back or feet against it. Uffffft. That always feels well nice and you can see the feeling come back into your hands because your little fingers can touch your ring fingers again.

I know he won't, but I hope Nouman comes alive at night and flies me away somewhere cool.

Sunday 4th January

Nouman didn't come alive overnight.

Maybe because in the cartoon there's only one boy who makes the snowman, so the snowman knows who to go to. Whereas because there were four of us he can't fly all of us away, he's too small, so he didn't want to pick a favourite and chose to stay frozen instead.

Or ... maybe it's because Nouman is a snowman and there-fore not real?

We'll never know.

Monday 5th January

Good news and bad news ...

Bad news:

They DIDN'T make me a prefect, man!

In class, Ms Williams was reading out the names of people who'd been made prefects. It was coming to mine and I was fully ready for 'Tehzeeb Ilyas'.

But she never, she skipped my name and carried on. I felt like everyone was looking at me.

'Shit, she didn't read your name out.' Thanks, Hassim, I'm right here.

'She didn't read yours out either,' I said.

'Yeah, but I don't give a shit.'

'Pfft. I don't either, man.' Lies. I had to act like I didn't care, but secretly I did.

Actually, I found out at dinnertime, out of all us mates, only Chucky got made a prefect. Shibz didn't, Was didn't, Mushy didn't, Haider didn't, obviously.

A few Indians, like Karolia, Ibby and Amina did (to be fair, that makes sense) and loads of goreh did as well, like Steven. It actually seemed a bit racist to me that they only picked one Pakistani boy out of our whole year to be a prefect.

At least Ammi can save money, as I won't be needing a new tie.

Good news:

There was good news today, though. It was proper weird. I was in English class and Mrs Place gave everyone some reading to do, and then she looked at me and goes, 'Can you please come outside with me, Tehzeeb?'

Everyone looked at me. Hassim mouthed, 'What did you do?' I shrugged. I had no idea.

Was I in trouble? I couldn't think of anything that I'd done. Maybe she's gonna make me a prefect? Do heads of department have that power?

She took me into the classroom next door, which was empty apart from Mrs Kirkpatrick (my English teacher in Year 8) and a girl and boy, all sat at a desk together. Mrs Kirkpatrick told me to sit down at the table and then she and Mrs Place explained that we'd been chosen out of the whole school to represent Witton Park in a public speaking competition against other schools in Blackburn.

WOAH!

'Do you want to do it?'

'Yes.' Obviously!

When I got home, I told Ammi, but I don't think she properly understood because she just told me to go and get ready for roza opening.

I'm proper excited, but.

Wednesday 7th January

Today was the first proper meeting of our public speaking team.

We're gonna meet at dinnertime twice a week until the competition on 4 February. That's wicked for me because I'm fasting all this month anyway, so I don't need to worry about dinnertime. Islam is the best!

So, there's me, Laura, who is this really clever girl from Year 11, and Neil, who's also in Year 11. I've seen them around but have never spoken to them before. They seemed really nice and excited too.

Mrs Kirkpatrick explained the rules. In each team there's a:

1. Chairperson. They have to say hello to the audience, introduce the team, our topic and why we think it's important. All in two minutes!
2. Speaker. They have to talk about our topic to the audience; they get six minutes for that. And then they have to answer one question from the audience, chosen by the chairperson.
3. Proposer. Lastly, they have two minutes to thank the audience, our team and ask the audience to thank our team. I'm not gonna lie, this member of the team seems like a weird one. When Mrs Kirkpatrick explained it, I thought, well the chairperson could do that, couldn't they?

I got picked as the chairperson. I was happy with that. I think it means I'm the team captain, although no one said that. But I'm sure that's what it means. That's crazy, that I'm the youngest in the team and I'm the captain. That made me happy. Who needs to be a prefect?

Laura is speaker and Neil is proposer.

Next job is to think of a topic. Hmmm ... We spent the rest of the meeting talking about what we're interested in. I thought summat about football, but Laura said no. She suggested talking about lowering the age of voting in elections to sixteen, but we couldn't think of enough reasons why that was a good idea. Neil said, 'What about flying cars?'

'What about them?' asked Mrs Kirkpatrick.

'I ... I don't know.'

I looked at Laura and we had to stop ourselves from laughing.

Hmmm ... What can we pick for a topic?

Monday 12th January

Oh my God! I was sat with Baj on the settee drinking our Ovaltines with Sports biscuits when this show just started on BBC 2.

I love Sports biscuits; I always try and find the football and cricket and snooker ones. They taste better than the rugby and golf ones, which makes no sense.

Baj laughs at me because I always nibble around the edges and then leave the middle till last. I do that with everything actually: Time Out, Jammy Dodgers, Twix.

Ammi always buys boring biscuits like custard creams and Pakistani rusks and rich tea. I mean, obviously I'll have them if there's nothing else, but if I go Tesco with her I always make her get party rings or pink wafers or chocolate digestives! Nothing better in the world than hot milk and chocolate digestives. Yummmm.

*

I'm getting distracted. On the TV these Asian people were sat round a table with a gora and they couldn't say his name, Jonathan, properly. Me and Baj started cracking up.

'That's like when no one can say Tehzeeb, Baj!'

'But they twisted it on the gora. That's well clever and funny.' I agree there, Baj. It was genius!

We were hooked the whole way through. There were four Asian actors doing different sketches. It was well funny. We were laughing so much, Ammi came from the kitchen, her hands wet from doing the dishes: 'Why are you making so much noise? Why haven't you gone to bed yet?'

I told her to watch it with us. She saw one bit, where the two men were pretending to be cool, and one of 'em goes 'Ras Malaaaaaai!'

And Mum just goes, '*Eh teh nera bekwaas eh*': Nonsense.

No, Mum! You just don't get it. Kiss my chuddies, innit! Obviously, I didn't say that to her.

Me and Baj have never seen anything like this show. We laughed our heads off. It's so good to see Asian people be on TV. Kasam.

Tuesday 13th January

Everyone was talking about *Goodness Gracious Me* in school today!

I'm so glad I watched it. The people who never felt well left out. Even some of the goreh watched it. Jack was saying that he loved the restaurant 'cheque please' jokes the best.

Also ... I solved it.

In *The Times* today, which I still buy and read every Monday, it said that the government wants to completely abolish (that means get rid of) the death penalty. I didn't even realise there was a death penalty in England still. But apparently there is for treason, and if you're a pirate and kill someone.

So, in the competition meeting, I said, 'How about we talk about the death penalty, because the government are trying to get rid of it completely this year?'

'And why that's a good thing?' suggested Mrs Kirkpatrick. Is it? I think the way she said it made me think I should say yes, but.

'Yeah, miss.' Everyone agreed, so that's what we're going to do our speech about.

That's why I'm team captain!

Saturday 24th January

Today was exciting.

So, we are looking for a new house, which means we have to go look at loads of houses. Today I got to go with Ammi and Abu to have a look at her favourite one. It was wicked, and much bigger than the house we're living in right now.

It's on Leamington Road, near the top. Outside, if you look down the street you get a top view of all of Blackburn and the countryside.

It's got a little front garden; we've never had that before. In 45 Hickory Street, which was our first house, we only had a front room, a living room and kitchen downstairs, and upstairs there was only two bedrooms and a bathroom. We had a back garden that had a toilet in it. I only ever used that when I was super-duper desperate and someone was using the bathroom upstairs. I was always too scared because it was dark in there and it was full of spiders.

I have such nice memories of Hickory Street. Just me, Ammi and Baji Rosey. It was simpler times. Sometimes I wish it was just the three of us again. But then I think of Saeeda, Zaheer and Tanveer and I would never give them up for anything.

Anyway, the council wanted to knock our whole street down, so we had to move to Edmundson Street. But now Edmundson Street is too small, so here we are on Leamington Road.

As well as having a front garden, the inside was big too. There was a long hallway, with a big front room and a big living room off the right side. At the back there was a kitchen and a garden. But upstairs was the best: there were three bedrooms, a bathroom and then an attic! I've always wanted to live in a house with an attic like Shibz's house. The attic had two rooms. Straight away I said to Ammi that I wanted the right-side attic, which looks out the front of the house.

'*Chup kar!*' – Be quiet! – Abu said really harshly. I didn't even know he was in the room.

I did go quiet. I understand: I shouldn't get too excited, we haven't actually bought the house yet. But he didn't have to say it so nastily.

Oh Allah, please let us get this house. Please please please.

Thursday 29th January

Today is Eid. After what happened last Eid, we cousins (sensibly) decided to stay home and play Mega Drive. No adventures this Eid ... No thank you.

Wednesday 4th February

Well.

That was ...

Damn.

Today was the big day.

The Blackburn with Darwen Rotary Club Public Speaking Contest 1998.

I feel like the team's worked really hard. I'm proud of me, Laura and Neil.

Mrs Kirkpatrick has been really good as well. Her main note to me is to slow down and make sure I breathe and make sure that everyone hears every word that I say. 'Annunciating', she called it. I have to annunciate.

I was ready ... even though I still didn't know what a Rotary Club is.

There was one problem. The competition was at Darwen Vale High School. That's well far. I told Mrs Kirkpatrick that I didn't know how to get there because my stepdad drives taxis at night so he won't be home and Ammi can't drive.

She was actually so nice, she said that she'll pick us up from home, take us there and bring us back. I asked Baj if she wanted to come but she had too much college work to do. She's studying to do nursery nursing.

That's well nice of Mrs Kirkpatrick though, innit? I think that's the nicest thing a teacher's ever done for me actually. Apart from when they give me good grades.

When we got to Darwen Vale, Ammi and Mrs Kirkpatrick went into the room where the competition was, and me, Laura and Neil had to sit in a separate room with all the other students from the other schools.

All the schools had a team. Darwen Vale were there obviously, St Wilfrid's, Pleckgate, Our Lady & St John, St Bede's, and QEGS (Queen Elizabeth's Grammar School).

I didn't think it was fair that QEGS was there. They're a private school. I thought they would definitely win. If I betted, which I don't because it's haram, I would've betted that they would win. I actually wanted to go to QEGS, but obviously we can't afford it. They have an exam you can take at primary school called the 11+ and if you pass that you can go without paying any fees. I was in Pakistan for Baji Shanaz's wedding when St Barnabas did the 11+, so I didn't even have the chance to pass or fail it.

That trip was so crazy. My whole family, Shibz's whole family and Dad and Was and Wadi Ammi all went to Pakistan for three months, September–December 1993. We were there for so long me, Shibz, Shiry and Muj had to go to the village school. They put us in reception class, where we learnt how to count and read the ABC in Urdu. Because I was learning alif, bey, pay I didn't get to take my 11+, which would've meant I could've gone to one of the best schools in the country.

I wonder how different my life would be if I went to QEGS. I wonder if I would've even been chosen to be on their team for this competition today. I looked at them; their team had the only other Asian guy in the whole competition. So maybe?

Seven teams, twenty-one team members, only two Asians, the rest were ALL goreh.

That's when I realised Beardwood wasn't there. They have an Asian population of 95 per cent in that school, so all their team would've been Asian. I wonder why Beardwood weren't there. Maybe it isn't just Witton Park that doesn't seem to give Asian kids a chance?

No one talked to each other in that room. The atmosphere was tense. Everyone just stayed in their groups and went over their notes.

Each team was called in one by one.

When the teams came back in, I couldn't tell if they had done good or bad. Their teacher was saying well done to them, but from the kid's faces I couldn't tell anything.

We were fifth.

We went into the room; it was smaller than I thought it was gonna be. But it was packed. There must have been about two hundred people inside, all goreh except about five people, including Ammi. They were sat in rows with an aisle in the middle splitting the two sides, like the weddings I'd seen on TV. Asian weddings aren't like that, but that's a story for another time.

There was a table at the front which we were told to go and sit behind. We each sat down. Me on the left, Laura in the middle and Neil on the right. I had my notes with me but suddenly I felt very nervous. I looked at them; I looked up and saw Mrs Kirkpatrick at the back of the hall. She gave me a nod, as if to tell me it'll be okay.

This buddah* got up and said in a posh voice, 'And now it's the turn of Witton Park High School, Blackburn.'

Everyone clapped and then I looked down, closed my eyes, took a deep breath and stood up. Looked at the audience and in a loud, clear voice said:

'Ladies and gentlemen, esteemed guests, thank you for joining us today. My name is Tehzeeb Ilyas and I am the chairperson for Witton Park High School . . . '

My time went so quickly, but I remember that I spoke clearly and confidently, and that lots of people were smiling when I introduced Laura and sat down.

I was trying hard to concentrate on what Laura was saying, even though I'd heard her speech loads of times already. She was doing well. We were doing well. I think.

About three-quarters of the way into her speech, Laura got a frog in her throat. Uh-oh. I looked up at her, she cleared it and then carried on. I looked back down, a bit worried.

The buddah who had introduced us was sat right in front of me. He looked straight at me and poured an invisible jug into an invisible glass. No one else saw.

What the—? This is not the time for charades, man!

That's when I realised there was a jug of water on the table and three glasses. I picked up the jug and poured out a glass of water. Just at that moment, Laura got stuck again, almost as if I had predicted it. I offered her the glass of water. She took it, took two sips, then carried on as if nothing had happened, and she was fine for the rest of her speech.

I stood back up, thanked Laura and then asked if there were any questions. One hand went up, this lady about halfway on the right. I said, 'Yes, madam.' And then this woman, yeah, stood up and asked the longest question I think anyone has ever asked anyone in the history of questions.

And then I said to her, and I'm not sure why, 'Thank you, madam. Would you mind repeating the question? I just want to make sure that I understand it before I ask Laura to give you her answer.'

Everyone started laughing. Brilliant. Even the woman laughed. Something about that made me feel really special. But I had no time to dwell on it. She repeated her question and I had to make sure I was listening properly.

When she finished, I turned to Laura and said:

'Laura, can you please tell our audience what you'd say to those countries that do still have the death penalty, and why they should take our lead on getting rid of it.'

Another big laugh, I think because I'd basically summed up this woman's really long and complicated question in a really good way.

Laura gave a good, short answer, just as Mrs Kirkpatrick had told her to do, and then that was it.

I stood back up, thanked her and then introduced Neil. Again, I'm not sure what the point of his role was, to be honest.

When he stood up, I poured him a glass of water and put it in front of him, just in case he needed it. He didn't, but the audience had all seen what I'd done.

Neil was great, to be fair to him. Very confident, and he kept their attention.

And then, just like that, we were done!

We left the room to a nice round of applause and went into the hallway and Mrs Kirkpatrick gave us all a big group hug and told us we were brilliant. It was such a nice feeling. It's amazing how good it feels when a teacher says something nice. I always get this funny tingling sensation in my neck when someone says something nice to me. I had that feeling right then.

After the other two teams were done, we were all called back inside, and the teams lined up at the back of the room.

The buddah stood up and congratulated everyone.

There were four awards. Three individual awards for each of the positions in the team and then the main award for the team that won.

First, it was best proposer. A girl from St Wilfrid's won that.

Second was best speaker. The Asian guy from QEGS won that. I felt weirdly proud.

Then the buddah said, 'The winner of best chairperson also belongs to the team that has won the overall prize.'

I looked up and down the line to see who it would be.

'And the winners are Tehzeeb Ilyas and Witton Park High School!'

My face! I was shocked.

Laura gave me a massive hug, Neil gave me a big high-five. We did it.

YES YES YES!

WE WON! I WON! WE WON!

YES YES YES!

I've never won anything in my life. I can't play football, or cricket . . . but I can bloody talk!

We went up and collected our trophy. I had such a big smile on my face. I could see Ammi, she looked so proud, that made me feel even nicer.

Afterwards, people came to congratulate us. I found the old buddah, I learnt his name, Robert. I proper thanked him for the water trick and he just winked at me and said, 'Good lad.'

Mrs Kirkpatrick took me and Ammi home, and I asked her if I could keep the trophy for one night and bring it into school tomorrow. She looked at Ammi and said okay. I'm looking at it right now and it feels amazing.

In your face to all those teachers who always said I need to be quiet! Actually . . . Why don't you shut YOUR mouth?!

Tuesday 10th February

I wish he would die. I wish he would die. I wish he would die.

Councillor Khan and Aunty came over from next door because the fight made that much noise. Ammi just stayed in the kitchen with Baji Rosey. I was sat on the settee in the living room, proper scared, Saeeda and Zaheer were upstairs and Tanveer was just crying on the floor. Abu was sat on a chair, opposite me, by the window, not saying anything.

Aunty and Uncle were on the other settee against the back wall. They asked if everything was okay.

NO IT ISN'T! PLEASE CALL THE POLICE! PLEASE TAKE HIM AWAY!

I wanted to scream and shout everything. EVERYTHING.

Instead, I said nothing. I'm such a soft bastard. A proper man would've defended his mum.

He told them that everything was fine. 'It was just some loud noises from the TV.'

LIAR!

After about ten awkward minutes they left and said, 'Let us know if you need anything.'

Abu went upstairs. I went into the kitchen and hugged Ammi. Baji Rosey hugged us both. They'd wiped the blood and glass up; it didn't look like anything had happened ... apart from the cut on Mum's lip.

Just before I wrote this, I prayed to Allah that he has a car crash and dies.

After that I listened to some Tupac. I needed it, but it didn't help my mood. It made me wish I had a gun.

That, I don't mean. I don't think.

Friday 13th February

Tomorrow is Valentine's Day. I didn't get any Valentine's cards. Was got one, Shibz got one and Hassim got one as well. Chucky got two. We don't know who any of them are from, but I reckon one of Chucky's is probably from Halima ... and that's nice. For him.

It's Friday the 13th and I feel like I'm the only one it's unlucky for.

Monday 23rd February

WE BOUGHT THE LEAMINGTON ROAD HOUSE!

£38,000. Wow. That's so much money!

Yes!!! Thank you, Allah, for answering my prayers.

Mum said we're gonna move in a few months' time because the family that live there haven't bought their new house to move into yet. I can't wait. I'm gonna have an attic room all to myself. Yes!

Hopefully, with a change of scenery, things will be better for everyone.

Wednesday 4th March

Obviously, we don't go on our dinnertime woods adventures any more. Actually, it's been nearly a year since the infamous shootout with the farmer – that's how I choose to remember it now, haha.

But that doesn't mean we behave at dinnertimes.

Our new thing is going to the chippy.

Every dinnertime, me, Shibz, Was and Hassim sneak (we're not allowed out of school) right to the bottom of the school, past the concrete netball court and through this little thicket of trees and up a path that brings us out of a little gap in the railings onto Buncer Lane. From there we cross the road and go to Redlam chippy.

I order the same thing every day, chip butty with loads of salt and vinegar. Yummm.

Then we sneak back into school and eat it on some steps near the south netball court where Ebrahim lot play footy every day.

Sometimes we shout encouragement at them; sometimes we laugh when they mess up.

'SIX POINTS FOR WIGAN!' I shouted today when Imran missed a sitter and booted it over the bar. We all laughed even harder, because he got more annoyed that we were laughing that he missed.

He turned around and goes, 'If you so good why don't you come show us then?'

And so we played with them and it was really fun. I think they had fun too because at the end Ebrahim asked if we'd like to play with them every day and Was said, 'Yeah.'

So now we're gonna play footy every dinnertime with the Indians.

Saturday 14th March

Today was the district final of the Rotary Club Public Speaking Contest. That means it's all the winners from towns in the whole of Lancashire and Cumbria. If we win this, we get to go all the way to the national final. Damn.

I'm writing this in the car on the way to Windermere School, where the final is. Mrs Kirkpatrick is driving and just telling me, Laura and Neil to enjoy it. Whatever happens.

Update: Well . . . we're on our way back. This is what happened:

When we got there, it definitely felt bigger than the Blackburn competition. There were fourteen schools competing. I was only one of three people who wasn't white. There was one black girl and another Asian guy.

I don't know why I always notice that wherever I go. How many Asian people or black people are there? The more there are the safer I feel. That's weird, isn't it? I don't think the goreh are gonna do anything to me or anything like that. But yeah, it's just a weird thing that if I see another Asian kid or even black kid, actually, I just nod at them and they nod back. We don't even have to say anything to each other.

I was less nervous this time. I didn't think we'd win in Blackburn (though I was wrong about that) and I definitely didn't think we'd win today (could I be wrong again?).

There was a big crowd today, about five hundred people. There was space for us to watch at the back of the room, so we sat on some tables and watched the other teams. Some of them were good. Really good. They were confident, funny, and most of them spoke without notes. I was impressed.

Suddenly I became nervous. I didn't think we'd win, but I didn't want to be embarrassed either.

I went outside. I felt like the more I watched, the more nervous I would get. After about half an hour, Neil found me and told me we were next. We went up and ... it was fine. It felt harder than the last time. The faces seemed less friendly, so it made it harder to work out if it was going well or not.

I did my pouring a glass of water trick for Laura, but the magic of the Blackburn competition wasn't there: she didn't need it and I don't think anyone noticed or cared.

We all did fine, but in the end we finished seventh. Which is okay.

I don't even know who won, to be honest. Probably some posh school from Lancaster or something.

Mrs Kirkpatrick was really nice about it and told us she was proud of us, which is still nice to hear every single time, to be honest.

I don't know if that night at Darwen Vale was a fluke, but my public speaking days are officially over. It was nice while it lasted.

Sunday 15th March

Home can be really scary sometimes.

Today Mum was just screaming and screaming at Baji Rosey. I just wanted to tell her to stop. It was really scary.

Ever since Baji Rosey came back from Pakistan, Mum has had a short temper with her. I don't understand why, because no one discusses anything grown-up with me. I know Mum's life hasn't been easy, but Baji Rosey's life hasn't been easy either.

When I came downstairs later, I could see Baj's face was swollen from crying, I asked her if she was okay. She just goes, 'I can't wait till I can move out and live my own life.'

I didn't know what that meant, but I wanted to give her a hug. But ... I ... I didn't.

I know I can't say it to your face for whatever reason, but I love you, Baji. And I hope you be proper happy when you grow up.

Parents can be proper cruel. Sometimes when Abu is checking Saeeda's homework he slaps her, proper hard in the face or on the back of the head, if she uses her left hand to write. But she's left-handed! It doesn't mean it's wrong. But he thinks if you write left-handed it's haram or something. Proper daft get. Just let her write with whatever hand she wants to write with, man.

If I wasn't such a scared soft pussy I'd speak up for my family. But I don't and everyone is just taking their anger out on everyone else. Sometimes I shout at Zaheer, or Saeeda too. Then I feel bad. But Mum shouts at me, and Abu bes horrible to her.

It's a vicious cycle. Allah jee, please let things be better in the new house.

Wednesday 25th March

In afternoon tutor group today, there was a present in Hassim's place.

Uh-oh, was I supposed to buy him a birthday present? We've never done that before. Are there different rules in upper school?

'Who's that from?' I said

'Fuck knows,' he goes.

'Well open it then!'

He opened it. It was an aftershave, but I was more interested in the card that fell out. I grabbed it.

'"Dearest Hassim. I love your eyes. Happy Birthday. From your secret admirer".'

I quickly looked around the class; no one was looking at us. Hmmmmm.

'Bro, who is this from? Tell me!'

'Kasam I don't know. It says "secret"!'

Hmmmm. Who is Boojo's secret admirer?

Friday 3rd April

I'll be honest. My life is hard. All grown-ups have to do is go to work, earn money, put food on the table, pay the bills and cook and clean.

I have to go to school and work! And my work is not safe. Especially when I hear a dog barking. And let me tell you, diary, I hate^ dogs! It probably comes from the time one chased me up Hickory Street when I was small, and I banged my head against the front door. Ammi was so angry, the gora goes, 'Sorry, my dog doesn't like Pakis.' What the hell? Why bring him to our street then?

Actually, there is one dog that I like. Me and Was used to see it sometimes at school, being walked by its owner. It was this massive fluffy golden thing. We used to call it a lion-bear. It was well cute.

Work is the most miserable when it's raining. It's so tiring having to carry two big bags of papers to Hope Street. And the pay is so bad compared to how much work I have to do.

Sometimes they send me the newspapers and a separate stack of leaflets. I have to put the leaflets in the newspapers, then the newspapers in the bag and then carry the bag and then deliver the paper. And do it all again for the second bag. All for £6.

It's good exercise, though, and I have saved about £50. I'm not sure what I'm saving up for yet. Maybe a new bike? The possibilities are endless!

^ Am scared of.

Sunday 5th April

Ufft. What a weekend!

It started yesterday morning.

'Wake up. Wake up. Start packing everything.'

All my clothes. My school books, my other books, my stationery, my Mega Drive, my games and my toys.

Baj and Saeeda helped Ammi pack everything up in the kitchen and me and Abu teamed up in the living room and front room. We didn't say that much to each other, but I made sure that I worked hard and followed his instructions.

By the late afternoon, every single room was in suitcases, black bin bags or boxes. I actually sat on the settees without the covers on for the first time ever. They're red with these flower patterns on! I'd only ever seen them blue, because that's the colour the covers are. We have covers on everything: settees, muras*, plastic covers on remote controls, jaalis on windows, even our hallway has a plastic lino on it to protect the carpet.

Tomorrow we're moving. We've already decided on our rooms.

Baji's got her own room, the small one at the top of the stairs, then the next room is for Saeeda and Zaheer, with bunk beds, and then the next room is the bathroom, which has got a cool massive corner bath that you can sit in – I've never seen that before! And then is Ammi and Abu's room, where Tanveer will also sleep, and next to their room is the attic stairs, at the top of which is two rooms. One is empty, which we're gonna use for storage, and the other one is my room!

Monday 6th April

Today, Shibz, Shiry, Muj, Mammu Saeed and Uncle came to help us move in. Uncle borrowed Taya's van to help us. Good job there was loads of us. Some of the stuff was proper heavy. We had to take the two settees from the living room, the fridge, the sofas from the front room, all the mattresses, all the beds, two big cabinets – they were proper complicated. The big brown one in the front room got stuck in the door and it took us ages to figure out.

We loaded up the van and then we drove to the new house and then had to take everything out of the van into the house.

THEN we had to go back and pick up more things. The TV, the TV stand, microwave, boxes and boxes of stuff, like paandeh* and clothes and random things. This was more fun, but, because me, Shibz, Shiry and Muj played pass-the-parcel from the room to the van and that made everything faster and felt good because we could have a laugh and work together as a team. I started going: 'To me, to you,' like on *Chucklevision*. That cracked everyone up.

Eventually, about 8 p.m., we had moved everything!

Well, everything except the sewing machine, which was also my dinner table. I sat there to eat most days, because the wooden coffee table is a bit low and I'm a messy eater and we didn't have a dining table. So, if I sat on the arm of the settee next to the sewing machine, it worked as a really good dinner table.

We're not actually selling Edmundson Street, so it doesn't matter that some stuff is staying there. Imagine if someone came to burgle it tomorrow and all they found was an old sewing machine! Haha. I would tell them that it works as a really good table too.

We finally collapsed on the sofas in the front room of the new house and then Abu and Uncle came in with pizzas! Yay! I LOVE pizza. It's one of my favourite foods.

We all sat on the floor eating the pizza, and for the first time all weekend there was peace and quiet because we were all so tired and hungry.

I'm about to spend my first night sleeping in my new attic bedroom, I love it! When you enter the room you walk in straight, but after about three yards the ceiling slants down and you have to bend down. The window is on the slant in the middle of the room. You can open it up and stick your head out, and you can put your hands on the tiles of the roof and see the whole street and sky. IT'S SO COOL!

I shouted 'Allah-hu-Akbar!' at the top of my lungs.

The one negative is that the window doesn't have a curtain, so the sunlight will proper hit me in the morning.

Just before I went upstairs to bed, I was watching the news and they said that Pakistan tested a long-range missile today and it was successful. I thought, that's good! But then they said that it's gonna increase tensions with India and that might lead to war. Uh-oh, that's not good!

I hope there's no war. Mammu Jamil (one of Mum's brothers) is in the army. I don't want him to go to war and I don't wanna stop playing footy with the Indians. Except they're Muslim, so they might be on Pakistan's side?

Wednesday 8th April

My first birthday in the new house!

I'm fifteen today.

It was really nice. I only got a small present (a set of Roald Dahl books) and a Kinder Surprise (which everyone else got too). Obviously because we were busy with moving, and I know Ammi and Abu spent a lot of money on the new house, plus it's big Eid tomorrow, so it's okay.

I did find out something today, though ...

Ammi is pregnant! That means I'm gonna get *another* baby brother or sister!

No wonder we bought a new house. That makes so much sense now.

Thursday 9th April

Eid Mubarak!

I got £40 on Eid today. That's the most I've ever had. I think it's because people knew it was my birthday yesterday too, so it was like a double present.

Friday 10th April

Today was a historic day. At least that's what the news said.

Basically, Mo Mowlam from Labour and Tony Blair made something called the Good Friday Agreement. I think it's called that because today is Good Friday and the agreement is between the UK and Ireland so there isn't any more fighting.

Catholic people in Northern Ireland want to be part of the Republic of Ireland, and Protestant people in Northern Ireland want to keep being part of Britain. They've been fighting with each other about it for a long time and sometimes the IRA, who are on the Catholic side, fight with Britain too.

I remember two years ago, there was a massive IRA bomb in Manchester town centre. Luckily no one was killed. I don't know how, there was so much damage!

But hopefully now there'll be peace and no more fighting and everyone will be happy. *InshAllah*.

Pakistan and India should do a Good Friday Agreement: the Achie Jumma Mohaeda (I had to ask Mum what 'agreement' was in Urdu). We could send Mo(hammed) Mowlam to Islamabad! Hahaha.

I'll be honest, today they might have done good, but usually Britain messes up a lot. Like Hong Kong and China. With Kashmir too, because when they did partition, splitting up Pakistan and India, they didn't make a decision about Kashmir and Pakistan and India are still fighting about it. And I heard that they proper messed up Palestine as well.

No, maybe we (Britain) should just keep our noses out of other people's business.

Tuesday 21st April

Baji Rosey told me a big secret today.

But first of all, happy birthday Baji Rosey! She's seventeen today. We did a little party for her, which was nice. After the kids had gone to sleep, Ammi was in the living room and me and Baj were in the front room. I was sat on one sofa, the one closest to the window, trying to get the hang of *FIFA 97*. I borrowed it from Shibz and Shiry. Baj was on the other sofa, nearest the back wall, reading a book. She loves reading.

She stopped at one point and goes to me: 'Oi, listen . . . I need to tell you a secret.'

'Are you adopted?'

'Shurrup. No. I'm . . . getting married.'

WHAT?!

'Wait . . . ' I made Kevin Gallacher shoot. He missed. Goal kick. Dammit. I paused the game.

'What?'

'Sshhh. Yeah.'

'When?'

'In the summer. We're going to Pakistan in the six-week holidays.'

'We? Am I coming?'

'Obviously. I can't get married if you're not there.' That was true. I am her brother. I have to be there. Then I asked the question, which should've been the first one I asked:

'To who?'

'Uneeb.'

'Who's that?'

'Maasi Rabia's son. The one that lives in Dhanyala.' I was tryna remember.

'Remember that tall guy?'

'I think so . . . yeah.' I had no idea.

'When, but? How?'

She explained that Uneeb's mum asked Wadi Ammi who asked Dad who asked Poupoh who asked Ammi, who asked Baj, who thought about it and decided it's a good match and so Baj told Mum okay, who told Poupoh okay, who told Dad okay, who told Wadi Ammi okay, who told Uneeb's mum okay. Who then probably told Uneeb.

'Why, but? You should've just said no.'

She just shrugged and goes, 'We all have to get married, don't we?'

I guess that's true, but she wasn't exactly enthusiastic.

'Plus I won't have to live with *him* any more.'

Great, leave me with him then, innit.

'Is that why Mum and you have been fighting so much these last few months?'

'I'm not sure, you know. I think it's part of it.'

I was so confused. Being grown up doesn't look like it makes any sense. I hope I'm happy when I get married and it's my choice. I want a love marriage (Martina Hingis), not an arranged one.

I don't know how I feel about it. I'm excited to be going to Pakistan, obviously. But I hope she's okay and happy.

Monday 27th April

I have a new route to school now because of the new house. My days of going to school and back with Was are gone.

Mostly I've been walking to school alone, but on the way back I go with Shibz, because most of it is in the same direction.

I noticed two things today. One was really cool: Marlon Broomes lives on Gorse Road! Me and Shibz saw him in his driveway on our way home.

As soon as I saw him, I said, 'Hey, man! Are you Marlon Broomes from Blackburn Rovers?'

And Marlon Broomes said, 'Yeah.'

Aaaaaaaaaaarrgh. I was too nervous to say anything else. I think I just said, 'COOL! Hi, Marlon Broomes.'

The other thing I noticed, also on Gorse Road, weirdly: the house right at the bottom, on the corner, had a flag in their driveway. The flag had a red background, and a blue diagonal cross with stars on it. As soon as I saw it, I knew I recognised it from somewhere . . .

When I went home, I opened up my encyclopaedia to the American history bit and I saw it. It was the Confederate flag. What the hell? The Confederate flag belonged to the southern states of America, who wanted independence in the civil war because they wanted to keep slavery. Evil.

What the hell is a house in Blackburn doing with a Confederate flag in its driveway in 1998? I would ask them, but they also have a massive bulldog too. Fuck that.

Shit. Marlon Broomes is black. I wonder how he feels about it. I hope he doesn't notice it. It can't be nice.

The only thing weirder than a Confederate flag in Blackburn in 1998 that I've seen is the yacht that's been on the corner of Devonport Road and Bromley Street ever since I can remember. Why is that there? Whose is it? Did they win it on *Bullseye*?!

Sunday 3rd May

I'm not gonna play in Dad's team this year – at least not in the league – because I'm going to Pakistan for Baji Rosey's wedding. Actually, so is Dad, but he's got an assistant manager who'll take over when he goes.

Also, Dad's only having one team this year, Whalley Range Tigers, no Cubs, so even if I wasn't going to Pakistan, I wouldn't fancy being a cheerleader all summer.

But he did ask me to play in the cup tournament which was this weekend … and … I … played … top!

Yesterday, it was the group stages and in one of the games the ball came to me. I high-chested it, flicked it over my head and the defender's head, then I ran onto it and took a shot. The keeper dived, got a hand to it and clipped it on the post, and then from the corner I won the header and it hit the bar. SO CLOSE. I didn't score, but we won, and I played well good.

Today, we won the quarters, but lost the semis. I was gutted because we were easily the best team in the tournament, we just didn't play as well as we can and so we're out. It would've been nice to win a trophy and get a medal.

In the changing room afterwards, Dad bollocked the whole team proper bad. I've never seen him that angry.

But he said, 'The only two fuckin' players who played any good were the ones I subbed off. The rest of you need to have—'

Wait, that was me and Shiry. I caught his eye and we smiled at each other.

That's the first time Dad ever said I played well at football. It feels good to retire on a high.

Tuesday 12th May

Today was a day of two halves.

On morning break, I went to the tuck shop and bought a Galaxy Caramel bar. Normally I like Crunchie, Time Out, Wispa, Rolos and mint Aero. But today I felt like experimenting and got a Galaxy Caramel, and guess what? There was NO caramel in there! I ate one piece, then a second piece, then a third piece. No caramel. I ate four out of the six pieces and then took it back to the tuck shop.

I got the dinner lady's attention: 'Excuse me, Miss. There's no caramel in my Galaxy Caramel.'

She looked proper confused!

'Look.' I broke the fifth piece to show her, and then the final piece: no caramel. It would've been proper basti if there was caramel in those pieces, but luckily there wasn't.

She looked confused but gave me a whole new Galaxy Caramel. I tried to give her the other one back, but she said it's okay, I can keep it. Get in. Two chocolates for the price of one. I tested the new bar and it did have caramel in it. I looked at the first wrapper to make sure there was no prize or something for finding the chocolate with no caramel in it, like I was Charlie Bucket and I'd get to win the whole Galaxy chocolate factory. But no, it was just a mistake. Just as well, I didn't want the Galaxy chocolate factory anyway, I prefer Cadbury's.

So, that was good.

But the afternoon was shit.

I was trying to get Mr Cooper's attention for a bit of work I was stuck on. I tapped him on the shoulder, and he turned around and pushed me to the floor!

Kasam.

And then he blamed me, saying that I tripped up, and sent me to the deputy head and I got put on report again! What the hell?

I remember when I got put on it the first time last year, I was proper shocked. Report is for bad kids. I'm in set 1 for everything. Has anyone in set 1 ever been on report once before, let alone twice? I really wanted to ask, but I didn't.

When you're on report, you get given this sheet and have to give it to every teacher at the start of every class, and if you misbehave they write it on there and every evening you have to get it signed by your parents.

This school is so unfair, man. Mr Cooper should be sacked for pushing me over, but instead he lied and I get put on report.

Tonight, I imagined Tupac was rapping about Mr Cooper:

First off, fuck your bitch and the click you claim—

I'm gonna do the same thing I did last year, though: I'm not gonna tell Ammi I'm on report and I'm gonna sign the report paper myself. Hopefully I won't get caught.

Two weeks of this because a teacher pushed me over and then framed me so he wouldn't get sacked.

Fuck 'em, we Bad Boy killers.

Monday 18th May

It's Ammi's birthday today! She's thirty-five.

By the time I'm Ammi's age, in twenty years, I'll be a surgeon, with a wife, three kids and a massive house and a brand-new Mercedes-Benz. InshAllah.

And I'll buy her lots of gold on her birthday. (This year, me and Baji chipped in and bought her a cardigan from BHS.)

Wednesday 20th May

I need to stop doing this job. It's taking the piss too much.

This week there was a special delivery I had to do.

PG Tips.

The tea!

The newspaper sent me hundreds and hundreds of boxes of PG Tips and I had to deliver them to everyone that I deliver my normal paper round to. Normally, I can shove loads of newspapers in one bag, and between two bags I can do the full round. But with the PG Tips, there's only so many boxes I can fit into one bag. Plus, since we moved, my walk to Hope Street is a lot longer.

It's taken me three trips of two full bags each day to do my whole round. Three evenings of my life. It was so hard and awkward.

The people on my paper round better appreciate their free tea!

It did pay £13, though, which is the most I have ever been paid for a job. So that was a nice consolation.

Friday 22nd May

I got my Year 10 Record of Achievement today ... and THANK GOD it's so much better than last year! For all my subjects – Mr Cooper must have been feeling proper guilty about putting me on report. Twat.

I don't think Ms Williams was happy that I got put on report without them talking to her about it, because she didn't mention it in her personal review. I'm starting to like Ms Williams. Obviously, I will never tell her that.

SUBJECT	YEAR 10	YEAR 9	YEAR 8	YEAR 7
Art	–	2	3	2
Business Studies	1	–	–	–
English	1/2	3/4	2/3	2
Geography	–	2/3	2	1
German	1	1	1	1
History	2	2	3	2
IT	1	1	1	1
Maths	2	2	3	2
Music	No music teacher	No music teacher	2	1
PE	1	1	2/3	2
RE	1	2	2	2
Science	1	2	2	1
Technology	2	1	1	2

You can see from last year that my report is much better. More like it was in Year 7. Actually, even better than in Year 7! I'm happy with that. Ammi was happy too.

Monday 25th May

Today I went to the cinema on my own for the first time ever! Basically, there was an offer to watch any film in the cinema for £1. One pound! No one else wanted to go. Not Shibz, Shiry, Was or Hassim. So I just went by myself.

I got a large sweet popcorn and a drink and a ticket all for only £5! I watched *Deep Impact*. When the film finished, I came out and no one knew I had been to the cinema on my own and I didn't tell anyone either.

It was my secret and maybe one day I'll do it again.*

Thursday 28th May

On the news today it said that Pakistan tested nuclear weapons and it was successful!

MUBARAK!

They showed scenes in Pakistan and everyone was celebrating, which makes sense.

The news said that India tested weapons ten days ago. Well, good that Pakistan has them, then. If two people might fight it's only fair that they have the same weapons, otherwise one can bully the other one, can't they? Obviously, I hope they don't fight. But maybe now they both have nuclear weapons they'll decide not to use them and just scare each other with them.

The thing I found curious, though, is that the news said Europe and America condemned the tests. But the UK, France and America have THEIR OWN nuclear weapons. So how can they tell another country off for having some? Sometimes politics makes no sense, kasam.

If I drank beer (*taubah taubah*), I can't tell someone else off for drinking wine. That would make me a hypocrite. I need to sort myself out first before I start telling other people off.

Friday 29th May [CONTAINS RUDE BITS]

Okay . . . I had to write this down, as it just happened.

Everyone had gone upstairs to bed. Quite often these days

---

* Going to the cinema on my own has been one of my biggest joys over the years.

I'm the last one to go to sleep. Sometimes I just sit there flicking channels, bored in my night-time salwar kameez.

I turned it to Channel 5 and I saw Mulder, so I got well happy thinking *X-Files* was on. That's actually my favourite show. But then I thought, no, that's not on 5.

I was curious and started watching it, and er ... it was a very different show to *X-Files*. More like *XXX-Files*.

It was very rude and showed this man and woman and they were naked and then ... they started doing proper rude stuff. The woman was so fit. She had ginger hair; I didn't even know that I could fancy someone with ginger hair.

Obviously then I got excited, innit. I didn't really know what to do.

The scene kept going on and on. I kept looking at the door because I was scared that someone might come downstairs for water or summat ... How much baisti would that be!

I would die.

After about ten minutes I got too uncomfortable and scared that someone would come down, so I switched over to channel 3 and then turned the TV off. I thought then whoever switches the TV on next won't know that I was watching Channel 5.

When I came to bed, I was still excited and couldn't get the images out of my head, imagining I was the guy and the girl was Buffy the Vampire Slayer.

In my head she goes to me, 'Have you got a wooden stake for me, Terry?'

Ufft! And then ... and then ... there was an explosion ... just like in the gym.

As soon as it happened, I could feel my kacheh* were wet and I felt proper guilty. Taubah.

I wish there was someone I could talk to about this stuff. Because it's gunnah, and what if it's not the last time it happens?

Monday 1st June

The World Cup starts in ten days!

Football World Cup, obviously. What other self-respecting World Cup is there? Well, cricket, but apart from that?

I'm so excited!

MICHAEL OWEN! He's gonna play at the World Cup and he's only eighteen. Imagine me playing for England in three years' time. The idea of that is crazy, but Owen is actually doing it! MashAllah, man.

Today I bought *FourFourTwo* magazine as it's got a proper wicked preview of all the teams and the tournament. Obviously, I'm most excited about England and Brazil, especially after the Nike Brazil advert where they're doing skills in the airport. It's too good.

The magazine came with a giant wallchart that has all the games on it and even which channels they're on. I've proper planned out how I can watch the most games and I'll be able to put the scores in and then fill it in once the teams get out of the groups.

I've mapped out how England can get to the final. We win our group (Tunisia, Romania and Colombia, that's easy), then we'll play Croatia in the last sixteen. They're a good team, but we can definitely win that. Then we'd play Germany in the quarter-finals and we'll get revenge for Euro 96, when they beat us on penalties. Then we'll probably play France or Italy in the semi-final; that'll be hard, but Shearer and Owen will get us through. Then Brazil in the final and who knows what could happen then?!

The other top thing about the wallchart? It's massive and covers my attic window, which means it'll make the room darker at night and block the sun in the morning. I love the World Cup!

Did I mention I'm excited?!

Wednesday 10th June

It's finally here.

I rushed home from school, dumped my bag in the hallway, said hello to Ammi, asked her to make me a keema sandwich (please) and went straight to the front room. I switched the little TV on and put it to BBC 1.

I was just in time to watch the end of the opening ceremony, which, to be honest, looked quite boring. It was in French, and no one said science in a weird accent, so I didn't understand any of it and I don't know anything about, or care for, the country of France.

Soon after, at 4.30 p.m., World Cup '98 kicked off! Brazil v Scotland. I'll be honest, I was supporting Scotland. Really I'm supporting England (Shibz is supporting Italy, Was is supporting Brazil, Hassim's supporting Germany (weirdo) and Shiry's supporting Holland), but today I switched allegiances: 1) because they have three Blackburn Rovers players (Colin Hendry, Billy McKinlay and Kevin Gallacher); 2) because Scotland are part of Great Britain, so they're also like a home team; and 3) because Brazil are England's biggest threat to winning the World Cup, so if they get knocked out early, the better chance England have!

Brazil scored after four minutes, so that enthusiasm didn't last long.

But after that, Scotland played really well, they only lost 2–1 in the end and Ronaldo didn't even play that good. Brazil won't win the World Cup playing like that.

The best thing about the World Cup? You get two or three matches a day! In the evening I watched Morocco v Norway. I was supporting Morocco because they're a Muslim team (I always support the Muslim team unless they're playing my team). It was a very fun game and finished 2–2.

I updated my wallchart curtain on the window of my attic

bedroom: 2–1, 2–2 and the goal-scorers. Two matches down, sixty-two to go!

Monday 15th June

Today was a special day as I watched a live football match in school for the first time ever. It was England's first game of the World Cup, but the kick-off was at 1.30 p.m. Mr Old (that's his name, not a nickname about his age. Although he is also old) and the rest of the technology teachers let us skive the lesson and watch the game instead!

They brought in a TV and the whole of Year 10 – who should've been doing woodwork, or electronics, or graphics (in my case) – got to watch England beat Tunisia thanks to Alan Shearer and Paul Scholes.

We were sat on stools, workbenches, some of us were sat on the floor. Even the girls were into it. When England scored, everyone cheered and hugged each other, even the people who said they were supporting other teams (*uhum* Shibz, Was, Hassim *uhum*).

And even better than England's sweet victory, ten seconds after the final whistle, the end-of-day school bell went off! What timing. It got the biggest cheer of the whole afternoon!

The magic of the World Cup is real.

Sunday 21st June

Tonight is the happiest I've been all World Cup! It was Iran v America. In real life Iran and America are enemies, from back in the 60s and 70s when America used to interfere in Iran's politics, and then in the 80s America supported Saddam Hussein's Iraq in a war against Iran. Even though America then turned against Saddam Hussein and Iraq too.

It must be hard being President of America. Every morning

they must ask their adviser, 'Are our friends from yesterday still our friends, or are we bombing them now?'

What was so funny was that at the beginning of the game Iran greeted America like they were a relative who's just come from Pakistan. They took one giant team photo instead of two separate ones. Iran gave them massive flowers and gifts just before kick-off, even though you're just meant to exchange a simple banner. Plus, all the Iranians had massive Pakistani uncle moustaches, which made it even funnier.

But when the game started it was very dirty. You could tell that neither team wanted to lose. But in the end Iran won! 2–1. Even Abu was happy, and he's paid no attention to the World Cup at all until this game. The best thing was, it looked like the whole world was supporting Iran. All the goreh (except actual Americans) in the stadium were supporting Iran and cheered when they scored.

No one likes America because they're bullies.

Wednesday 24th June

I walked past St Mark's church today (it's opposite our school).

There was a sign which I'd never noticed before, but it says in big writing JESUS SAVES! Underneath, someone had graffitied 'and Owen scores the rebound!'

I couldn't stop laughing. But I felt bad as well. We shouldn't disrespect other people's beliefs and cultures. I hope an apna* didn't do that. To be fair, a gora might have done it. They proper don't respect their religion, is really weird.

The first time I realised that was in primary school. I was sat in assembly and we were belting out a hymn:

Sing Hosanna, sing Hosanna, sing Hosanna to the King of Kings!

What a tune, bro. I used to feel funny about singing hymns, because it's Christian and we're Muslim, but then Ammi told me that Muslims and Christians (and Jews, actually) believe in the same God. That made it okay in my head to sing the hymns about God then.

Still, it was strange that in St Barnabas and St Paul's Church of England Primary School they'd get the kids, 60 per cent of whom were Muslim, to belt out these Christian hymns and we just took it as normal. I don't remember anyone ever complaining. Imagine if all the goreh in our area had to go to mosque in the evenings and even if they didn't believe in Islam the molbi saab made 'em pray kalimeh! That'd be hilarious. Smacking 'em and calling them 'mouldy sheep' if they got it wrong. Hahahaha.

Anyway, 'Give Me Oil in My Lamp' ended and an entire assembly hall of goreh and apne kids are belting out 'He's Got the Whole World in His Hands', and Kyle, who was sitting next to me, was changing the words to '*He's got my poo-poo in His hands, He's got my stinking poo in His hands . . .*' and he was laughing and I remember thinking he was crazy because we're talking about God here. Is he not scared of the consequences and getting gunnah? What are his parents teaching him?

I knocked on for Kyle for my very first day of Witton in Year 7. His dad answered the door and I remember thinking he looked at me a bit funny. But anyway, Kyle was my friend, we walked to school together and talked about how exciting high school is. That was the only day I ever knocked on for him. We don't even talk any more.

That's what this school does to you.

Friday 26th June

We beat Colombia. Thank God.

We're through. But we play Argentina next. That's gonna be hard.

Today's the last day of school for two weeks because all the

Year 10s are going on work experience. I'm going to Johnson Street Pharmacy. I applied to go to the hospital because I wanted to see some surgery. But the hospital weren't up for a nosy fifteen-year-old watching people being cut open. Shame. The pharmacy will be good, though. It'll be fun learning about what happens after I send patients away with their prescriptions.

Was is going to Burton's clothes shop. Shibz is going to Henry Ibbotson, the building company, and Hassim is going to the pharmacy on Preston New Road next to Harry Fu's Chinese restaurant.

Karolia got the best one, but. He's going to the cinema! Lucky git.

Monday 29th June

I had never heard of methadone. Until this guy came in, taubah I shouldn't say this, but basically, he looked like a tramp, innit. Uncle Professor, the owner and pharmacist,* he's really nice, recognised the guy straight away.

'Wait here, Simon.'

The guy did as he was told. Shuffling on the spot, he looked really awkward standing next to the Farley's Rusks.

I went to the back, behind the counter where all the magic happens. Well, science, not magic. Uncle Professor put this horrible green liquid into a cup, he comes out and gives it to Simon, who goes, 'Here, sir, can't you put it in a lickle bockle so I can have it later?'

'You know I can't, Simon. Now drink up.'

I think they'd had this conversation before, because Simon didn't argue. He drank the liquid in one go and then gave the cup back to Uncle Professor, who threw it in the bin.

---

* Everyone called him Professor, but it felt rude to not call him Uncle as well. Even though Uncle Professor is a weird name, looking back.

When Simon left, Uncle Professor told me that it was metha-done, which they give to smackheads (he said 'recovering heroin addicts') to help with their withdrawal symptoms. I think Uncle has to watch them have it there and then, so they don't sell it for money to buy drugs. I felt well sorry for Simon. He looks like he's had a hard and horrible life.

In the afternoon Fozia, who works in the pharmacy as an assistant, told me to put some tablets in a bottle. I was counting out all the tablets and it was taking well long. At one point I lost count. Fozia came to the back to check on me. Straight away she started laughing. 'Terry. What are you doing?'

'I'm counting the tablets.' She couldn't stop laughing.

I mean, how was I supposed to know that there's something called a triangle tablet counter? Am I a pharmacist? No.

Once she showed me how to use it, though, I proper buzzed off it. Kasam.

But to be honest, most of the work is boring. It's like working in a shop. I have to make sure all the nappies and toiletries look neat and that there's enough out on display, and if there isn't I have to go to the back back, past all the medicines and drugs (haha) and go get some packs of nappies out of the nappies box and then bring them out and put them on the shelf.

Nine more days of this.

Tuesday 30th June

I FUCKING HATE FOOTBALL!!!

Wednesday 1st July

Argentina knocked us out last night.

At least I'm not at school, otherwise Was and everyone would laugh at me because my team's out now and all their teams are still in.

I was watching the news before bed last night and there was a story about Stephen Lawrence. The evil men who killed him were in court giving evidence for an inquiry. There were lots of people outside tryna get into the courtroom and then the Nation of Islam turned up, looking all smart, and they barged in and then they had to stop the court session for the safety of those evil bastards.[*]

I wonder if there'll ever be an inquiry one day into Shehzad's murder. Someone needs to expose the truth.[†]

Saturday 4th July

Even though England are out, which I'm still so gutted about, at least I'll have Owen's goal in my memory for ever. I'm still watching every single game of the World Cup and I'm so glad I am, because DENNIS BERGKAMP!

Friday 10th July

Today was the last day at work experience and what I have learnt in the last two weeks of working at Johnson Street Pharmacy is that I do not want to be a pharmacist.

It's SO boring.

Actually, everyone I spoke to said their job was boring. Hassim didn't have it better at the pharmacy he was in. Even Karolia, and he was in the cinema!

Maybe being a grown-up just means life has to be boring.

---

[*] Two men, Gary Dobson and David Norris, were eventually convicted of the murder of Stephen Lawrence in January 2012.
[†] No one was ever convicted.

Saturday 11th July

I was in my room listening to the radio and doing my history homework (we owe Alexander Fleming a BIG thank you!) and there was a knock on the door. Ammi was standing there.

'*Mera puttar ke kardeh pya?*': What is my boy doing?

I switched the radio off. Ammi doesn't need to get into an argument with Brandy and Monica about whose boy I am.

'Nothing, Ammi, just my homework.'

'Good, good. I need to talk to you.'

Uh-oh. I instantly panicked. Does she know what I watched on TV that night? Shit. Shit. Shit.

'It's about Rosey.'

Er . . . what the hell has Baj been watching at night?

'I'm not going to Pakistan with you for Rosey's shaadi*.'

Huh? What? Why?

She explained that Wadi Ammi and Dad are taking care of the wedding arrangements and so she can't be part of the celebration as she won't go to Dad's house in Pakistan.

But that's not fair!

Ammi has sacrificed SO much – everything! – to bring me and Baji up. Especially in her marriage to Abu. If it had been up to him, he would've packed me and Baj off to live with Dad, but Ammi put her foot down and insisted we weren't going anywhere. I think that's a big reason for some of the problems in their marriage.

And after all that sacrifice, blood, sweat and tears, she's not gonna be a part of her eldest daughter's wedding.

I'm shocked, sad and angry.

And what do I say or do to make Ammi feel better?

'Okay, Ammi.' That's the best I can manage for the most important person in my life. Shame.

'You'll be there to represent me, okay? With your naani ammi and mammus and khalas. It'll be okay.'

'Okay, Ammi.'

Then, in even badder news ...

'How much money have you saved up from your paper job?'

Yesterday was my last day of my paper round. Thank God! And with that pay packet, I have saved 'Exactly £104, Ammi.'

'Very good. Give me £100 so I can buy Rosey a nice wedding gift from you.'

Er ... What?

So the first ever £100 that I earned from working, I have to spend on Baji Rosey's wedding present?

Cool. Cool. Cool. *Really happy* about that. I love my Baji after all. So ... yeah ... top.

I *happily* handed over my entire life savings.

Sunday 12th July

What the hell?

France won the World Cup final 3–0. Easily, like it was a group game against Saudi Arabia.

I was happy that Zinedine Zidane scored two goals, because he's Muslim and it's nice that a Muslim player won France the World Cup. But what the hell happened?

At the beginning of the game Brazil said that Ronaldo wasn't playing because he wasn't feeling well. Then suddenly Brazil changed their minds and Ronaldo *was* playing. Like me, the presenters were proper confused.

Ronaldo did not play well. He looked lost and tired and ill, and it looked like whatever happened before the game affected the whole Brazil team, because they looked proper shell-shocked. What a weird ending to an amazing month of football.

Monday 13th July

At school, everyone was talking about what happened to Ronaldo. Nearly everyone thinks he was poisoned.

Think about it. The World Cup was in France. France wanted to win because they're at home and they've never won the World Cup before. As host country, they control everything. So it probably would've been easy for them to get someone to put some poison or something in Ronaldo's food or drink.

The final should be replayed.

First they killed Diana, and now this.

Fuck France, man.

Sunday 19th July

I'm on a plane!

I'm writing my diary on an aeroplane thirty-five thousand feet in the air. What a crazy world.

I love going to Pakistan. This is my fifth time, which I think might be a record in my family for my age. I know none of my friends have been this many times. I'm proper lucky!

Who's with me is: Baji Rosey (obviously), Shibz, Poupoh, Jaffer, Dad and Wadi Ammi.

We've got SO much luggage. Asians always pack way too much, kasam. Like we're moving house and taking all our belongings with us. Plus, too many people dropped us off at the airport. It's like for every one person that goes Pakistan, five people have to come to drop 'em off. Okay, so thirty-five people didn't drop us lot off, but there was still like ten people!

Ammi didn't come airport and actually it was very emotional leaving without her. Her and Baji Rosey hugged for a very long time on the doorstep and they were both crying loads. Then that made me cry because I'm soft. Ammi told me to look after her. I said *I will*, and I meant it.

Packing for Pakistan is always interesting. I don't take that many clothes because I don't wear English clothes there, only shalwar kameezes. And usually I just get new ones made for me when I get there. But I always have a suitcase full of gifts for Ammi's family. At the airport, when they say to me, '*Did you pack your suitcase yourself?*' I always say, '*Yeah.*' But Ammi could've put anything in there ... Good job I trust her!

Dad only has one big sister in Pakistan, with most of his family in England, whereas Ammi has both her parents, brothers and sisters and loads of uncles and aunts and cousins over there. I'm related to like half the village! I love them all, but Mammu Abbas is my favourite uncle. Because he's funny and always takes me on rides on his motorbike. Oh yeah, everyone has a motorbike in Pakistan. No one has a car. Some people still ride bicycles too. I remember when we first went to Pakistan, we didn't have a motorbike in our family and my mammus would take me everywhere on their bicycles. The bikes there all have racks, so you sit on the back of them while the rider cycles around. I used to love looking at all the fields, riding past the villages and houses that look so different to England, wondering *who lives there?*

Shibz, Baji Rosey and me got loads of sweets for the eight-hour flight: Starburst (the new name of Opal Fruits), chocolate mice, giant strawberries, fizzy belts, jawbreakers, double lollies, Double Dip, mini eggs and cola bottles (I always bite the top off first and then pretend to drink it). We shared everything with each other. Swapping and mixing and matching so we can all get a bit of everything. Lucky for me, those are all my favourite sweets.

I've got a window seat which is great when the plane takes off. Everything looks like the beginning of *EastEnders*. It's night-time right now, but, so I can hardly see anything!

Monday 20th July

I'm in Pakistan!

We arrived at Lahore airport in the morning.

As soon as I stepped off the plane, I knew we'd arrived. The air felt so thick and muggy and it took about five minutes to get used to how to breathe. Ahhhhhhh.

After filling out the immigration forms and going through passport checks we got our luggage. Which took AGES. Because we had so much of it!

When we came out of the baggage bit into Arrivals, it was so busy. I was pushing a trolley, looking at all the faces of people who were awaiting their loved ones. There was only one face I was looking for, though.

I scanned the crowd and ... then ... there he was! Pushed up against a railing, he gestured for me to go the end, then he disappeared behind someone and so I pushed my trolley as fast as I could till I reached the end of the waiting area and there he was, right in front of me: my Mammu Abbas. Stood there in a blue shalwar kameez, with his long face, big hair and even bigger smile decorated with that classic bushy Pakistani moustache. He gave me the biggest hug. I'd missed him a lot. Though he's not as tall as I remember him being!

A few other people from Ammi's family were there to greet us too and I wondered if it was awkward for them to greet Dad. If it was, no one showed it. Good.

We loaded two vans with the luggage and then me, Shibz and Baji Rosey got into one van with Mammu Abbas, Khala Fozia and Mammu Shama (Ammi's brothers and sister), while all the other grown-ups went in the other van. It was a fun ride back. We were all chatting away, catching up about everything. It didn't feel like we'd just been on an eight-hour plane ride.

The Pakistan countryside is so beautiful. It takes about four hours to get from Lahore to our village in Jhelum, so I had lots of time to see it. In England, when you drive in the countryside it's very leafy and green, whereas in Pakistan it's much more sandy and yellow. Plus, most of it isn't built up like in England. It's so different.

Halfway home, we stopped at a petrol station to fill the vans up and eat some food. Mammu got us all some bun kebabs, which I guess is what you'd call a burger on *Catchphrase*. Whatever its name, though, it is SO tasty!

I had my first bottle too. A bottle basically means a 250ml glass bottle of fizzy drink.

I asked, '*Bottle kitne dee eh hoon?*': How much is a bottle these days?

'*Maingay oh gai eh. Saat rupayeh*': Things have gone expensive. Seven rupees.

Woah! That's well expensive! I mean, seven rupees is about 3p, but for Pakistan that is a lot.

When I used to come to Pakistan, having a bottle always seemed like a luxury and a big deal. Nevertheless, me and my cousins always had competitions over who could drink the most bottles in one day. My record is five. When you finish with them you send them back to the shop, who send them back to the factory to be cleaned and reused. Recycling ... which I've heard is a good thing.

Then there was a fight between Pai Naseer and Mammu Abbas over who was going to pay for the food. Obviously. This ALWAYS happens in Pakistan. Everyone wants to pay for everyone. And then there's a big argument (a friendly one) over who actually pays. Mammu Abbas won this time (or lost, depending on your perspective), and so he got to pay.

We eventually arrived in Boken (the village where Ammi was born) just after midday. There was a huge crowd of people there to greet us. To me it looked like half the village had turned up!

So many people to hug and so many wet kisses from old women I barely recognised.

After eating again, Dad and Wadi Ammi got ready to go to our home village of Jahangir, which is about a mile and a half from Boken. Technically, you're from where your dad is from, so I'm from Jahangir. But the first three times I came to Pakistan were with Ammi, and we stayed in Boken, in her parents' home. So when people ask me where I'm from in Pakistan, even though I'm supposed to say I'm from Jahangir, I say Boken.

I asked Dad if I could stay in Boken for the night. He didn't look too pleased, but he said yes, though I had to go to Jahangir tomorrow.

I spent my first night back under the stars of a clear Pakistani sky, sleeping on my favourite manji*. It's hard to believe that Pakistan shares the same sky with England, because there's always SO many more stars in the Pakistani night sky. It's beautiful. Especially when a jugnoo* flies past.

Wednesday 22nd July

The wedding is next week, so there's so much to do. There's been no time to rest, everyone's been running around non-stop. Mainly going to Jhelum sher* and shopping!

Sher is incredible. Is SO busy. The streets are lined with so many different types of shops: women's clothes, men's clothes, juice stations, jalaibi, cassettes, sandals, sports equipment and household items to name a few. Most of the shops are really small. The whole centre is like Blackburn Market, but bigger, smellier and noisier, with motorcycles ready to run you over every three steps.

We had to buy so many clothes for everyone. That means getting your measurements taken by the tailor and picking out three different outfits and three different pairs of sandals or khusseh*.

I mean, it's fine when it's your clothes, but the amount of time spent in the women's clothes shops . . . I thought I was gonna die of boredom. I understand that it's important. But they take forever!

And then they have to haggle for everything. Every shop that we go to, either Poupoh or Dad or Wadi Ammi or Naani Ammi have to argue with the shopkeeper about the price. EVERY SINGLE TIME. He'll say a thousand rupees. They have to scoff and ask him if his brain is working. They're fully ruthless. The shopkeeper laughs and says something like, 'Look, you're like my own mother, for you I'll do the best price: seven hundred rupees.' That's 30 per cent below what he said before. Still not good enough, though. Naani Ammi will say something ridiculous like 'We saw this for four hundred in the shop down the road.'

No, we never. I was there, I don't remember that.

The shopkeeper will laugh again.

This will go on for ten minutes. Until we start walking out of the shop (and I'm thinking, but I actually want these shoes – don't walk away), and then eventually we'll get it for five hundred rupees. Half price. Sometimes even better. It's a ridiculously stressful system.

And that's just shoes and clothes. It's a wedding: there's so much to buy!

Jewellery. Flowers. Gifts. Then there's the samaan*, Baji's dowry. We bought furniture. So much of it. Sofas, bed, wardrobe, dressing table, dining table, chairs, manjis, TV, dinner sets etc. It's like we were furnishing her husband's entire house. Dad explained that because we're from England, we can't look cheap.

The whole thing was confusing and tiring and exhausting, to be honest. What is good, though, is we got a bottle in nearly every shop. I think I had four today.

Sunday 26th July

After a week of shopping and catching up, the wedding festivities start tomorrow. A week-long celebration, at the end of which Baji Rosey will be married!

Damn.

I say that, but it kinda felt like it started today. Pai Abid (my new brother-in-law's neighbour and cousin) came over to our house in Jahangir this evening with his mum. There's a custom before the wedding where a representative from the boy's side comes to finalise the dates of the wedding.

Er ... the wedding is next week! SHOULDN'T THIS HAVE BEEN DECIDED MONTHS AGO?!

Anyway, there they were, sat with Dad and Wadi Ammi. While they were talking, Big Poupoh called me into the kitchen to tell me that there was another custom that went along with this. She gave me a bucket full of coloured water and told me I had to spill it over Pai Abid.

What?!

I mean, okay. If you say so.

I took the bucket out but he spotted me straight away. He got up and started running to the other side of the yard ... I ran after him ... the bucket was a bit heavy ... The yard is big, but it's just a big square and so there's nowhere to hide.

'Nah karee!' Don't do it! I could hear Wadi Ammi shouting behind me.

'Get him, son!' Dad's encouragements came from the same direction.

I caught up with Pai Abid and launched the bucket, draining him in a mix of red, blue and yellow. Everyone started laughing ... but I'd let my guard down. Abid ran at me, grabbed the bucket and poured the remainder over my head!

Urrrrrgh.

I didn't know what was happening, or why, but it was a proper good laugh. I like Pai Abid. Tall and wide. He's a big cuddly bear sort of man.

Sunday 2nd August

What a week! Damn I'm tired!

Baji Rosey is officially married to Pai Uneeb. I have a new brother-in-law! I always wished I had an older brother and now I do.

So, what happened?

1. Monday 27th: Dholki 1. This was the first event, at our house in Jahangir. It's one for the ladies really. Basically, a whole load of women got together around a drum (the dholki) and sang songs (in the most terrible voices I've ever been unfortunate enough to hear) and took turns dancing. Poupoh, Naani Ammi and Wadi Ammi were proper into it. It was the funniest and worst thing I've ever seen in my life, all at the same time. Baji Rosey looked so embarrassed, which made me and Shibz laugh even more.

2. Tuesday 28th: Dholki 2. It was the women on the boy's side's turn to do their terrible singing and dancing. Allah da shukr eh* we didn't have to sit through that. It's bad enough when you know the women doing the horrible singing.

3. Wednesday 29th: Mehndi 1. The mehndi, basically a henna party, is another one of those things I don't understand the point of. We all met up in another person in the village's house, ate some food and then were led by a procession of girls and ladies carrying trays of candles and henna back to our house. Then they set the trays down and did a dance around them that they were all too embarrassed to do properly.

Then Baj had to sit in a chair on a stage and, group by group, people came up and gave her some money, while putting some henna in her hand and feeding her some mitai* (sometimes with the same hand they used for the henna – yuck!).

It went on for way too long. Me and Shibz got so bored. At one point the electricity went out (that happens two or three times a day in Pakistan) and we had to carry on by candlelight.

4. Thursday 30th: Mehndi 2. This day was the henna party for the boy's side. Similar to yesterday, we started off in some random house in Dhanyala (the boy's side village, about thirty minutes on a motorbike from Jahangir) and made our way back to the boy's house before we were subjected to some more bad dancing.

But this procession was a bit different. Me and Shibz were with Pai Abid and Mammu Abbas, and they told us about a tradition ... to smack the boy's best men whilst on the procession. Sorry, what?

You get to smack the boy's best men? And if you have sewing pins you stab them! Fortunately, we didn't have any sewing pins(!); I know what I'm like. I would've got carried away and I didn't wanna be responsible for spreading hepatitis C in Dhanyala.

But let me tell you, with Pai Abid and Mammu Abbas's encouragement, me and Shibz got some proper licks in. Teamwork, as well. Shibz would smack one and hide behind Pai Abid, then when the guy turned round to see who hit him, I would hit him from the other side and hide behind Mammu Abbas, and then Shibz would do it again. It was too funny. And cruel. But mainly funny. Pai Abid couldn't stop laughing. Him and Mammu Abbas basically protected us, because me and Shibz were going well over the top.

At one point, one of the best men turned around angrily and goes, '*Tudhe te neena maar sakde!*': They're not allowed to kick! Oops.

*

5. Friday 31st: This was the wedding day! A proper long and full day. We spent all morning running around getting ready.

I caught a glimpse of Baji Rosey ... I had to do a double-take, I barely recognised her!

Her eyebrows were thin lines and she was proper white, like a ghost. I'm not sure what the idea of beauty is here in Pakistan, but they made her look like one of those Japanese ladies from TV. I didn't think it really suited her. But today was not the day to say anything. And actually, after I got used to the look, she did look beautiful.

After we all got ready, we had to wait ages for the groom's side to arrive. How it works is, the groom's side bring their procession and guests to our village. We feed them and then there is the rukhsti, which is the tradition where the groom takes the bride away from her home and back to his. That part can get very emotional.

The groom's side eventually came (classic Pakistani timing), but before we could let them enter the village, he (or rather his dad) had to pay a price. Some girls from our side formed a barrier with a rope and the boy's side had to barter to be allowed in. Which basically means giving our girls money. And the girls are encouraged to hold out! The boy's side can't look cheap, so the girls ended up making a few thousand rupees! It's mad.

As Pai Uneeb came into the village on a horse, there was a long and loud procession behind him. Drummers, dancers, people throwing money in the air which the poor people in our village were either catching or collecting off the floor like it was the giant dome in *Crystal Maze*, and then we finally got to make our way to the wedding dinner.

Which was ... chaos.

I've heard that in goreh weddings, everyone is told where to sit and then waiters come over to give them food and there is only one sitting. Not here.

There were over five hundred people and only so much space in the tents that we'd put up. So people had to wait their turn, and when it was time to eat there was no patience. The food would get put on the table and people would attack it. Me and Shibz were a bit uncomfortable. In England our weddings are fun and chaotic, but there was a desperation here that made me think a lot of the guests were really not used to eating well regularly, and so they were making the most of the opportunity.

After that was the nikkah*. Which is the actual wedding bit. The imam asked Baji Rosey to pray, then asked her three times if she wanted to get married, before making her sign the official registration form. Then the imam went to Pai Uneeb and did the same thing. And *dieses*, we have a wedded couple!

Then they both sat on the stage for ages, while everyone took turns for pictures and gave their gifts. Now, I have to say something here about how Pakistanis take pictures, because it is the funniest thing ever! They're all happy, happy, happy, and then as soon as the camera is on them they make the straightest face in the world. It's such a straight face that they actually look sad, which makes me laugh so much because the wedding album is gonna be full of pictures where everyone looks miserable, even though they're not. Just smile!

This is when I gave my gift to Baji. A lovely gold ring. She said she loved it. She bloody better, it cost me my entire life savings!

After all that is finally done, it's the rukhsti. And it was emotional! My Baji Rosey is leaving our house and becoming a woman. The next time she comes to visit, she'll be a guest. Something about that made me cry a lot. When it was my turn to hug her, I wouldn't let go; we were both crying so much. I think we were both thinking of everything we'd been through together and how we wished Ammi was there. And now we were at this moment where we had to say goodbye, and it was ... it was too much. Eventually I got pulled off her by Dad and Poupouh. Both of whom were also very emotional.

And then she left with Pai Uneeb.

6. Saturday 1st: Walima*. PARTY TIME!

A day of eating, more gifts (mainly money, to be honest) and posing for pictures. I drank seven bottles, breaking my personal record. So that was something.

Towards the end of the day, I managed to speak with Baji Rosey for a bit. She said she was okay and was having a nice time. GOOD.

Then, in the evening, it was all over.

It's been an amazing week. But God, I am so shattered!

Tuesday 4th August

Ah ... this is more like it.

Today I did nothing. Well, almost nothing.

I woke up scratching my hands, arms, legs and feet, because of the mosquito bites. No matter what we try – the fan, medicine, special light – the little bastards always find their way to my skin. Naani Ammi says it's because our English blood is really sweet, that's why the machar* love it so much.

After a good scratch, I got up and went into the yard. Our house in Jahangir belongs to Dad and Taya. They built it about five years ago. It's huge. It's got a big courtyard in the middle, with Dad's side on the right and Taya's side on the left.

It's massive, but the standout bit is the football tank on the top of the fourth floor on Dad's side. Every house has a tank, which gets its water pumped from a well. Because Dad is football obsessed, the tank on his side is a massive football, which you can see from miles and miles around. It looks well cool. I'm proper proud of it.

I had a shower, with cold water, because that's what you do in Pakistan. Also, it's already so hot by the middle of the morning, a nice cold shower actually feels proper good.

After getting dressed and eating breakfast I said goodbye to Wadi Ammi and Dad and walked to Boken. There are two routes out of the village: one is through this forest with a graveyard in it and one isn't a forest with a graveyard in it. I chose the non-death route.

It's a twenty-five-minute walk along a dirt path that winds through fields that grow corn in the spring, or pateh* for buffaloes and cows. Most roads around here are not very good. They're either made of bricks, or just dirt. Because there's no proper drainage like there is in England, when it rains it can get proper messy!

I got to Boken, take the lefts and rights through the narrow alleys of the village and arrived at my grandparents' house, which is on the outskirts of the north side. It's currently getting done up. There's a big yard, which is divided into a courtyard for sitting in, then some plants and trees that split the middle and behind that a yard where we keep the animals. We don't have animals at our house in Jahangir, because no one lives in that house when we're not there. But here in Boken we have one buffalo, its baby, two goats and some chickens.

In England, farmers have cows and sheep. In Pakistan, people have mainly buffaloes and goats. Some people do have cows, but the only people that have sheep are Pathans*.

I love being here. I chilled all day. I had some grapes with Naana Abu while he smoked and practised his broken English on me: 'How do you do good gentle man? English gentle man is best gentle man.'

Ammi tells me that Naana Abu is proper strict and can have a temper, but to me he's so sweet and is always making me laugh.

I asked him to tell me my favourite story about Ammi. Which he always loves telling.

Basically, when Ammi was six, she and her big sister, Khala Shakeela, went to the mosque to get some water out of the well. They threw the bucket in, and then little Ammi peered over the edge to have a look at the bottom, slipped and fell in.

SHE FELL INTO THE WELL!

Khala Shakeela started screaming. Obviously. Everyone came running out of their houses to help. The imam's son climbed down into the well to get her. And apparently, on the way up, Ammi was shouting, '*MERI JOOTI MERI JOOTI!*': MY SHOE MY SHOE!

One of her shoes had fallen off and she was really upset and thought she'd get into trouble at home for it! That's so funny, because that's exactly how I would be. Like when I got hit by a car and was more worried about my Skips! It made me smile that I was like Ammi in that way.

By the afternoon it was too hot, so I had a little lie down in the baitak*, and when I woke up a few hours later I had some mangoes. Pakistani mangoes are heavenly. Then me, Shibz and Shama went to the khooh*, which is basically a farmyard that Shibz lot own, but they've got this ultra-power shower with water that comes straight out of their well. It's the most amazing thing you can do in this weather. You get knocked back by a storm of cold water and the moment it hits you it's too much, because you feel a shock, your breath leaves you, for about three secs and then you get used to it. It's incredible and you feel so clean afterwards.

We headed back to ours just as Mammu Abbas came home dragging a bale of pateh on his back, that he'd cut himself using a sickle. He was absolutely drenched in sweat.

Me and Shibz chilled as the sun set and started hearing the frogs and the crickets. Our house is at the edge of a chapra*, where the buffaloes can bathe, but it means it's full of very noisy insects!

I got up to see what the others were doing. Khala Shaheen and

Khala Fozia were by the little brick stove, where they used dried buffalo dung as fuel to cook our chooza* saalan and roti for dinner.

We ate in the yard, while we watched a drama on TV, which was on the veranda. My eyes kept wandering to the three little lizards that had gathered on the wall behind, running near the tube light. Occasionally one of them would disappear underneath it and then reappear out the other end. Mammu tells me they're harmless. Maybe. It's still a lizard in your house, though. Like a fly or spider. It's weird!

At bedtime, everyone's manjis are lined up outside, with big fans on either side. Even though it can get a bit cold at night, we need the fans to keep the mosquitos at bay. God, I hate mosquitos SO MUCH!

I'm about to go to bed now, the stars are out, I can hear frogs and crickets, I can see some fireflies. Whoosh!

Ooh! I just saw a shooting star. I've just made a wish. Marry Buffy the Vampire Slayer when I grow up.

I love this place.

Tuesday 11th August

Ammi rang today. I have a new baby brother! Tauqeer. I think that's how you would spell it.

I told Dad, he gave me mubarak and then he told me he had news too: 'Your Aunty's expecting. So you're going to have another brother or sister in a couple of weeks.'

Woah. Thanks for the heads up, Dad! You only had eight and a half months to tell me. But it's so cool, like a buy one get one free on siblings.

'Mubarak, Dad!'

I can't wait to go home and meet them both. That'll be eight siblings I have then.

Sunday 16th August

Because our house in Boken is getting done up, there's builders around and loads of sand and cement and equipment and stuff. Me, Shibz and Shama have realised that the sand in part of the garden is deep enough that we can jump off the roof into it. It's pretty cool, to be honest. It's still quite high, so a bit scary, but safe. And even though we kept getting told off by Naani Ammi, we carried on doing it.

Late afternoon, one of the trailers was going to the river to collect more sand, so me and Shibz jumped on the back of the trailer. Shama told us not to go, but because me and Shibz had got on the trailer he had to get on too because he couldn't just leave us.

It was a fun, bumpy ride. After about twenty-five minutes we arrived at Jhelum River. Me and Shibz threw our kameezes off and jumped in the river. Shama can't swim and he kept shouting at us from the side to get out of the water and that kids always drown in the river.

'Yeah, kids who can't swim, Shama! Me and Shibz can both swim.'

'Yeah. Chill out, Shama.'

Me and Shibz were having so much fun we told the trailer guy to leave and to get us on the next round.

While we were floating in the river, soaking in the evening sunshine, Shibz asked me if I thought about what college I wanna go to for A levels.

I said, 'The only ones I know are Blackburn College and St Mary's.'

'No, you can't go Blackburn College, man. That's for dossers. Go Mary's, that's where people with better grades go in Blackburn,' Shibz said.

'Are you gonna apply there?'

'Yeah. Definitely.'

'Safe. I'll apply there as well then.'

Thanks, Shibz. Yeah, I wanna go somewhere I can learn, not where all troublemakers be. I've had enough of that at school.

We carried on swimming and splashing about and tryna get Shama to come in the water with no luck.

About forty-five minutes after we sent the trailer guy away, Mammu Abbas and Chacha Farooq (Uncle's younger brother) turned up. Uh-oh. They looked proper pissed off.

They told us to jump on the motorcycles. It wasn't a negotiation.

Shama and me got behind Mammu Abbas, and Shibz got behind Chacha Farooq.

'I told you not to go, didn't I?' Shama whispered to me.

'It'll be okay.' I told him. We're fine, aren't we?

They drove back, and instead of going to our house, we ended up at Shibz's house where we got shouted at by Mammu Abbas and Chacha Farooq so much. It proper reminded me of the bollocking we got last year for going to Preston on Eid. Actually, it was worse, because Shama got a beating off Chacha Farooq, and that was really unfair because he was just following me and Shibz.

I felt well bad. He's gone to sleep now. I'll buy him a bottle tomorrow, hopefully that'll cheer him up.

Friday 21st August

I was watching *Captain Planet* on PTV, which is the one show I recognise in this country. When it finished, the news came on and it said that America had bombed Afghanistan. That's right next door to Pakistan. Ufffft.

What the hell, man? I didn't understand why because the Urdu on TV is too posh for me, but America does whatever it wants. I wish someone would teach their army a lesson.

Monday 24th August

I had an argument with Mammu Jamil today. It was well funny.

He didn't know that my name is not Tahir.

Basically, when I was born, Pua Said kept my name as Tehzeeb. Ammi hated it, but that's what got put on my birth certificate. But Ammi insisted on calling me Tahir. I mean, that's a completely different name. Tahir then became Terry.

Anyway, Mammu Jamil didn't know that Tehzeeb is my actual name. He wouldn't believe me. I had to get Shibz to convince him. He looked so confused. Haha.

Thursday 27th August

I've just been attacked! I thought I was gonna die. Seriously.

Okay, for like seven seconds. I'm being a drama queen. But it was scary!

I was messing about in the yard at Naani Ammi's house and then I climbed the stairs to go up on the roof and I noticed, right at the top of the stairs, this small little blob. It looked really strange. I went closer to have a look, and it had a face!

I'd never seen anything like it. It looked so helpless. I got closer and realised it was a baby bird. It looked up at me. Awww. I was about to kneel down, when WHACK!

What the hell was that? Someone just smacked me on the head. I looked around but there was no one there.

So, weird mayb—

WHACK!

Heh?

WHACK!

I thought there was something behind me (a djinn*, maybe?), so I did the most stupidest thing I could at that point: I took a step on to the roof.

WHACK WHACK WHACK!

I looked up and then ducked just in the nick of a time as a crow swooped down, trying to take my eye out.

WHACK WHACK WHACK!

There were about ten crows circling overhead, all taking turns to have a whack at my head!

I'm not proud of this, but I started yelling. No, that's not true. Screaming. I started screaming. 'HELP! HELP! HELP!'

No one in this village speaks English; who was I calling to?

People did start coming out of their houses, though. To watch the spoilt British boy running around his grandma's roof as birds circled overhead, waiting to take chunks out of him. It must have been well entertaining for them! They must've thought, thirty years ago, his mum fell into a well and now Tahir's here being eaten by birds. What a family.

After about half a minute of screaming, Naani Ammi came to my rescue. She was at the top of the stairs, yelling at me to go over to her while she waved a stick over her head to keep the crows at bay.

The stick did the trick. I ran over and hid behind her as the crows came low and then flew off again to avoid the stick. Pussies!

Just before we went down, Naani Ammi used the stick to push the baby crow off the ledge of the roof! Which I thought was unnecessary, but I guess a message had to be sent to the crows. Fuck with my baby and I fuck with your baby, innit!

She checked my head to see if I was bleeding, which I wasn't. To be honest, it was all over so quickly, I suddenly felt embarrassed.

But then again, what if no one was home? I'm sure there's a horror film about murderous birds. I wonder what it's called. Put it this way, I'll never be able to watch *Dumbo* the same way again.

What a crazy trip.

Monday 31st August

I'm on the plane back to England. It feels so different to the trip here. It's just me, Shibz and Baji Rosey. Baji would've liked to have stayed longer, but she has to go back to college. She's gonna apply for Pai Uneeb's visa in a few months, then he'll join us in England.

All the grown-ups are staying a bit longer. Well, it's not like they have school to go back to, is it?

It was proper emotional saying goodbye to everyone. I stayed over at Boken because Shibz was there too, so it's easier to leave together. I said bye to Naani Ammi, Naana Abu, Mammu Jamil, Mammu Habib, Mammu Shama, Khala Fozia, Khala Shakeela and Khala Shaheen. Plus Neelam (Khala Shakeela's daughter, my little cousin) too.

I told them I'll see them all soon. Although to be honest, I don't know when that will be.

Mammu Abbas and Kafait (Neelam's older brother) came with us to the airport: it was even more emotional saying goodbye to them. I had a suitcase full of stuff again, and my own stuff was probably less than half of what was in there. Most of it was stuff for Ammi and other people. When they checked our suitcases, the airport workers asked us for money, then realised we were kids on our own. They looked a bit frustrated but had to let us go. Serves you right, you corrupt gits.

We made it on the plane and now I'm gonna sleep till I get home.

Tuesday 1st September

England is freeeeezing!

The weird thing is that the sun was shining. But a warm day here would be a cold day in Boken.

Ammi gave me a big hug when we got home and said, '*Itna kamzor augeyeh*': You've gone so weak/thin.

Yes! I needed to lose weight!

Then her and Baji hugged for a long time. They were both crying like it was Baji's wedding day all over again. I went into the living room and grabbed Saeeda and Zaheer and gave them big hugs.

Little Tany smiled when he saw me. Yes! He hasn't forgotten who I am. His eyes lit up when I gave him the little somersaulting dog I picked up in a shop in Jhelum.

But best of all was when I got to meet my new baby brother, Tauqeer. He smelt like baby powder. He was so pale and small. I love him.

Abu came downstairs and just nodded at me. I nodded back. He put his hand over Baji's head and said, 'Mubarak.'

That was it. The most minimal of acknowledgements he could muster.

We had different guests coming all day. Mainly to meet Baj because she's married now. Pua Said and Uncle came with Shahid. So I got to hang out with Shahid, which was nice. While I was thrashing him at *Street Fighter II* I asked how his dad's takeaway, Goodfellas, was doing.

'Really good, man. You should come more. You know we'll always sort you out.' Shahid, always the kindest person in the room.

Wednesday 2nd September

I have ANOTHER brother! Today Suliman was born. He's Dad's third child with Aunty. That's eight brothers and sisters now! Rosey, Saeeda, Saira, Zaheer, Yasmin, Tanveer, Tauqeer and now Suliman. That's enough, I think.

*

Today was my first day as a Year 11. Shit gets serious now, man. I have to say, though, the first day of school is always one of the nicest days of the year. And today was no different. Witton Park actually looks proper pretty in the sunshine, with its green fields and trees and woodland backgrounds.

In every class we had, the teacher said the same thing. Pay attention, work hard and do the best you can do.

I need six As to get in to do medicine at uni. I'm gonna do everything I can to get 'em!

Sunday 6th September

Babies are so cute. My new baby brother Suliman is no different.

I wondered two things: 1) Will him and Tauqeer grow up to be friends,* seeing as they were born only three weeks apart? And 2) How does the baby of a family feel when a new baby comes?

Suliman was laid down on a baby mat; Yasmeen and Saira were cooing at our little brother. They both seemed really happy, to be fair.

The room was packed. Dad, Taya and Tayi were sat on one settee and me, Was and Nads were sat on the other. 'It's not often you see teddy bears playing with a baby, is it?' Was obviously thought this scene was as cute as I did. Teddy bears is what me and him called Yasmeen and Saira.

Dad was telling Nads about the latest with Baaji: 'They're saying he's got Alzheimer's now too. So it's not looking good, to be honest. He's really starting to forget basic things, and even names.'

'*Allah rahm kare ne*' – May Allah show mercy on them – Taya said softly. His voice cracked a bit.

'Ameen.'

---

* They did not.

We all fell silent, feeling sorry for Baaji and Wadi Ammi while we quietly watched these cute little things playing together.

'What we gonna call him?' Nads asked innocently.

Good question. Cos we all got nicknames: I'm Terry, then there's Nads (Nadeem), Was (Waseem), Muj (Mujeeb), Shibz (Shabaz), Shiry (Shiraz), Jaffa Cakes (Jaffer) etc.

'Sully?' Was suggested.

Suddenly from the door of the kitchen, my stepmum said, '*KHABARDAR! Kake da na Suliman eh!*': How dare you! The baby's name is Suliman. She continued, 'So you'll call him Suliman. I don't want to hear no Sully-Shully from anyone!'

A room of ten people went quiet. I guess that's us told.

Suliman it is.

Tuesday 8th September

I got two new teachers. Which is good news and bad news.

Bad news first: Mrs Blake has left. Which I'm gutted about. She's taught me German for four years and she always gives me really good marks. I'm gonna miss being in her class.

Now we have Miss Rose instead. Which is really bad news. Because Miss Rose is the fittest teacher in our school. She's SO FIT! Too fit. How am I meant to concentrate in her class?

I heard she's got a black belt in tae kwon do and can do the splits. That last bit is information that I didn't need to know man.

The second new teacher is actually a new teacher in the school. Mrs Fisher, my new RE teacher. And she's wicked, man. She was telling us that she's Greek Orthodox, which I don't think means that she's Greek, I think she's a type of Christian, like we have Sunnis and Wahhabis.

Anyway, she was telling us how much she likes and respects Islam and that made all us Asians feel well good. Maybe she'll convert one day?

Thursday 24th September

The news was really interesting today. It said that Iran had stopped supporting the fatwa against Salman Rushdie.

That's a name I haven't heard for years and years.

Basically, Salman Rushdie wrote a book called *The Satanic Verses* in which he insulted the Prophet Muhammad (Peace Be Upon Him) and Islam in general. Which is obviously really bad! What a crazy guy, it was like he was in a rush[to]die.

Islam, Allah and the Prophet Muhammad (Peace Be Upon Him) are THE MOST important things to a Muslim. We don't let anyone insult them. We're taught to defend and uphold their honour. So, when Salman Rushdie wrote his daft book, Muslims all over the world were proper angry and some of them wanted to kill him. I don't understand: his name is Salman, so he must be Muslim; he should've known to not write something so stupid.

Then Iran actually did a fatwa, saying that they'd give a reward to whoever killed him, like he was a pirate or outlaw in the olden days.

I remember when I was at Cedar Street Infant School, when we were living in Hickory Street, probably in 1988 or 1989, there was an actual Muslim strike. In the whole of the country. Muslims didn't go to work and didn't send their kids to school in protest about Rushdie's book. I remember that day, I didn't go to school. Imagine that, all the Muslims in the country, together, taking action as one. Amazing.

Anyway, now because Iran wants to do business with England they're saying they don't support killing Salman Rushdie any more.

As much as I hate Salman Rushdie, the stupid bastard, I think that's right. I don't think you should kill someone for writing a book. The Prophet Muhammad (Peace Be Upon Him) was insulted by his enemies all his life, sometimes with words and sometimes people would actually harm him physically. *Taubah*

taubah. It makes me shake with anger just thinking about the people that would dare do that. But the thing is, the Prophet (Peace Be Upon Him) always dealt with those people with patience and never retaliated.

And I think because we love him and respect him so much and he was our greatest teacher, we should take those teachings from the Prophet (Peace Be Upon Him) and use his example to deal with this.

Because whatever Salman Stupid Rushdie wants to write, it doesn't actually change even one tiny ounce of how great the Prophet (Peace Be Upon Him) is, that Allah is THE Greatest and that Islam is the right religion. Nothing will change that. Ever.

We Muslims need to remember and be happy about that. Because he used words, we should use words that explain to everyone why Rushdie's wrong. If we act violently towards him, people will just think we're janglees* and that our religion teaches us to be violent. We should leave it to Allah to deal with him, which He will when the time comes.

Tuesday 6th October

AHAHAHAHAHAHAHA!

So, we had a special PSE class today. They split us into boys-only and girls-only classes. For the first time ever in a lesson (tutor group not included) I sat next to Was.

Mr Barker, normally our maths teacher, was taking the lesson. He wanted to talk to us about growing up. He set us a task: discuss with the person next to you and describe your perfect partner.

So, me and Was discussed it and we thought of all our friends and we thought, right, if you take the best things about each of our friends, that'll be the perfect partner, innit?

I thought about all my friends, like Was, Shibz, Hassim, Shiry etc. and the best things about each of them and then wrote it out. My perfect partner would be a boy, around my height, tough, clever, a good laugh, who likes pulling pranks, football and cricket.

That sounded pretty perfect, I thought.

After about ten minutes, Mr Barker asked us to stop and asked who would like to read out their perfect partner. I was pretty confident about ours. So I put my hand up.

A couple of other students put their hand up too. Mr Barker went to Lee. Lee said, and I'm not making this up ...

'BIG TITS!'

Everyone started laughing. Mr Barker tried to get everyone to calm down.

Me and Was looked at each other, proper confused.

'Anything else?' Mr Barker goes.

'Yeah, a wet minge.'

Me and Was looked at each other, horrified. We had definitely misunderstood this task!

We scribbled over what we had written. And I started thinking about Fiona and Halima and Martina Hingis and Buffy. And wrote down: fit, nice legs, pretty face, makes me smile, fights vampires, good at cooking, Muslim.

Mr Barker then went to someone else. They had a more sensible description than Lee.

Anyway, the point of the exercise was for us to start looking at girls as more than just how fit they are, to see them as real people like we do our friends and mums and sisters.

That's a good point ... but bloody hell ... Allah da shukr Mr Barker didn't come to me. I can't even imagine what I would be being called all day and probably for ever.

Thursday 15th October

I've been thinking long and hard about what I want to do for my GCSE graphics project.

Definitely harder than Kelloggs.

Today, before we started on our own, Mr Old got us to sit in a circle on our stools in the middle of the long workshop.

The graphics class is actually crazy. Most of my other classes are with the same people because I'm in set 1 for everything, but in graphics it's a mix of people from the whole year. People I'm not in any other class with. Like Haider, Kelloggs, Lee, Tommy etc. It's also different to my other classes because we're not doing or learning the same thing; everyone is working on their own projects. That means the class can get really disruptive and out of control.

Mr Old went around and asked everyone what their project is. I wasn't really paying attention because I was thinking about mine. But when Mr Old asked Kelloggs, he goes, 'A scope.'

'Sorry, Fesser, a what?'

'A scope, sir. I'm making a scope.'

The whole class burst out laughing. Even Haider, his cousin.

What the hell is a scope?

Kelloggs tried to explain it, mainly by making an okay sign and putting it over his eye and going, 'You know, a scope.'

The more he explained it, the more we all laughed.

I didn't know where to start with mine. I want to create a foldable pocket fixture list for Rovers.

'Why don't you start off by getting some examples, so you know what already exists and then you can analyse them and decide how you want to make yours different and better?'

That was a really good idea. Except, 'Where do I get that from? They don't sell different teams' fixture lists in the newsagents.'

Mr Old suggested that I write to football clubs and ask them to send me their fixture list. That's actually a sick idea!

'But, sir, I don't have the addresses of any football clubs except Ewood Park.'

'Don't worry about that. You write the letters, I'll get the office to find the addresses and send them off.'

So I wrote and printed off ten copies of the same letter, addressed each one to a different Premiership team and asked them to please send me their fixture list. I put my address on there.

Mr Old took them off me and told me he'd sort it. It's weird, I always thought he was useless. But people can really surprise you.

Unless he just took the letters and put them in the bin and told me that he got them sent. In a way, I would actually find that quite funny.

Friday 23rd October

I have a new crush!

Britney Spears. She's this new singer and she's got this song that goes 'Hit me baby one more time'. It's a really good song *and* she looks like Miss Rose, which is gonna make concentrating in German class even harder!

As well as loving music, I have so many favourite shows on TV now. I have to be careful to make sure that I still have time to study properly and do my homework. In no particular order, they are:

1. X-Files
2. Match of the Day
3. UEFA Champions League
4. Football Italia
5. Blue Peter
6. Buffy the Vampire Slayer
7. The 11 O'Clock Show
8. They Think It's All Over
9. Bernard's Watch
10. Sabrina the Teenage Witch
11. Clarissa Explains It All
12. The Queen's Nose

13. Byker Grove
14. The Demon Headmaster
15. Gladiators
16. Big Break
17. Art Attack
18. GamesMaster
19. The Fresh Prince of Bel Air
20. Rugrats
21. Hey Arnold!
22. Aquila
23. Goodness Gracious Me
24. Pokémon
25. Animaniacs
26. The Simpsons
27. Robot Wars
28. Funhouse
29. You've Been Framed
30. Catchphrase
31. Who Wants to Be a Millionaire?
32. 999
33. Crystal Maze

Is that too many? They're not all on one after another, though!

Thursday 29th October

Today was Saeeda's tenth birthday! We had a big party in our house, and invited all of Shibz's family. I love it when we have big family gatherings. It's so nice when everyone bes together.

The evening was so fun. We put a big mat out on the floor, which everyone sat on to eat. Even though it wasn't my birthday, I felt like Ammi made all my favourite foods: kebabs, samosas, chaat and cholay chawal. I also love her keema sandwiches, but my biggest secret is that I love Mum's daal! Not with chawal, though, I'm not Indian. With roti. That's the meal I can eat the fastest. I just wolf it down!

Saeeda got lots of presents and money, which was good. I got her a stationery set, which she seemed to really like.

But the best part of the whole evening, though, was this amazing prank that Saeeda pulled on everyone.

Everyone was chilling in the living room, chatting and joking. Then Jaffer came in and without any warning he switched the light off. It went dark and everyone was shouting at him to switch the light on. About three seconds later he did . . .

'AAAAARRRRRGGGHHHHHHHHH!!!'

SCREAMS!!!

When Jaffer put the light back on, Saeeda was standing by the door in a Halloween mask making a horrible monster-growl noise and everyone – and I mean EVERYONE in that room – screamed!

Oh my God. It was so funny. She nearly gave us all a heart attack.

'*Baghairateyeh!*' Ammi shouted at her: Shameless!

But it was too funny, and I could tell that she was proud of herself. As she should be!

Happy birthday, Saeeda!

Wednesday 4th November

Witton Park doesn't have a sixth form, which means that after our GCSEs all the Year 11s have to leave and go to college – or get a job, I guess.

This month all the colleges have open days. That means we get to look around and decide which one we want to apply to. I definitely don't wanna go to Blackburn College after what Shibz told me. St Mary's would be all right. But, actually, I don't want to go there either.

Mrs Place told our class about Clitheroe Royal Grammar

School. They have a sixth form that accepts you if you get really good GCSE results. Like six As, for example. That's where I wanna go.

But everyone from the school was going to St Mary's open evening today, so I went. What a laugh! I know St Mary's because it's where I used to train for Whalley Range Tigers (Cubs) with Dad. I'd never been inside, though.

Me, Shibz, Was, Hassim, Haider, Kelloggs, Mushy and Chucky made a plan to meet up outside St Mary's and go in together about 7.30.

Only problem ... security wouldn't let us in.

They said you had to come with a parent. Huh? We weren't told that. So we went back to the road and discussed what to do next.

'That's proper racist, man.' We all agreed with Shibz. Then Halima, Deela, Asma and Amina turned up.

'Why aren't you inside?' Asma asked.

'They're racist. They won't let you in unless you're with your parents,' Hassim told them. We all nodded along.

(Meanwhile, Halima and Chucky went to the side to have a little chat. Weird.)

They looked gutted. They went to the doors to try and persuade the security guards to let us all in. Amazingly, they let the girls in almost straight away!

What?!

'Oi, that's, that's ... ' Mush's face was going red. 'What's that word Miss Fisher called me because I said girls should do the cooking at home?'

'Sexist, Mush.' I remember that lesson.

'Wait, don't you only have brothers?' Was obviously needed some answers.

'Yeah. Sexist. They can't treat us different cos we a different sex to the girls. Isn't that what she taught us?'

That is what Miss Fisher had taught us.

I said, 'I think it was more about our attitudes towards the girls, thou—'

'Come on, let's tell 'em.'

So we went back and again security stopped us.

Kelloggs was prepared. Sort of. 'But you just let in our friends who weren't with their parents! That's sexy.'

'Sexist,' Hassim thankfully corrected Kelloggs.

'Sexist! Yeah.'

They didn't budge.

We started arguing and shouting and tried to force our way in. But during the arguments I realised I could sneak in. Security was distracted by the shouting, so I just took three steps to my left, snuck behind them and went in.

Was noticed I was in. I signalled for him to follow me, but instead he distracted the security so I wouldn't get caught. What a guy.

I was inside, but I didn't really know what I wanted to do. I just started walking around. Eventually I came to a big open space that had a balcony with tables around it, and downstairs was a canteen and more tables. It was the students' common room and study area. This seemed to be where most of the activity was taking place. There were stalls explaining all the subjects that were being taught and then a stall about all the extracurricular activities, a stall about their sports facilities, and then a stall for the army, which was a weird one.

On the stairs I bumped into Amina and Deela, and I don't know what came over me, I think I was just feeling so confident after sneaking in, I just went, 'Hello there, ladies.' They started giggling and walked away. Well, that was new.

After a while I got bored, but then I saw Shibz and Was, who told me that eventually they all just stormed the entrance and forced their way in. Security were chasing some of the lads around the building. I love my friends.

I know one thing: I am not coming to this stuck-up, sexist (possibly racist) college.*

Sunday 8th November

I'm writing this with my left hand. Damn, my handwriting is terrible.

It's all Was's fault, he's such a sore loser. If I was as good at football as he is, I'd be a much better sport. Ruined a perfectly good game, made me spend four hours in hospital and now my hand is in a plaster.

Me, Was, Shibz, Shiry and a few of our friends were playing football in this empty warehouse on Preston New Road† (we were using empty oil drums as posts, it was actually pretty cool). It was a really good game. Even I was playing good, which, as you know, diary, doesn't happen very often.

Typical, Was was getting more and more aggressive as the game went on, especially when his team was losing. He tried to dribble the ball past me and I tackled him; the ball popped up and hit his hand.

'HANDBALL!'

'Fuck off, it was accidental.'

'Doesn't matter. Handball.'

'Penalty,' Shibz joined in.

In frustration he kicked the ball REALLY hard, like full whack, and I was only two yards from him and the ball smashed my right hand.

'ARRRRRGH!'

Damn it hurt. Straight away I knew something was wrong. It was the most pain I could imagine and I've been hit by a car.

---

* St Mary's is closing down next year. Owing to a lack of students and thus funding. No comment.

† Where Texaco-Morrisons petrol station now is, for those that like local references.

Shibz and Shiry came over straight away. I couldn't bend my wrist. It hurt way too much. That was it, game over. As we were leaving, I turned to Was, tears in my eyes: 'I hope you're happy now!'

I mean, I don't think he was happy, but he didn't say sorry. Which upset me.

Dad was at Lancaster Place visiting Poupoh. So he took me to hospital. I explained what happened.

He said, 'I'm sure Was didn't do it on purpose. These things happen in football. Eh, the amount of injuries I've had playing football. It wasn't anyone's fault, you know.'

I knew he was right. But in that moment, I was thinking, *Was broke my wrist!*

I mean, I've calmed down now and I know he didn't do it on purpose. But ... also, not *not* on purpose.

The X-ray showed that I have a fracture in my wrist. And they put a plaster on. Ammi was not impressed! I told her it was an accident. She hates me playing out and I didn't want her to ban me.

The plaster's actually quite cool. Except I have to wear a bag over it when I have a bath and I have to write left-handed. This is my life now for six weeks.

Monday 9th November

This cast has got magical powers.

I got so much attention and sympathy today. Everyone wanted to know how it happened and if I was okay. In tutor group, Fiona asked me if she could sign it. OH MY GOD, YES!

'Yeah, cool, whatever. If you want.'

She got a marker pen and signed it: *Get well soon mate, love Fi x*
I fully nearly died.

After that, loads of people wanted to sign it. I'm already running out of space.

Was signed it: *Handball*.

That did make me laugh, and he did say sorry, which he was too proud to say on Saturday.

I can't stop staring at Fiona's message.

Wednesday 11th November

Tonight was Blackburn College's open day. I didn't go. Because of my arm and also because I know I don't want to go there anyway. I deserve better than Blackburn bloody College.

Wednesday 18th November

This evening was Clitheroe Royal Grammar School open evening.

From my school, only a handful of people were going. From my friends, just me and Hassim. They told us in advance that you had to take a parent with you, so Hassim's dad took him, me and Ammi there.

I know it's an obvious thing to say, but it was just like a school. I liked it. It didn't feel too grown up and I liked their uniform too. They had blazers! I always wished I could wear a blazer to school, but Witton Park doesn't have them.

The teachers were really nice too. I talked to one for a while and she asked me about what I wanted to do. I told her medicine and she said, 'The school sends a lot of students to medical school and, actually, to Oxford and Cambridge, if you'd be interested in that?'

I wasn't. I know who I am and kids where I come from don't go to Oxford and Cambridge. But I didn't say that to her. Instead I said, 'Oh right, that's well cool.'

I really want to come here. Only people who want to learn come here and everyone competes with each other to get good scores, something I keep getting told off for at Witton.

'What marks do I need in my GCSEs to get in here?'

'You'll need four Bs, and at least a C in each of English, maths and science.'

Is that it? I'll definitely and easily get that.

I looked at Hassim. 'We're definitely coming here next year, man.'

Monday 23rd November

I wish I was a bully.

Today, at dinnertime, I was on the field and this little gora from Year 7, 8 or 9, fuck knows, and who I had never seen in my life, goes to me, 'Oi, how did you break ya wrist? Were you wankin'?'^ Ha ha ha.

I said, 'Piss off, man.'

I turned around to try and see my friends and he fuckin' sucker-punched me in the face and ran off with his friends! Bastard. It didn't hurt that much, but I started crying, probably more because I was feeling sorry for myself and wondering, where are my friends? He's lucky they weren't there; they would've killed him.

Afterwards, Mr Garrison asked me what happened. I told him, but I couldn't explain what he looked like – all these little kids look the same to me – and when I explained that he was like Year 7 or 8, Mr Garrison made a weird face. I realised how it sounded. So I just left it.

I didn't tell Hassim or Was or Shibz, or anyone, what happened. The story makes me sound too soft and I'm ashamed.

^ Loads of kids say this to me. I've never had a wank, unless you count what happened in the gym or when I watched Channel 5 that night. Is it that dangerous, that you can fracture your wrist from it? No wonder it's haram.

Friday 4th December

The inside of my plaster STINKS! I can smell it because there's a small gap where my thumb pops out. Uffft. Smellier than Was's socks. Ewwwww.

The plaster's looking cool, though. So many people have signed it, and no one's said anything rude. I get to take it off in three weeks and I cannot wait! But I'm gonna miss having Fiona's signature on my arm.

Oh, also, I got my first qualification today – RSA CLAIT – I have no idea what it stands for, but I do know it's an IT qualification and one of the most baby tests I've ever done. Too easy.

But still. Well done me and everyone else who passed.

Monday 7th December

Mocks start today. I don't think I'm gonna do that well in them. I haven't revised properly, plus I can't write that fast with my left hand, so that's gonna be a problem.

But they are important because it's what the teachers say my predicted grades will be based on. As long as they predict me at least four Bs and at least Cs in English, maths and science I should be okay. That shouldn't be a problem, though. I'll definitely get at least all Bs and Cs in everything. It's how many As or A*s I can get. That's the question.

Friday 11th December

I feel like I'm being left behind.

All my friends are growing taller. Some of them even have little moustaches now. Some of them have girlfriends. Some have started smoking cigarettes. Some even smoke weed. Some of them hang around with each other after school, or with other boys in their area.

The goreh do even more. Drinking, partying. Hassim was saying that he heard that Laura's had five abortions already. That's crazy.

I'm still short, just go to school, do my lessons, play football, come straight home, do my homework, play my Mega Drive and watch TV. Even when I do go out, it's only to play football, or cricket in the summer. I never go to just hang out with people in the park or summat.

Even if I wanted to ask out Halima or Fiona, I wouldn't dare. They're too fit for me and they'd definitely say no, and then everyone will laugh at me. How do you even ask a girl out?

Oi, will you go out with me?

That's proper awkward.

ME: Halima, do you wanna go out with me?
HALIMA: Yeah.
ME: Oh, wow, wicked.
HALIMA: Where?
ME: Er . . .

Where do you even go? Fair enough in school, you can go pavilion or the woods or summat and hold her hand there. But outside of school, I can't go to her house, and she DEFINITELY can't come to mine. If we go town, some nosy uncle or aunty will see us and grass us up to Ammi or her mum. Plus, I don't have any money, so what would we even do?

It's weird, because at the moment Chucky and Hassim and Haider and Mush have girlfriends, but we never talk about how you're supposed to be with them or what they get up to or whatever. How are you supposed to learn any of that stuff? Boys, we never talk to each other except about football or taking the piss out of each other.

Now that I think about it, I'm the lucky one. It's haram, actually, and it sounds like too much trouble. Who needs all that stress and headache?

Thursday 17th December

'It's time for us as a people to start makin' some changes.'

Tupac's making even more sense than usual today. I'm listening to him as I'm writing this.

In English this term we've been reading *Roll of Thunder, Hear My Cry* and *To Kill a Mockingbird*. Aye aye aye. These are the two best books we've read in school. Wow. We proper learned how bad America was and how they treated black people so bad.

Christian goes, 'At least England's not bad.'

What a daft thing to say.

'What about Stephen Lawrence?' Everyone looked at me.

He didn't have anything to say to that.

Mrs Place seemed to agree because she said, 'It's easy to look at other people and find their faults. But actually, it's important to examine ourselves and find our own faults too. We've got problems in this country. We're not perfect.'

'Never mind this country, miss, we got problems in this school.' This time everyone stared at Mushy.

'Ay oy, Mush,' Hassim broke the tension. Everyone laughed.

'Okay. Let me ask you . . . Who thinks our school is racist?' Mrs Place was going for it today.

Every apna put his hand up. From the goreh, only Jack and Steven put theirs up. Respect. The other goreh just looked down. I could tell they were uncomfortable, but it's the truth.

The bell rang. Just as it was getting interesting.

I'm so glad Mrs Place makes us read these books, because even our school can be proper racist sometimes and so hopefully this will make everyone think differently.

Friday 18th December

Today is the end of term and was the last exam in our mocks. I was right, I wasn't properly prepared for them at all! I can't be this lazy for the actual GCSEs, man. Come on, Terry, do you want to be someone who goes to Clitheroe Royal Grammar School, gets wicked A-level grades and then does medicine? Or some dosser who ends up at Blackburn College smoking weed and has to do some shit degree at Man Met?*

Sunday 20th December

I got my plaster taken off today. Finally. My arms are skinny anyway, but my right arm is even skinnier now, it looks like a baby's arm. The doctor said it should go back to normal in a few weeks, and that I should carry stuff with it instead of my left arm to get it stronger again.

It felt SO good to wash my arm. The smell was way too much!

It was proper good timing, because I can do wudhu* properly now, which is important because Ramazan started today!

This year and next year is the easiest Ramazan we will ever have, because December has the shortest days of the entire year.

We have to close our fast at 6.30 a.m. and we break our fast at 3.50 p.m. – that's only nine hours and twenty minutes. Some of that I'll be sleeping anyway because it's the Christmas holidays, so I don't have to worry about going to back to sleep after closing fast, because I don't have to wake up again for school.

I was looking at the yearly namaaz timetable and when Ramazan falls in June, which it will in 2015, we'll have to close our fast at 2.55 a.m. and we break the fast at 9.45 p.m. – that's eighteen

---

* Manchester Metropolitan University

hours and fifty minutes! Damn! I don't have to worry about that for another eighteen years, but. I'll be thirty-three then. Proper old! I should be used to it by then.

Saturday 26th December

I've been well excited for Christmas TV for weeks. But this year, it's not lived up to the hype. It's Boxing Day and the only good film I've seen so far is *Casper*. Yesterday I watched *Super Mario Bros.*, what a piece of shit.

Why is it that whenever there's a film about a computer game, it's always rubbish? *Street Fighter, Mortal Kombat* and now *Super Mario*.

They also put on *Babe*. *BABE*?! I'm supposed to watch a film about a pig in Ramazan? Get lost.

At least I can concentrate more on fasting and praying. But it would be nice to record a good film and then watch it at night.

I was talking to Baji Rosey about what she would want as a Christmas present if we did celebrate it. She said she would love to get driving lessons. I said I'd like a computer. Ammi told us to be quiet.

1999

Friday 1st January

Happy New Year!

1999. Wow. It actually looks so cool. 1 9 9 9.

InshAllah I will live for another 365 days, and then I'll be lucky to have lived to see the end of another year, my second decade, a century and a millennium! How many people can say that? Well, everyone who will be alive on 31 December, when the clock goes from 11:59:59 to 12:00:00 midnight. But SO many people who like me will be excited about that, but are gonna die this year. God will decide to call them back and they won't get to see it.

Imagine you were born on 1 January 1900 and you died on 31 December 1999. You never experienced a different century and, in this case, a whole new millennium!

I wonder what it would've been like going from the year 999 to 1000? Obviously so different to now. If I was alive then, I'd be in Pakistan. Although it wouldn't have been called Pakistan. It would've been India. I wonder if they were excited about it like me. Or if they celebrated it . . . or even knew about it?

Yeah, a lot of people might not have even known about it, because the calendar we have is a Western calendar; back then they probably weren't using that in India. It's crazy to think about how different life was for people back then and how much things have changed. No electricity, no taps for running water, no Kinder Surprise.

Makes me think how much life will be different in 2999. I wonder if they look back at our times and think, damn, them lot had nothing, I wonder how they survived. Maybe they'll all be living in space! Or ... maybe, it'll be Judgement Day before then and human beings won't even get that far.

Anyway, inshAllah I do get to see the new millennium and all my family do too!

Oh, the news said that the euro currency starts today. It means that all the countries in Europe that are part of the European Union are gonna share the same currency. The euro.

All of them except us. We're gonna keep the pound, even though we're part of the EU. Apparently because the pound is so strong, it won't be worth scrapping it and joining in with everyone else.

Maybe we should join, because we are in the EU, but so far Tony Blair's been wicked, so he's probably right about this as well.

Tuesday 5th January

We had to do this stupid test today that would tell us what career we are suited for. It was daft and a waste of my time, because I know I'm gonna be a doctor. The daftest part: the test was under exam conditions in the main hall. It made no sense.

Towards the end of the test I sneaked over to look at Hassim's answers, to see what he wrote. Not because I wanted to copy (Hassim wants to be a businessman and I don't really know what that means), I just wanted to see what he'd put. Mr Cannon caught me looking at his paper and threw me out of the hall.

Luckily, I had already finished. It was still proper baisti, though, leaving the hall in front of everyone. But, kasam, a bit of me felt proper cool! I had to go to the headteacher and everything.

WHO RANG AMMI?! What the hell? It wasn't an exam!

I was so scared on the way home, thinking, what will Ammi say? When I came home I braced myself for some shouting or even maybe a slap.

Nothing.

Heh?

It was normal. I was proper confused and on edge.

Baji asked me if I was all right. I said yeah. Then she told me she answered the phone and just pretended to be Ammi.

What a lifesaver!

Thursday 7th January

OH MY GOD.

I COULD CRY!

I got a computer today. YESSSSSSSSS! Thank you, Ammi, SO SO much!

Mammu Saeed works for Time Computers (a company who make and sell computers and who are owned by Asians from Blackburn!) and so he gets a discount. It's gonna be in my room and will help me with my homework and stuff.

Mammu helped me set up the monitor, base, keyboard, mouse and printer. Mammu said it's top of the range:

- Windows 98
- 400Mhz
- 64MB RAM
- AMD K6-2 processor (I asked Mammu why he didn't get me an Intel one, but Mammu said that AMD is better. Intel is just a fancy name)
- 8GB hard drive

- CD-Rom
- 3.5" floppy disk drive

I've been playing on it all evening. Changing the desktop picture, icon colour and sizes, screensaver (TERRY IS COOL!!!) and playing the games. There's Solitaire, FreeCell and Minesweeper (though I don't know how to play any of them) and 3D pinball!

I can do my coursework on here from now on.

Thank you so much, Allah, for giving me such a top ammi. I'm so lucky!

Friday 15th January

Mushy made the whole class burst out laughing today.

Everyone, that is, except Mrs Place. Unfortunately for Mushy, she doesn't know who Ali G is.

Basically, Shibz was telling me about Poupoh being in i'tikaaf*. That's basically like a retreat for the last ten days of Ramazan. Men do it in the masjid* and women do it at home. It means Poupoh can't leave the front room, where she's retreated to for ten days! Except to go to the bathroom, obviously. No one is allowed to disturb her. I wonder if I could do that. Sounds hard!

Anyway, Mushy overheard us and goes, 'Are you talking about i'tikaaf? My dad's doing it at Randal Street Mosque and—'

'Mustaqeem, be quiet please. Concentrate on your work.'

But Mushy didn't listen. He kept tryna talk to us and eventually she made him move and sit on his own at the table by her desk, and as he was walking over to it, that's when he said it: 'Is it coz I is black?'

'HOW DARE YOU? GET OUT!'

She flipped! What a guy, man. Is it coz I is black? No, Mushy. IT'S BECAUSE YOU AIN'T BLACK! But then neither is Ali G, actually.

Tuesday 19th January

Eid Mubarak!

Another Ramazan has finished and it's another Eid.

This one was pretty quiet. I mean, it was full on: I prayed, ate, changed, ate, went to Shibz's house, ate, went to Was's house, ate, went to Dad's house, ate. Came home, watched a film, ate and went to sleep.

It was quiet. And filling.

Friday 22nd January

I got taught a lesson today.

It was our first coursework assignment in English and only two people got As in our class. Me and Jack. Well I got A–, Jack got A.

Except, I did twenty pages. Jack did four.

I don't understand how he only did four pages and got an A and I did twenty pages and got slightly less than him.

Wow.

I was gonna ask if I could read his. But I didn't. I think my pride got the better of me.

Tuesday 26th January

I got my final Record of Achievement today. This is what I got, with the predicted grades they gave me in brackets:

SUBJECT	YEAR 11	YEAR 10	YEAR 9	YEAR 8	YEAR 7
Art	–	–	2	3	2
Business Studies	1 (B)	1	–	–	–
English	1 (B)	1/2	3/4	2/3	2
Geography	–	–	2/3	2	1

SUBJECT	YEAR 11	YEAR 10	YEAR 9	YEAR 8	YEAR 7
German	1 (A–B)	1	1	1	1
History	2 (A)	2	2	3	2
IT	1 (B)	1	1	1	1
Maths	2 (B)	2	2	3	2
Music	No music teacher	No music teacher	No music teacher	2	1
PE	2	1	1	2/3	2
RE	2 (A)	1	2	2	2
Science	1 (B)	1	2	2	1
Technology	2 (B)	2	1	1	2

Ms Williams proper smiled when she gave it to me. She said that I'd worked really hard and I should be proud of myself. Awww ... Thanks, Ms.

When I read it, I wasn't as pleased as she was. They only predicted me two As. I need six! For example, I don't understand how in business studies my predicted grade is B, when I got 88 per cent in my mock exam!

Something did cheer me up, but ... I heard a new rap song today on the radio. It was well funny! They said he was a gora and that Dr. Dre was saying he was gonna be a star.

The song was so funny, though, he was talking about his teacher and he goes,

> Chased him with a stapler,
> Stapled his nuts to a stack of papers ...

HAHAHAHAHA! I hope M&M does more stuff.

Thursday 4th February

I've made good progress with my graphics project. Most of the teams wrote back to me, including Rovers, which was so wicked. The worst thing was that Man United wrote back to me, and they were really helpful and included loads of nice pictures and stuff too, including a photo of the whole squad, signed by all the players. Which I hadn't asked for. God, I hate them so much.

I didn't make a lot of progress today specifically, because Mr Old left the class for like twenty minutes and me, Haider and Kelloggs had a stool-throwing playfight against Lee, Slim and Kyle.

Why? I DON'T KNOW.

There's lots of places to hide in the workshop so none of us got hit, but we were properly lobbing them hard. The girls ran behind Mr Old's desk. Smart.

Luckily, we stopped before Mr Old came back. Imagine if he walked in and I was just lobbing a stool full whack, like it was a grenade, at another student?

I love my graphics class. It feels like such a break from the rest of my classes.

And . . .

Still none of us know what a scope is. Hahahaha.

Although Haider and Kelloggs are laughing more at me these days. Haider's got this annoying new nickname for me: Terry with the Leopardskin Specs On. It's a long nickname.

I got these new glasses from the opticians, and they're leopard coloured. I only realised when I got them and took them home that it says 'for girls' in them. I never showed that to anyone. Proper embarrassing.

Why the optician didn't stop me, I don't know. Idiot.

Anyway, Haider always sings it: 'Terry with the Leopardskin Specs On.'

I pretend I don't like it, but to be honest, I've had much worse nicknames:

- Terry: this is what everyone calls me and is wicked.
- Elephant: Taya called me elephant for ages, because I was a bit fatter than I am now. I must've got a bit taller, because I wouldn't say I'm skinny now, but I'm not fat any more.
- Tahir Tahir gandeh pair: this was the worst one. Hassim called me this once in Year 8 and all day all the boys were just calling me this. Tahir Tahir gandeh pair, which roughly translated means Tahir Tahir dirty feet, but in Punjabi it rhymes, which it doesn't in English. That's the beauty of Punjabi: it is the best language to swear in. Some of the swears that Wadi Ammi comes up with. *Taubah.* She says stuff like *rani chaudiyah!* Wife-fucker! Which I don't understand as a swear. Isn't that what you're supposed to do?

To be honest, Blackburn is the home of nicknames. The best ones I can think of are:

1. Latchie or just Latch: This is Dad's nickname. Because apparently he wouldn't take the elaichis* out of rice, he would just eat them.
2. Mithu: Muj's nickname. Mithu means parrot and it's what Baeji Aish (his grandma) calls him. He hates it if anyone else calls him it, though.
3. Chucky: Wajid's nickname. Because he's got big hair like the doll in *Child's Play*.
4. Kelloggs: This is Fesser's nickname. Because he likes cereal. WHO DOESN'T LIKE CEREAL?!
5. Chyna: This is a boy who lives in my area, and we call him Chyna, because, even though he's Pakistani,

    him and his whole family have got Chinesey kind of
    eyes. So . . . Chyna.

6. Peggy: A boy who lives on Lancaster Place, he's
    got a problem with his leg, so he's limped his entire
    life. We called him Peg-leg, which became Peggy or
    Peggy Mitchell.

7. Granny: This is an older boy who lives four doors
    down from me. I have no idea why he's called
    Granny, or what his real name is.

8. Daley: A lad on Lancaster Place who's a couple
    of years younger than us. The older boys started
    calling him Daley, because he's dark . . . like Daley
    Thompson. That's well bad.

9. Shampoo Man: My single favourite one. Shampoo
    Man is a gora who lives near Was. One day Was said,
    'Look, there's Shampoo Man. There's all sorts of
    crazy stories about him.' Never mind the stories – my
    question was, 'Why in the hell is he called Shampoo
    Man?' Was looked at me and without hesitating said,
    'Because he's bald.'

10. Quiet Yasin: We call Quiet Yasin Quiet Yasin because
    his name is Yasin and he's quiet.

Monday 8th February

In tutor group today, the seat next to me was empty. Then this
happened . . .

'Tehzeeb?'

'Here, miss.'

'Hassim?'

No answer.

'Hassim?'

'He's not here, miss.'

The class laughed.

'Yes, Tehzeeb. Do you know why?'

No miss, I don't. Is what I should have said. What I said instead was ...

'Oh, miss, he's broken his neck.'

My brain actually shouted at me in my head. WHAT?!?

'Really?'

'Yeah, miss.'

'How?'

Go on.

'I'm not sure, miss.'

Wow.

'That's really serious.'

Shaabash.

'Yeah, miss.'

'A broken neck?'

'Yeah, miss.'

'That's ... wow. People get paralysed from that.'

Gasps in the class.

Shit.

'Yeah, miss, it's really serious.'

'Oh God. Poor Hassim.'

Why did you have to say neck?! You could've said ankle, knee, dick. Anything else. NECK!?!

Everyone in the class started asking me questions, like I was a neck doctor or something, and I just had to keep going with the story.

The worst thing was, I then had to tell every teacher all day that Hassim had broken his neck, because a lot of my tutor group are in the same lessons as me. So even when I didn't say anything myself, Fiona goes, 'Oh, Tehzeeb knows what happened to Hassim.'

Fuck sake.

'Yeah, sir, he broke his neck.'

'Really?'

'Yeah, sir.'

'How?'

'I'm not sure, sir.'

'That's really serious.'

YEAH, I'VE HEARD.

'Yeah, sir.'

'A broken neck?'

'Yeah, sir.'

'God, wish him a speedy recovery from us all, won't you?'

'I will, sir.'

It's got to the point where I'm hoping he has broken his bloody neck. Otherwise, I have a lot of explaining to do. I don't dare ring him.

Tuesday 9th February

Hassim came back into school today.

Obviously, a broken neck isn't as serious as everyone thought it was.

No one was impressed with me.

Wednesday 24th February

Wow. Today the Macpherson Report came out, which was the inquiry into Stephen Lawrence's murder. The report said that the POLICE ARE RACIST. Institutionally racist, it said. I don't know what 'institutionally' means, but it must mean like all of it, top to bottom.

I wonder if that's the reason that Pai Shehzad's murder didn't get solved properly.

I remember once, I was staying at Shibz's house and me, Shibz, Shiry and Muj were talking to Uncle, and we asked why he sends so much money to buy houses and shops in Pakistan, and Uncle said, 'One day the goreh might kick us out.'

And I laughed, and said, 'They can't do that, Uncle, we're British in the law.'

And Uncle said, 'Maybe, but maybe one day it'll be such an environment that you will want to leave.'

Today made me think of Uncle's words.

Well, at least now they've said it out in the open they can change it and make the police better and not racist.

Friday 19th March

This term we did *Macbeth* for English literature. A play by William Shakespeare. It is sick. Kasam, Mrs Place has fully smashed it. Witches, battles, murder, betrayal, revenge. What an amazing story. This is definitely my favourite Shakespeare book. Out of the two that I've read.

Though the *Macbeth* film was shit compared to *Romeo + Juliet*. It needed more black people in it, I think.

I'm feeling rubbish this evening, but. Rovers lost AGAIN today. We actually might get relegated. I mean, we won't get relegated. It's my team, that won't happen. But the thought of it is so scary. I wish we weren't so shit. How did we win the Premier League four years ago and now we're eighteenth?

Tuesday 23rd March

In the least-ideal preparations for my GCSEs ... I'm back on a plane!

I'm off to Pakistan again.

Ammi surprised us last week. Mammu Habib and Khala Shaheen are getting married and Mum didn't wanna miss her little brother's and sister's weddings. So I get two trips to Pakistan in the space of twelve months!

When I told Ms Williams last week, she looked like she was about to faint.

'Just so I'm clear, two months before the start of the most important period of your life, you are going on holiday to Pakistan for four weeks?'

'Er . . . Yeah, Ms.'

I've taken all my books and notes with me. I'll just have to make sure I revise in Pakistan.

Our full family is going: me, Ammi, Baji Rosey (she can see her husband too!), Abu, Saeeda, Zaheer, Tanveer and Tauqeer. Imagine how much luggage we had? Uffffft.

Plus, Mammu Saeed and his family (Baji Shanaz and the two babies, Zara and Safa), and Uncle and Muj have come too. It should be a really fun trip!

Ooh, also Wadi Ammi is already in Pakistan, so it'll be nice to see her.

My family is so big I can barely keep up. Haha.

Wednesday 24th March

We've arrived in Pakistan.

Mammu Abbas (who feels even less tall than last year) was there, of course, to meet us at Islamabad airport, as well as Mammu Shama, Pai Uneeb and Naani Ammi.

It was nice to watch Baj see Pai Uneeb. I'm happy that they're together again.

We had to have two vans again as there were too many people and luggage.

Ahhhh. Breathing in that fresh, smelly Pakistan countryside

air again. So beautiful, man. There's nothing like it in England.*
Even though England is home and inshAllah always will be,
Pakistan is *home*, you know? I know what I mean.

The all-familiar entourage greeted us on the borders of Boken.
Naana Abu, mammus, khalas, cousins and an assortment of my
mum's cousins and aunts and uncles. I went to grab one of my
bags. To be polite, to be honest: I knew what was gonna happen.

'*Ey ey. Tu rendeh*': Oi oi. Leave it.

Mammu Shama shooed me away from the bags and told me
they were his responsibility.

It was Tany, Tauqeer, Zara and Safa's first visits to Pakistan so
they were very smothered. Did I mind that I didn't get as much
attention as normal? Only a tiny weeny bit. But to be honest,
as much as I love Pakistan and all my family here, they proper
treat you like a baby, like you can't do anything. I try not to take
advantage of that. It would be well easy to. Easy, but wrong. So at
least now they can do the babying to actual babies.

This trip already feels different. Like I've crossed a threshold
into a different age group. I'm no longer a child to be smothered
and spoilt. Good. I think.

After greeting half the village (I wish that was an exaggeration)
I eventually went into Naani and Naana's house and the first
thing I did was grab a fresh shalwar kameez off Khala Fozia and go
to the bathroom. I quickly stripped off, did my business, watching
the ants crawling along the wall. You're never alone in a Pakistani
loo. Then I had a quick cold shower ... Brrrrr ... they always take
getting used to. I got changed into my shalwar kameez and then
came out, closed my eyes, soaked in the amazing sunshine and sat
on a manjee and tried to relax.

---

* Actually, having now driven extensively around Britain, our countryside is vastly underrated.
Britain is fit AF.

Impossible. People wanted to say hi. They always ask the same questions about school and everyone back home. And then someone else comes and repeats the same cycle of questions.

Eventually people left and it was just the family. Mammus Shama and Abbas put a mat out for us, and everyone except me sat down to eat. I ate, as per normal, on a manji. Naana Abu kept me company, which was nice.

'England weather good? Rain, sunshine? Yes?'

He always makes me laugh.

'Yes, Naana Abu. Sometimes rain, sometimes sunshine.'

'How's your daada?'

Oh man. What a question. I explained to him in my not-quite-fit Punjabi that Baaji wasn't well. At all. What's the Punjabi for stroke and Alzheimer's? I'll get Baji Shanaz to explain it to him later.

After our meal, Mammu Abbas and Shama and a couple of their cousins started grabbing Ammi, Abu and the kids' suitcases to take them to the other side of the village. That's where Abu's family home is.

'*Chaal tu rest kar leh,*' Ammi said: Okay. You rest. 'I'll see you tomorrow.'

I never go there; I don't feel welcome and Ammi doesn't ask me to come.

'*Jee teek eh Ammi*': Yeah, okay Ammi. I gave her a hug.

I said goodbye to Saeeda, Zaheer, Tany and Tauqeer, and I especially made a point of saying Khuda Hafiz*, to Abu, because I know he has to be nice to me in front of so many people. He's so fake. I wish they could see the cold-hearted robot he actually is.

Baji Rosey left with Pai Uneeb and then Uncle and Muj went to their house. I could finally relax. I asked Mammu Habib if he was looking forward to his wedding.

'*Shaadi karni eh. Teek eh*': You have to get married. It's fine.

Always the same response. No one ever seems happy to be getting married! I would laugh if it wasn't so serious.

Just before bed, we were watching the news and even though my Urdu isn't amazing, I understood most of it. It said NATO, which is a gang of Western countries, they're bombing Yugoslavia to help save the Albanian Muslims there. The West helping Muslims? I looked up to the sky just in case there were pigs flying. Then I thought, we're in Pakistan, there are no pigs here. Maybe they are flying in England, though.

Friday 26th March

COCK-A-DOODLE-DOO!

That's the alarm in Pakistan. Every morning at 5 a.m. It's nice on the first day, because it's so different.

But it wasn't today. I woke up really ill. And being ill in Pakistan is no joke.

While Naani Ammi and my khalas and mammus were doing their daily morning chores – milking the buffalo, getting the eggs from the chicken coop, cleaning the yard, feeding the animals etc. – I was taking turns to shit out half my body and vomit the rest out straight after.

In the afternoon Mammu Abbas took me to see a doctor in Chak Jamal. I don't know if the doctors here learn things differently to what they learn in England, but he gave me an injection! And four different tablets! I have never been given an injection for being ill in England, only for immunisation. And I've never been given tablets, only ever liquid medicine.

This better not make me worse.

'*Kaileh kah*' – that was Naana Abu's advice. Eat bananas. He was actually right. It calmed the diarrhoea right down.

I'm just resting in the baitak, on the nice big bed, and hopefully

I'll feel better by Eid at least. I opened my history book and the first thing that I saw I had to revise was the history of medicine. Haha. I'll never forget this. Allah bless Alexander Fleming. And, of course, the hundreds of Muslim doctors who pioneered medicine hundreds of years before, that our syllabus never covered but Mrs Fisher told us all about in RE.

Sunday 28th March

It's Big Eid tomorrow. My first one ever in Pakistan. I'm proper excited!

Plus, I'm feeling better. I can't wait.

Monday 29th March

Er ... Eid in Pakistan is bloody boring!

Big Eid is known as bakra Eid in Pakistan. Which literally translates as goat Eid. I'd never truly appreciated what that meant until today.

Small Eid, Eid-ul-Fitr, comes after Ramazan; it's to celebrate the end of fasting. This Eid, Eid-ul-Adha, comes after hajj (pilgrimage to Makkah), and it's to celebrate people performing hajj but mainly to celebrate when Prophet Ibrahim (Peace Be Upon Him) was going to sacrifice his son Prophet Ishmael (Peace Be Upon Him), but then Allah sent a ram instead for Prophet Ibrahim (Peace Be Upon Him) to sacrifice.

So, to celebrate this sacrifice, every Eid, every Muslim who can afford to has to contribute to the sacrifice of an animal (goat, sheep, cow, buffalo etc.), whose meat is then shared between family, friends and poor people. It's called Qurbani.

Now, in England, Ammi and Abu and presumably all the grown-ups send their contribution for Qurbani to Pakistan or a poor Muslim country, because we don't really have the means to do Qurbani in Blackburn. So, obviously, if we are sending money to Pakistan for the Qurbani, then that is where the Qurbani takes place, which I learnt first-hand today.

So, after Eid namaaz, the ENTIRE day is spent sorting the Qurbani out. A butcher man goes around house to house and sacrifices the animals. That's his job. Okay, so that bit was fun. Watching him do the zaba, which is what we call the method of killing the sacrificial animal, is actually cool and it's very interesting to see where the meat I eat comes from. In our house we sacrificed one cow (a cow or buffalo equals seven people's portions) and two goats (a goat or sheep only equals one person's portion). So, we had nine portions from our house. One for each adult.

The butcher guy made sure the animals were kept away from each other, so they didn't see what's happening. He laid the animal on the ground, then the man prayed, stroking the animal, calming it down, till it relaxed. Then he slit the cow's neck with a really sharp knife. Blood went spraying all over, the cow wriggled a bit, and then very quickly it was dead.

After that, my mammus took over. They have to cut the animal open, skin it, chop it up, and then put the meat in different portions and deliver it to poor people and friends and family. It's a very important job and obviously a big part of our religion, but man, it takes all day. But that is basically Eid here.

As I said . . . boring!

Wednesday 7th April

Mammu Habib and Khala Shaheen got married this week. To different people, obviously. Actually, they got married to a different brother and sister in the village. So Mammu Habib married Khala Uzma, and Khala Shaheen married Khala Uzma's older brother, Mammu Abaid.

Not that I'm getting married any time soon, but I would hate to share my big day with someone else, and especially my little sister! Saeeda, Saira and Yasmeen can have their own days, thank you very much!

The wedding days were really fun. Not as extravagant as Baji Rosey's (but that's because we're from England and have more money, and have to spend more money because people expect it), but still really fun with all the colour and shit dancing and food and stupid serious pictures and laughs.

I'm so glad I came, GCSEs or no GCSEs. Family is everything.

Thursday 8th April

IT'S MY SWEET SIXTEENTH TODAY!

Today was Mammu Habib's and Khala Shaheen's walima as well, so I thought everyone would have forgotten about my birthday, but then in the evening when the guests had left and it was just family, Mammu Abbas brought a cake out and everyone started singing 'Happy Birthday'!

It was so sweet and embarrassing, because I know they don't really celebrate birthdays in Pakistan, but they made such an effort. I knew this was Ammi's doing. She's the best.

Oh ... but the cake was shit. I mean, thank you. But ... also, it was.

Wednesday 14th April

I'm so dumb.

Baji Rosey needed to go back to Dhanyala today from Boken and no one was free to take her. So I volunteered. TO TAKE HER ON THE MOTORCYCLE!

Now, I've driven a motorcycle once. In 1995, Nads took me and Was for a cruise and let us both ride it. He taught us the basics:

put it in neutral, kick start, clutch, gear one, race and let go of the clutch . . . keep your balance, speed up, gears two, three, four, brakes, gear three, two, one.

We were twelve.

It's been four years. But how hard could it be?

Well . . .

It *was* going well. I left the house with her on the back (in Pakistan, men sit on the motorcycle with one leg on either side of the seat but women, when they're passengers – and I've only ever seen them be passengers – they sit with both legs on one side, like it's a swing. Women do ride motorcycles in the big cities, but not here in the pind*).

We went through the dirt roads up onto the sark*, I turned left, and it's going FINE! I am sixteen and I'm riding a motorcycle in Pakistan, in my sandals, with no helmet or licence. I am basically everyone else here.

We were going along, talking, laughing . . . and then we came across some divots. The sark always gets damaged, no matter how much they fix it. Every time I come back to Pakistan, it has more potholes. I tried to go around them and I ended up slowing down too much, the bike wobbled, Baji panicked and just before I could put my foot down to stop us from falling, she jumped and fell on her ass.

I threw my older sister off a motorbike!

I panicked, but luckily, she was fine.

And then I laughed. Because as you know, diary, that's who I am.

She hesitated to get back on, but we had gone too far for her to walk back to Boken and we were still too far away for her to walk to Dhanyala, so she had no choice. The rest of the journey, on the rest of the broken sark, through the sand road, onto Chak Jamal sark and then right past the big army depot straight to Dhanyala was wicked.

I drank a bottle at her in-laws and then I rode back. I was

thinking, *shit*, imagine if I have an accident when I'm on my own? Mammu Abbas shouted at me, and at Naani Ammi for letting me go by myself, when he got back home.

But I didn't care ... I rode a motorcycle all by myself and I am very proud. How many of my friends in England have ridden a motorcycle in their Easter holidays? Zero, 0, none, that's how many.

Friday 16th April

I'm in awe of Mammu Abbas. I've never met anyone who works as hard as he does, or who does as many favours for people. He never complains and he's always laughing and joking.

It's harvest season in Pakistan. Our family and all the families around the village are farmers; we have animals, but also we have land that we grow crops on. At this time of year we grow wheat, which we turn into flour for making chapatis. We keep what we need, give a bit to the needy and sell the rest to other families.

Mammu Abbas and his cousins and friends have spent every day since the wedding out on the land harvesting each other's fields. Using a tractor and then gathering all the wheat and carrying it back home. Every evening he's come back fully sweating and stinking. Today they finally finished. This is proper work, what they do. I couldn't do that. I'm not made for how they have to live. It's made me even more motivated to do well in my GCSEs.

Baaji left Pakistan forty years ago, so I didn't have to have a hard life like this. Even though he doesn't recognise me any more, I'm gonna make him and everyone in my family proud.

Sunday 18th April

Well ... today was ... weird. Surreal, even.

I couldn't believe what was happening and had to double check in the back of the car on the way to Dhanyala. 'Muj, are you sure?'

'Yeah, cuzzy. Don't worry about it, man. It's wicked.'

I looked at Baj; she just looked down.

'You're only seventeen, but?'

'Exactly. I'm eighteen next month. Baeji wanted it to happen. I want to make her happy.'

'Okay. I mean . . . Yeah okay.'

I love Baeji Aisha. She's my grandma's mum and Muj's dad's mum. She's the best and most adorable woman in our village. And she's put the idea in Muj's head, and I guess it's in there now.

I whispered to Baj later on when Muj was on stage with Seema, 'He's still got the mindset of a kid. Do you think he's mature enough?'

Baj just goes, 'I'm not saying anything. It's up to him.'

I looked at the stage; he was grinning ear to ear. He looked happy enough. I looked round the room and everyone was smiling. I felt guilty that I wasn't more happy for him.

Uneeb was particularly happy because Muj just got engaged to his sister. Seema was looking down, no expression on her face, as I've learnt Asian brides do on their wedding day. I guess an engagement is no different.

Then I found out when I got back to Boken . . . Wadi Ammi told Naani Ammi today that someone was asking for my rishta*! What the hell? Naani Ammi asked Ammi and Ammi said over her dead body.

TOO RIGHT. I'm sixteen. SIXTEEN!

The grown-ups in my family are proper crazy sometimes.

Ammi and Dad got married proper young, had Baji Rosey and me and then they were divorced while they were both still teenagers. And then they got Ammi another arranged marriage and he . . . well . . . the less said the better.

But have they learnt any lessons from these marriages? Have they hell. It looks like they're repeating the same mistakes for our generation.

I AM NOT GETTING MARRIED (OR EVEN ENGAGED) IN MY TEENS! PISS OFF.

Thursday 22nd April

I'm back on the plane.

Leaving Pakistan is always so emotional and today was no different. Saying goodbye to my mammus, khalas, grandparents, other relatives. You never know if you will see them again.

But actually, for the first time ever, I was glad to be getting away. It seems like the older you get, the more complicated trips to Pakistan are.

It was only me, Baj and Muj who came back together. Ammi and the kids and Abu and everyone else are coming back next week.

Everything went smoothly enough. I asked Muj if he was happy. He said he was. Good. As long as he's happy, that's the main thing.

It always feels SO cold when we land in Manchester compared to Pakistan. But it's good to be home AND STILL SINGLE.

And now it's hit me: my GCSEs start in a few weeks. I have work to do.

Saturday 24th April

Bloody hell. Allah have mercy on us all.

A LOT happened while I was in Pakistan. There was a bomb today in London. THE SECOND ONE. Last Saturday there was a bomb in a place called Brixton in south London, where mostly black people live. And today there was another bomb. This time in east London, a place called Brick Lane. Where is mostly Bengalis.

It must be the same guy, innit? He's obviously targeting

innocent people who are not goreh. Lucky only thirteen people got injured today and no one died. The police have to catch this racist motherfucker before he does it again.

Not only that though ... Taubah, on Tuesday, two days before I came back from Pakistan, there was a bad shooting in America. At a place called Columbine High School. Two kids from that school went in and killed twelve students and one teacher, injured twenty-four others and then killed themselves. It was like Dunblane, but this time it was actually students who did it! That's crazy. Imagine two students from Witton Park, just coming to school with guns and trying to kill other kids. Kids they had lessons with, who they had lunch with, who they did PE with. Proper evil, man, kasam. I can't even imagine it.

Actually ... if I think about it, Tommy would definitely do that. There's defo summat wrong with him.

I hope America bans guns like we did after Dunblane. I'm sure they will. That's a good way for President Clinton to do something right after his mistakes.

Oh, and NATO is still bombing Yugoslavia to help the Muslim Albanians. I've asked, and no pigs flew over England either.

Rovers are still in the relegation zone.

Thursday 29th April

In RE today, we were talking about Jill Dando, who got horribly killed on her doorstep on Monday and Mrs Fisher was saying how sad it was.

'Just imagine her final moments. What was the last thing that went through her head?'

At that moment, my mind had a thought, but before I could stop it, my mouth, the dumb bastard, decided to say it ...

'A bullet.'

Everyone gasped; some boys laughed. Sometimes my voice acts

quicker than my brain and it'll say something, and my poor brain will say: Bro ... why?!

Mrs Fisher sent me out of class.

Fair enough.

Friday 30th April

What the hell is going on?!

There was ANOTHER bomb in London today. The news thinks it was the same racist guy from the last two. This time he did a bomb in a gay bar in Soho. So, basically, this guy just hates anyone who is different to him. Pathetic.

The news said three people died, including a pregnant lady and her two friends. Seventy-nine people got injured. It's too sad, man. I'm so angry. I hope they catch this evil guy and execute him. Well no, I just argued against that last year, didn't I? I hope they lock him away for ever. I'm so glad that Muslims don't behave like this. Bombing innocent people. Obviously it's against our religion, that's why.

In the Qur'an it says *'whoever kills an innocent life, it's as if he's killed all of humanity'*.

Monday 3rd May

'You're such an idiot, man.' It was hard to argue with Hassim.

'Do her face again.' I pulled a face like someone posing at a Pakistani wedding. He couldn't stop laughing.

'I said, everyone line up in your tutor groups!' Mr Garrison was not happy that he had to say the same thing five times. I'd just finished playing footy on this pitch ten minutes ago and now we're back outside again.

'You lucky Ms Williams didn't put you in detention. She's already pissed off with you that you went Pakistan for four weeks.'

Shibz was right. I was lucky, I thought, as him and Was went to line up with their tutor group away from me and Hassim.

I pulled a prank, another prank, on Ms Williams today. In after-noon tutor group the fire alarm went off. I had only just come in, so I was nearest to the door, and I went back out to have a look . . .

'Oh my God, Ms, I can see smoke!'

Ms Williams's face fell; she came running over. Except . . . there was no smoke. The look she gave me. Kasam. I thought she was gonna give me a backhander!

I mean, in hindsight, given there had just been three bombings in London, a big school shooting in America and a famous person getting shot in the head, all in the space of three weeks, I can see why she might have been on edge.

I'll say this, though: for someone who dropped drama two years ago, I'm a very good actor.

Oh . . . They arrested someone for the bombings! Thank God.

The devil was called David Copeland. Rot in jail, you evil bastard!

In better news, my favourite player, Stephen Hendry, won the World Snooker Championship! For the seventh time! That's a brand-new record. He shared the record previously with Steve Davis, but now it's all his. I reckon he could win ten champion-ships. He's easily the best. I love how calm he is under pressure. He never shows emotion until he wins. He's like my favourite Formula One racing car driver, Michael Schumacher. I know he's German, so I shouldn't support him, but I love him too!

When someone is that good at the thing they do, you HAVE TO respect that. Like Muhammad Ali, Maradona, or me at annoying teachers.

Tuesday 11th May

This school, man. Proper takes the piss.

I got put on report ... AGAIN! My third time. I must hold the record for being put on report the most times and being all top sets for everything. Well, I got away with putting a fake signature on it the last two times, so that's what I'll do this time too. Ammi (and everyone else) got back from Pakistan on Sunday; she doesn't need to know about this.

It's the last week of my school career, of course I'm gonna mess about a bit and talk to my friends in class. This is the last time we'll be in this environment together. It's history. Our history. And the teachers just wanna ruin it by telling us to be quiet so we can concentrate on our revision and get good GCSEs.

How can I get put on report when everyone's been wreaking havoc these last few weeks, man? School is proper unpredictable right now.

During breaks and dinnertimes, our gang, like twenty of us, stand on either side of the south corridor, and when someone walks past, the first people in the row start pushing the poor bastard to each other, proper violently. Basically, the person gets pinballed down the line till they come out the other side, some-times on the floor, sometimes still standing.

Boy, girl, doesn't matter. Never a teacher, though. Obviously. We don't have a death wish.

I'm still wearing my jumper to school, even though it's really hot, because a new game has been created, where if you've got your front shirt pocket exposed, it's fair game and someone will just rip it off. And here's the thing: sometimes it comes clean off, other times, half the shirt comes off with it.

We had to pack that in when someone ripped half of Dawn's shirt off and you could see her bra and belly. That was tight. One of the other girls lent her a jumper. But that was the end of that game ... or is it? I'll keep my jumper on in case.

Oh, and then there's the pile-ons ... Someone will trip someone up, shout 'pile on!' and then everyone, and I mean EVERYONE who heard it, has to come on and pile on. I counted twenty people on Slim last week. He's a big guy, to be fair, he can take it. But still!

And with all that going on, I GET PUT ON REPORT?! Just for being a nuisance and talking and interrupting the teacher in class. Same old story.

Wednesday 12th May

Rovers got relegated tonight.

Obviously, it was against Man United, because that's the worst team for me it could be against.

AAARRRRRRRRRRGGGGGGGGGGGHHHHHHHHHH!!!

Thursday 13th May

Was and Hassim didn't even laugh at me in school, they knew it was too tight. Your team getting relegated is NOT a joke!

Friday 14th May

Today was the last day of school!

I can't believe it. Five years ago, I started as a young boy and now I'm leaving as a slightly taller boy.

We still have revision classes and exams next week, so it's not truly the end. Though everyone got their shirts signed today and Golly brought eggs in and everyone had a big egg fight. At dinnertime, we went to egg Karolia and he said don't, because he has to go read Jumma*.

What?

Apparently, the Indians have been reading Jumma every Friday with Mr Kala (that's not a nickname, we're not racist. It's his actual name). I didn't even know he was Muslim! How is the last Friday of being in school ever the first I'm hearing about this?!

I asked Was how come we haven't been reading Jumma with them this whole time, and he said, 'They're wobblers,* innit.'

Now was probably not a good time to mention to Was that I've started praying at Al-Asr mosque, who are, as he would say, wobblers.

It was emotional saying goodbye to everyone. All the lads gave big hugs to each other. We were even nice to the girls. I'm gonna miss everyone:

Hassim, Chucky, Mushy, Haider, Kelloggs (and his scope), Golly, Karolia, Ebrahim, Geery, Quiet Yasin, Zed, Imran, Gabah, Lee, Jack, Asma, Halima, Faiza, Amina, Deela, Fiona, Farhana, Andleeb, Stacey, Vicki, Dawn. Even Ms Williams. Everyone. Not Tommy.

Sunday 16th May

Today I asked, 'Is it wrong to pray at Al-Asr, Baj?'

I was thinking about what Was said to me.

'How do you mean?' Baj looked up from the copy of *Pride and Prejudice* she was reading on the sofa in our front room.

'They wobblers, innit? So does our namaaz count if we pray there?'

All my life I've been going to Sunni mosques (Madni Masjid, Lancaster Place; Islamic Education Centre, Devonport Road; and Masjid-e-Raza, Randal Street), but over the past few months I've started going to Al-Asr (on the corner of St Silas and Preston New Road) and Masji-e-Anwaar (on the corner of New Bank

---

* Which is a rude way of saying they're Wahhabis. That's a different sect to what we are, like Catholics and Protestants.

and Granville Road), just because they're closer to home, by ten metres.

Baj said, 'When you pray there, are there any differences?'

I thought about it ... And you know what ...

'Not really. They read namaaz in exactly the same way we do. Maybe a small difference in how they do dua* afterwards, that's it.'

'Exactly. I teach there, don't I? And I spent three years in dars*. So who knows more, me or your friends?'

That's true. If it's good enough for her, I guess it's good enough for me.

'Who do you think's gonna win the Cricket World Cup?' I pointed to the TV, which was showing the highlights of the first weekend's games.

'Pakistan?' She shrugged her shoulders and went back to her book, making it clear that the conversation was over. Is she missing her husband? Is her college work hard? Who knows? I was distracted by the cricket.

A distraction I really don't need this summer. England beat Sri Lanka in the first game, but obviously, I'm supporting Pakistan, who beat West Indies today.

Pakistan won the World Cup in 1992, which was wicked, but I was only nine then. I hope Baji's right and we do win this one, because I'm old enough to appreciate it more now.

Friday 21st May

It was near the end of the school day. I was in South Building, in Miss Rose's room. In a revision class for German.

'Oiiiiiiiiiiiiii!'

The silence was broken by a sudden burst of shouting from outside.

I looked out the window and I just saw boy after boy running past our window. First goreh boys and then apne boys. Miss Rose went to the window to have a look. She turned around in a panic and told us to stay where we were.

I looked at Hassim sat next to me, then we turned behind to look at Shibz and without saying anything we all sprang out of our chairs and legged it out the class. Turned left, left again, out the double doors into the stairs corridor and then bolted straight through the double doors and outside.

There were still boys running past us. I looked to my right and down the hill, and there was basically a Royal Rumble going on. Oh great. Another race riot in our school.

Asians v Goreh II.

'What the hell, man? Wh—' I suddenly realised I was talking to myself. Shibz and Hassim were already halfway down the hill.

For a split second I considered joining them. Then Shoaib, Faiza's older brother, ran past me with a bat! Mr Cameron, who I only just noticed, yelled after him,

'You're a disgrace, Shoaib!'

Shoaib, who doesn't even go to our school any more, turned around and, looking a bit embarrassed, said, 'Sorry, Mr Cameron!' And then carried on running down the hill. I couldn't spot Shibz or Hassim, but I decided to stay put. Especially now Mr Cameron had seen me.

The school bell rang for the end of the day and everyone got released from their classes. Which I'm not sure was the best thing to do: putting all the students outside, considering what was happening.

Straight away I could hear girls screaming. They must've been so confused about what was happening.

Hassim and Shibz suddenly came back up the hill. 'We're leaving. Come on.' Shibz wasn't asking me, and I didn't need telling twice.

The walk home was fuckin' scary. As soon as we got out of south gates we saw a group of Asian boys just chasing two goreh lads down Buncer Lane and across Redlam. It was chaos. Proper anth*. None of them were wearing uniforms, so God knows who they were.

As we went up Buncer Lane, being careful to keep to ourselves, we just saw lads running in different directions and police cars zooming past.

'What the hell is happening?' I was sure that Shibz knew more than I did.

He explained there's this boy called Faheem who joined Witton a few months ago. He's a bit of a nutter who loves fighting. He got expelled from his last school – that's the level we're talking about here.

I don't know him, Shibz doesn't know him. He's in Year 10, though, so Shiry knows him a bit. But ever since he's joined us, he's been itching for a fight and he's given a lot of aakar* to a lot of goreh.

Yesterday, he got jumped near pavilion by four or five lads. They gave him a proper beat down, apparently. Everyone got suspended, including him, which to be honest seems a bit unfair.

So ... today, near home time, the school got flooded with loads of apne from Beardwood and Pleckgate, and lads who'd left Witton. They came with cricket bats, baseball bats and God knows what else and just started laying out every gora they saw.

Bish bash bosh. I hope no one got badly hurt.

I guess the one good thing that came out of it is that Tommy got it good again.

Fuckin' mental. Kasam.

Sunday 23rd May

Pakistan beat Australia today!

Australia are the best team in the world. That's wicked! We can definitely win the World Cup!

Revision is going well. Despite all the distractions. If the right questions come up, inshAllah, I can definitely achieve my goal.

Monday 24th May

I can't believe that nothing about Friday's riot at school is in any paper! The police came, boys got arrested. But nothing.

Scabbed it.

What was in the news, but, was a story about a horrible tragedy yesterday. So sad, man. Owen Hart from WWF died. He's Bret Hart's little brother. So horrible.

There was a big pay-per-view event, and for his match, he was being lowered to the ring from the ceiling, and the harness he was wearing broke and he fell about seventy feet into the ring. Ufft. Taubah.

The crazy thing is, they took him to hospital, announced that he had died and then CARRIED ON with the event. Have they not got ~~hearts~~ Harts? How must their family be feeling? How must Bret Hart be feeling? He already hates WWF, which is why he's at WCW now.

If my friend had died, like if Hassim died when he got hit with the iceball, there's no way I could carry on doing whatever I was supposed to be doing that day. Poor Owen. He was only thirty-four.

Wednesday 26th May

How is life fair? I don't understand.

Manchester United, who relegated Rovers two weeks ago, won the Champions League today, even though they were losing until the ninetieth minute. Then they scored two goals in injury time to win. HOW IS THAT FAIR?!

Friday 28th May

I was in revision class today in IT and Mr Garrison let us put the TV on. I watched the India v Sri Lanka game. Ufft. India battered them.

I saw on the news, India and Pakistan are fighting at the moment in Kashmir. Which makes me really worried about my family back home. Pakistan HAS to win the match against India. Has to, has to, has to.

Tuesday 1st June

A.M.: After five years of school, thousands of classes, hundreds of homeworks, tens of pushing in the dinner queue, three times put on report, one time chased by a farmer with a shotgun, zero prefect duties . . . today is the beginning of the end.

I've worked really hard these last few weeks. I've stuck to my revision timetable, I've listened to my teachers' advice and I've practised lots of past exam papers. I feel like I'm ready. This afternoon I'll go to school and sit my first GCSE exam. English literature.

P.M.: Well . . . I think that went okay. It's hard to tell with English, cos it's not right or wrong like maths or science. But I answered all the questions, the things I revised came up and I made sure that I gave more than one point of view in my answers.

It's gonna be a long month.

Tuesday 8th June

I'm no fun to be around sometimes. I feel sorry for Saeeda, Zaheer and Tany when that happens. Which is usually when my team loses, like today. Pakistan lost to India!

Full baisti, man. Losing a cricket match to someone you're fighting a war with. Probably got paid to lose, or were told to by Pervez Musharraf. Some politics bullshit that I don't understand.

We won the first four games, but we've now lost three in a row. If we lose our next game to Zimbabwe, we're out!

WE HAVE TO WIN THAT ONE!

Anyway, I lost my temper at Saeeda and Zaheer and Tany, who were only playing, but I felt like they weren't taking the situation of the cricket seriously enough. Zaheer made a face like he was about to cry. I felt bad. To make up for it I took 'em to Patel's and let them buy a chocolate and crisp of their choice. I could tell it made them feel better, and then we had a race up Leamington Road. I was about to let Saeeda win, but then I sped up at the last second to show her that life isn't easy. Hahaha. For a second I forgot all about the cricket and my GCSEs. It was fun.

In good news, but: *mein deutschsprachige Prüfung verlief sehr gut.*

Friday 11th June

WE BEAT ZIMBABWE!

Thank God.

We're going to the semi-finals, baby!

Oh, and India's out! They beat us for no reason!

You're not singing any more; you're not singing any more!

HAHAHAHAHAHAHAHAHAHAHAHAHAHA!

Oh, and I did well in my chemistry exam today. That revision is paying off, Alhamdulillah*.

Oh, also, the fighting in Yugoslavia and Kosovo has stopped! Yugoslavia are gonna leave the Albanians alone and let them have their own country. SubhanAllah.

I'm glad that England helped. On the news it said thousands of people died and that the Yugoslavian side killed so many

Muslims. Taubah. Taubah. InshAllah they'll catch the guilty people and put them in jail like they did with the Nazis after World War II.

Sunday 20th June

Allah doesn't want me to be happy about sports. Pakistan lost the final. Australia won.

Actually, we didn't just lose. We got twatted. Bad style. We got all bowled out for 132. One hundred and thirty-two. What the HELL?

Australia made that score in twenty overs.

Full baisti.

Ammi goes, 'They must have got rishwat*.' (Famously, Pakistan never lose unless they take bribes.) But, I said, 'Mum, if they were trying to lose on purpose, they'd at least make it a bit close, not this obvious. They were just shit today.'

I don't know what's worse, England losing on penalties after playing top, Rovers getting relegated, or Pakistan getting absolutely demolished in the World Cup final?

Actually, I know the answer to that. Rovers getting relegated. That's my team, week in, week out. It's just sunk in. They're gonna be playing Division One next season. Against Grimsby Town. Who the hell are they, man?

Wednesday 30th June

'Time! Put your pens down. Close your papers. Everyone remain seated until all the papers have been collected.'

I could just about hear Mrs Fisher's voice in the background. All I could think is, *I've done it. We've done it.*

Witton Park High School Class of '99 is done.

I looked around the hall at my friends. Hassim, Shabaz, Was,

Karolia, Ebrahim, Asma, Amina, Halima, Fiona, Jack, Steven, Christian. I wondered what they were thinking.

I suddenly felt a bit emotional. We've officially left now. I'm no longer a schoolchild. No more revision classes, no more exams. No more of these stupid teachers telling me to shut up! But also, thank you for everything!

As I left the hall, everyone was talking excitedly about their summer plans. We have two months of summer holidays, then our GCSE results and then (*inshAllah*) the rest of our lives, which for me starts at Clitheroe Royal Grammar School.

Everyone, in their own heads, has an idea of what they wanna do and what they wanna be. But not everyone does it. I wonder who, from the boys and girls leaving this hall, are gonna achieve their dreams and who's gonna end up being disappointed with their life. Who's gonna live the longest? Deela: she's Hindu, so vegetarian. Who's gonna get married first? Definitely one of the apnia*, ip-tip-dog-shit-you-shall-be-it – sorry, Faiza. Who's gonna die first? Tommy, inshAllah.

Oh, shut up, brain.

I distracted myself by watching Asma chase Haider and Mushy just in front of South Building. I think they smashed an egg over her head. I couldn't help smiling.

I'm really gonna miss school.

I walked home slowly, up Buncer Lane, cherishing every moment. This is the last time I'll be doing this: past the weird Confederate flag, past Marlon Broomes's house, across Preston New Road, into our area. It suddenly dawned on me: I don't need this uniform any more. This navy-blue jumper with a green crest has been a part of me for five years and today is the last time I'll ever need to wear it in my life.

Damn.

Might wear the shirt again, but. My front pocket's still intact.

Thursday 1st July

I wasn't here last summer, because of the Pakistan trip, so this is the first summer I get to spend as a New Bank boy.

New Bank Road is the road in our area that has all the shops on it: Patel's (the corner shop that's been there as long as I can remember), Asim's chippy, the post office, a butcher's, Spar and, just round the corner, Faisal's barber's. There's also two primary schools (St Silas and Sacred Heart), four mosques and Corporation Park.

It's still all terraced houses here, but I think this area used to be posh because the houses are slightly bigger and more expensive than other parts of Blackburn. There used to be a lot of goreh who lived here, but they moved out and more and more apne moved in.

I always found it weird when goreh at school asked, 'Oh, how come all you lot live together in the same areas in Whalley Range and Little Harwood and Audley?'

My answer was always the same: 'Do you lot not live together in Mill Hill and Cherry Tree and Roman Road?' Also, maybe if the white people who lived in those areas before didn't sell their houses because they didn't wanna live with Asians, then maybe it'd be a more mixed area.

I love living here, but the one bad thing is that there's nowhere to play sport. There's no proper pitches. In Was's area they've got St John's, which has a massive AstroTurf pitch where at any one time there might be five separate footy games going on, and a game of cricket. Here we have to play in either Hargreaves, which is basically a factory yard, or the St Silas or Sacred Heart playgrounds, both of which we have to climb over the railings for. So basically breaking and entering.

Our footy games are legendary. Shibz, Shiry, Muj, of course. And then the new friends I've made: Rizzy, Deemy, Nasir, Nisar, Zak, Big Riz, Saki, Asghar, Pats, Kes, Chyna, Bilal, Abdulla,

Faisal, Shazad etc. We battle it out, first team to twenty goals wins. When one team gets to ten it's half time and we swap sides, which is only fair because every 'pitch' we play has slightly different ends, with different walls and goal dimensions. So it's important that we switch sides.

Today's game was sick. One of those rare games that gets to 19–19 and then it's next goal wins. My team won 20–19, but what was so good was that I scored such a top goal. Nasir was in goal and he threw it out to me,* it came over my shoulder and I hit it first time with my left, side-footed, on the volley and into the opposite top corner.

Everyone's jaws dropped. I didn't know what to do myself. It's what I had wanted to do, but so rarely in football do my mind, body and soul work together. I'm usually one of the last picks, so to score a goal like that was absolutely wicked!

Tuesday 6th July

Did I mention that we're not actually allowed to play in St Silas? Well, we're not actually allowed to play in St Silas.

The cops came today. Again. It's SO frustrating. There are boys our age and older dealing drugs, smoking, drinking, getting girls pregnant and God knows what else. We just want to play football! And the cops come and tell us off. It doesn't make any sense. It's so stupid.

The boys I play with are generally good lads.

This isn't the first time this has happened, though, and we have a plan now. Thank God, because I got caught today.

What generally happens is someone who turned up

---

* Nasir would later admit that the only reason he threw the ball to me was that he was so frustrated at being in goal, he thought by throwing the ball to me, the worst player on the team, I would mess up and then I'd be asked to swap with Nasir and have to go in goal. Baist.

late – today it was Pats – will be standing outside the railings watching the game, and if they see a police car they shout, 'MAAMEH!': Cops!

When this happens, no matter what is happening in the game, we scatter. For some people it's the fastest they've run all afternoon. We climb over the railings and then run left, right, up and down the street, into alleys or other streets. About fifteen minutes later we come back and finish the game.

Usually someone gets caught, and today . . . it was me and Shiry.

The police separated us for questioning. Smart. But we're smarter. We had just enough time to whisper a few things to each other before they got to us.

'Did you know that you're not allowed to play in this yard?'

'No, officer.'

'You've never been told?'

'No, officer.'

'Who were the lads you were playing with?'

'I don't know, officer. I'm not from here.'

'Where are you from?'

'Manchester.'

'What's your name?'

'Shah Rukh.'

'That your full name, is it?'

'Khan. Shah Rukh Khan.' Ha! Shah Rukh Khan is a legendary Bollywood actor.

'And what's your friend's name?'

'Shahid Afridi.' HA AGAIN! Shahid Afridi is a legendary Pakistani cricketer.

And Shiry would say the same thing, and eventually they'd let us go with a telling off. I'm not gonna let the police stop us from enjoying our summer. All we do is come out and play and go home to eat and sleep. Stop wasting our time and go and arrest some criminals, innit, you institutionally racist pigs.

I mean, I don't know if these police officers are racist, but that report said that the whole police is institutionally racist, so . . .

Thursday 15th July [CONTAINS RUDE BITS]

I've been waiting for this day for a long time.

About seven years.

When I first ever read it in the green book.*

All Muslims (men and women) must remove the hair from their underarms and from in and around their pubic area.

It's time.

I don't have enough hair on my face yet to justify shaving it, but I do now have hair in other areas and so I need to remove it.

I've bought a ten-pack of Bic disposable razors. I have one with me, and off to the bathroom I go.

Update: Well . . . it looks very . . . different.

Bigger?

I started off by wetting my armpits with hot water, then I took the lid off the razor and just went for it. Right armpit first. In Islam you always start things on the right-hand side.

I was surprised how easily the hair came off. I don't know what I was expecting, to be honest. I was too embarrassed to talk to anyone about it beforehand. I heard Was talking about it with Shibz a few weeks ago, but I was too shy to ask for advice myself.

After a few strokes of the razor all the hair was gone. I felt the area with my hand; it was so smooth! I did the same with the left side.

Then for the . . . er . . . pubic area?

I got in the bath (we have a big corner bath with a seat now

---

* The green book was a textbook I had in mosque, which went through some basic Islamic practices for kids and teenagers.

and that really helped). I sat on the seat and poured water all over my bits and thigh area, and started shaving. Upwards, downwards, left to right, right to left. Pouring water over the area to get rid of all the hair. And repeat.

Then the top of my right thigh, then the top of my left thigh, then I bent over and shaved the inside of my ass! Haha. I'm just laughing as I write this. What a crazy sentence. Then last I did my balls and my actual dick. That was tricky. I poured cold water on my balls, so they became like hard domes instead of floppy, and that way I could see and shave the hairs properly.

It must've taken me about forty-five minutes altogether. But by the end, my pubic area, top of my thighs and all my bits and bats were as smooth as my favourite type of peanut butter.

SO MUCH HAIR, BUT ...

Because I was concentrating so much, I didn't even realise that the water in the bath was rising because my pubes and ass hair had blocked up the plughole. I took all the hairs out of the hole and threw them in the bin. And then normal service resumed, and the water drained away.

I washed myself and then finished up, making sure that the bath was as clean as when I first got in it. I don't want anyone to know what I was doing ... even though Ammi, Abu and Baj must do the same thing too?

Urgh! Urgh! Urgh!

Anyway, I'm back in my room, admiring my work. I did a good job. Well done, Terry, you're a man now. A man with less hair than when you were just a boy.

Tuesday 3rd August

I was praying Maghrib* at Al-Asr and I saw something I've never seen in our mosques: a jamaat*.

It's where a group of boys and men travel round the country, going to different towns, staying in mosques and learning more about Islam. Basically, like a travelling i'tikaaf, or a summer camp for Muslims.

Yesterday I met a group from London who are staying in Al-Asr for two nights. There's twelve of them. Most of them are only a few years older than me and there's a couple of adults with them to teach and probably make sure they don't mess about too much.

I was talking to them after Maghrib yesterday. There's this one guy called Atiq, who seems really cool; he reminds me of Was, the way he talks and cracks jokes. Plus, he's the only Pakistani in the group, the rest are Indian. He invited me to sit with them and share their food (pizza, so obviously I said yeah), and he explained to me all about the jamaat and what it is and what they try and learn and stuff. It sounded really cool.

He explained to me that they're Sunni too! Even within Sunnis there's slightly different varieties. They're just a different type of Sunni to what me and my family are. What he said made a lot of sense to me. Then he invited me to join the jamaat, because they're going around Blackburn mosques for the next week. I wanted to say yes straight away, but I had to ask home first.

I explained to Ammi what it was, and she said, 'Yeah, go.'

So tomorrow I'm going on jamaat!

Friday 6th August

Oh my Allah.

I have learnt SO much in just two days.

They've corrected my namaaz technique, I learned loads of technical things about praying, like what to do if you miss a rakat* in congregation etc. AND apparently the way I pronounce Arabic has been wrong my whole life! I've been pronouncing it like it's Urdu because some of the letters are similar, but actually those letters are supposed to be pronounced completely differently. It's not *alif bey thay say*, it's *alif baa taa saa*! Damn.

I feel like I'm only really learning about Islam now. That's crazy. There is so much to Islam. It's a whole way of life. There's little prayers when you enter the house/leave the house, when you enter the mosque/leave the mosque, when you enter the bathroom etc.

So much to learn. Maybe I did leave mosque too early. I actually feel like a child again.

Monday 9th August

I think I might've outstayed my welcome.

I overheard a couple of the lads talking about me, saying that I haven't given any money to the kitty for food and that I haven't contributed. I feel well bad. Obviously, it makes sense, because they're feeding me and stuff, but I wish someone had told me to bring some money, then I could've paid for my share. I just didn't think of that. I think they were being unfair, but I didn't say anything because I don't like confrontation.

Atiq is still being really nice to me. He did a speech today about praying and how we should pray as much as we can, well five times a day – it's a pillar of Islam and it's the minimum we are expected to do. He told the story of how when the Prophet Muhammad (Peace Be Upon Him) visited Heaven during the Night Journey, he was told by Allah that we have to pray fifty times a day!

As he was leaving Heaven, Prophet Musa* (Peace Be Upon Him) stopped him and told the Prophet to go back and ask for less, that people wouldn't be able to do fifty, that it would be too much for us. So, the Prophet went back to Allah and the number was lowered to forty-five. Prophet Musa again told him it's too much, so the number was lowered to forty. But Prophet Musa continued

---

* Musa: Moses

to send him back, till the number was five. At that point, Prophet Musa still thought it was too much of a commitment for us, but the Prophet Muhammad told him he was too embarrassed to go again, and so the number of times we have to pray each day is five.

It really hit home that: 1) five times a day is not that many times to worship our Creator, surely; and 2) thank Allah for the Prophet Musa! Because fifty would've been WAY TOO MUCH.

I am Muslim, why don't I pray every day? From now on I'm gonna pray every day, inshAllah five times a day when I can!

I've had fun and I've learnt so much, I think it's actually changed my life. But I told Atiq I'm gonna go home tomorrow. In my head it was because I don't want anyone to say anything else about me not paying my way, but I told him it's because I'm homesick.

We said we'd pray for each other and he gave me advice on not listening to other people when they talk bad about you. I wondered if he knew that his friends were talking about me, or if he was just saying it anyway? Either way, I appreciated it and it made me feel better. Top guy, kasam.

May Allah make him happy and grant him success both in this life and in the hereafter. Ameen. I hope I meet him again some day.*

Thursday 12th August

I went to see Baaji today. Obviously, he's been ill for a while. He's completely bedridden and he doesn't even remember anybody any more. He even calls for his first wife, who died about fifty years ago.

It's really sad. Especially because he used to be so formidable. Everyone respected him and looked up to him. He was the first

---

* I never did. If you're reading this, Atiq, hit me up on the 'gram, man.

person in our family to come to England. I'm here, my entire family is here, because of him.

He fought for England in World War II and as part of his 'reward' he got to come and rebuild England. After a while he called Taya over and then Wadi Ammi and Poupoh and Dad. Big Poupoh stayed in Pakistan because she was already married.

It was hard for them in those days. They didn't have halal meat shops or a mosque or a community like we do now and goreh were even more racist than they are now. Dad told me that when Baaji first came over, he used to work in a factory and twelve people would be sleeping in the same room. Six would work the day shift, while the night-shift people would sleep, then when the day-shift people came home, the night-shift people would go to work and the day-shift people would sleep. They worked six days a week for only a bit of money compared to what people earn now. Everyone who came did that.

It made me think of Mammu Abbas and how hard he works. He could do that. I couldn't.

And now look, we have a thriving community. People have made businesses and we have respect. That generation, we owe them EVERYTHING. We can never pay them back.

There's one thing I can do, though. From now on, every day, I'm going to come and visit Baaji, sit by him and pray Surah Yasin* out loud to him and give him company.

It's sad seeing Baaji in his bed, so helpless. Just a shadow of the magnificent man he used to be. I remember him chasing us out of the house once, because me, Was, Shibz and Shiry and Muj were laughing in namaaz. I think Was actually got a smack because he was last!

I miss the man he used to be.

---

* This is a short, eighty-three-verse chapter in the Qur'an. Often described as the heart of the Qur'an.

Wednesday 25th August

It's been a busy summer!

Playing football or cricket nearly every day. Getting chased by the police, hanging out with my new friends (the Maliks), going on jamaat and becoming more religious, tryna convince my friends to come to namaaz with me (this was never very successful) and going to see Baaji every day.

But tomorrow ... tomorrow my GCSEs come out!

I'm so nervous. As I was leaving Baaji, I told him to pray for me. Even though I know he can't understand me, I was hoping deep down he's still there and could hear me. The reason he brought his family here is because he wanted them and his future grandkids to have a better life, and obviously the biggest part of that is to get a good education.

'Baaji, I hope I do you proud tomorrow.' InshAllah.

Thursday 26th August

Baaji ...

Ammi woke me up this morning at 7.30. Baaji's passed away. My granddad's died.

She gave me a hug and told me to come downstairs.

I was numb, I'll be honest. Shocked. He's old, around eighty-eight, so it's not a tragedy, and the man we knew had already gone because he was so ill, and it's good that he's not suffering any more, but ... still ... I'm really sad.

I had a quick bath, changed and then went downstairs. I had a bowl of Rice Krispies (only one small spoon of sugar now) and I was about to set off for Randal Street – Baji Rosey had already gone.

Ammi stopped me and told me to go get my GCSE results first. MY GCSE RESULTS! Shit. How could I have forgotten about them?! Ammi explained that there was nothing I can do for anyone right now. 'Go get you results, come back home and then go.'

I got to school and Mrs Livesy, our head of year, was there. I said hello. She asked me how I was feeling; I didn't tell her about Baaji because I would've started crying. I told her I was nervous.

She told me that Witton Park had only got an A*–C pass rate of 35 per cent, though the average in the whole country was 56 per cent. Was that meant to make me feel better? Or is she tryna tell me I did crap, but it's okay because our whole school did crap?

I got my results envelope, said Bismillah* and opened it ...

Graphics	C

Shit.

English	A
English Literature	A
German	A
Science	AA
IT	A

Six As!!!
I did it.
I DID IT!
ALHAMDULILLAH, I DID IT!

I got Bs in maths, business studies, RE and history. I was so stunned and happy and sad.

I saw a few people, but no one I would call a friend. I was one of the first to arrive, I guess, and knowing my friends, they wouldn't be there till a bit later.

I looked around for Ms Williams, but I couldn't see her. I was a bit sad about that. I wanted to say thank you to her. She's been really encouraging this year and I feel like she helped me believe in myself.

I couldn't wait, though, I had to be somewhere else. I left school and rushed home. I told Mum and she gave me such a big hug, and we both cried. She told me how proud she was of me. Then I walked to Randal Street and all sorts of emotions were entering my mind.

As soon as I stepped onto the street I saw Dad, who was outside Wadi Ammi's house with Taya and Nads. I didn't have the words. I gave Dad a hug and then passed him the results envelope. I'm not sure he knew what it was. I gave Taya and Nads a hug, everyone seemed to be coping okay. That was good.

I turned around and Dad's jaw had dropped. He looked at the results, looked at me and looked at the results again. His face was beaming and then his eyes got watery, he grabbed me and gave me a huge hug. It lasted a long time. He told me how proud of me he was.

I was so happy that on the saddest day of his life I was able to offer him some hope for the future.

The rest of the day was a blur of hugging, praying, telling everyone my results and listening to the grown-ups as they worked out who was taking Baaji's body back to Pakistan. Wadi Ammi, Dad, Taya and Poupoh are all gonna go.

Tomorrow's the funeral.

Friday 27th August

Today was very emotional.

We said goodbye to Baaji. The mosque was packed with worshippers all wanting to pray for a man the whole community knew and respected. I've never seen Dad cry so much. Jaffer and Nads were crying a lot too. It was very hard to watch.

After the funeral, they left with the body to go to the airport. That was that.

Later in the day we let off some steam. Me, Was, Shiry, Shibz and Muj went to St John's to play football and there was this Indian boy there who looked at me funny. I asked him what his problem was and he swore at me. Before I could answer him back, Shiry, Shibz and Was had pounced on him and were twatting him.

After like ten seconds, they pushed him to the ground and told him to fuck off. He did.

Then we played 60 seconds and Wembley.[*]

It was fine today, but life can be cruel sometimes.

And by life, I mean my cousins.

In 60 seconds, one person goes in goal and the other people have to try and score on the volley. So you can only score if the ball is passed to you and you kick/head it in before it touches the ground.

If you're the keeper, there's two ways you can get out of nets: if you get to sixty seconds (the last person who touches it has to go in nets, unless you get unlucky and the keeper is the last person who touches it, then you have to stay in), or you catch a pass, or shot. Then the person who you catch it from has to go in. A couple of years ago, Was, Shibz, Shiry and Muj kept me in nets for sixty minutes! A full hour. It felt like forever. It was the biggest baisti of my life.

The worst thing was, it was like they were doing it on purpose. Usually, if the keeper gets to 54, 55 seconds, then no one wants to touch the ball, and the person with the ball is stuck and has to end up going in. But for me, they played extra hard. It was well tight. At one point, I saved the ball at 53 seconds and threw it at Was. Now, normally Shiry, Shibz and Muj would run, so he couldn't kick it at them, but instead they all stayed to risk it and try and score, and this one time they scored on 59 seconds! You feel dead in that moment. I mean, it was fair and square, but it also felt like bullying. I didn't cry that day, but I wanted to.

---

[*] One keeper, and everyone else plays a knockout tournament.

Today was better. It was about coming together and healing, by twatting a stranger and having a kickabout.

Tuesday 31st August

I did two big things today and I don't know if either of them was the right decision.

I called Clitheroe Royal Grammar School up and told them that I won't be joining them. They were very surprised.

I've thought about it a lot over the weekend. I think it's too far and I have to get a bus there, which means I have to wake up really early every day, plus the uniform is really expensive too and I don't wanna ask Ammi for the money for it. I know how hard it is for her already with Abu.

After that, I called St Mary's and asked them if I can join them and they said *no, we're full.*

SHIT.

I should've maybe rung them before I rang Clitheroe.

Well, Blackburn College it is. It's a good college, actually. And anyway, it's more about if the person wants to learn. If they do, it doesn't matter where they are: they'll be fine! Right?

The second thing I did, and this was because Shibz put the idea in my head, I burnt all my schoolbooks. Every single one. I made a little bonfire in the garden and one by one I put my books in there. I had loads from Years 7–9 as well.

I was proper ruthless. I don't really know why I was doing this, though. Was I tryna be cool like Shibz? That's probably what it was, to be honest. I think a part of me was definitely sad, but I'm moving into a new phase of my life now. Time to leave the sentimental kid behind.

English, science, history, maths, RE, German, IT, business studies, all burnt to a crisp. Nothing left of them but ashes.

I kept my graphics project, though. That's different. I created that. I'm gonna keep my National Record of Achievement safe too. That's got all my certificates from Year 7 up to now in it and all my end-of-year reports too. Who knows when they might come in handy?

Hopefully I don't need my maths or science books for my A levels at ~~Clithe~~ Blackburn College.

Wednesday 1st September

'Is he fucks like!' Nisar is arguing with Zak again.

'Yeah he is, tell me then, who's better? Go on, I'm listening.'

One of the highlights of the summer, and actually since moving to this new house, has been making friends with the Maliks.

They're a big family who moved to New Bank last year, they ran a shop for a bit, but the shop is closed now and they use that room as their front room, in fact it's almost like a Pakistani baitak, and us boys hang about in it all the time after footy games.

There are three brothers who I hang out with. Zakria, he's my exact age; Nisar, who's one year younger; and then there's Nasir, who's a couple of years younger than him but very mature for his age and a top football player.

One of my favourite things about them is how passionate and emotional they are. They have such short tempers with each other. They always shout at each other and look like they're about to fight, it's so funny, but with us lot, they're always proper sound.

Today's argument was about who's a better striker than Anelka in the Premier League. Zak supports Arsenal.

Every day after a footy game, me, Shibz, Pats, Kes, Chyna and sometimes Shiry chill with the Maliks in their house, watching TV, practising free kicks with a little football or just chatting loads of crap about footy and stuff.

It's really fun and like our den.

Saturday 4th September

I start college next week, so I have loads of things to buy. I had some money saved and Mum gave me £20 so I bought: two jeans, three tops, some new trainers, a new jacket and some new stationery too. The main thing was a graphing calculator. That's different to the scientific calculator that I used in my GCSEs, in that it costs more and does lots of stuff I don't understand.

I also bought some new pens and pads. Unlike school, you have to bring your own writing pads, because they don't give you exercise books. I'm gonna miss those.

I'm actually a very neat worker. I use either a black or blue pen depending on how important the subject is (black for English, maths and science), I double underline my headings using a red pen, and I use a green pen for sub-headings. It really helped for revision.

I liked school exercise books because they had nice space between the lines and really good margins to make other notes in. The pads that I've bought from Stationery Box don't look as nice.

I wonder if Clitheroe Royal Grammar School give out exercise books. I bet they do. They are a school, after all.

I told Shibz that I turned down the place at Clitheroe and I'm going to Blackburn College instead. I thought he'd be proper disappointed, but he's going to Blackburn College too.

One thing I noticed in the shops was that I was alone. Almost everyone was with their friends or family. Especially kids my age, who were all with their friends.

I don't like asking people to come with me to town. Or asking them to hang out with me. No one's asking me to hang out with them, so if I ask them, what if they say no? Or if they just say yeah to be polite . . .

I actually just realised, I spend A LOT of time in my own company. Am I okay with that? I think so.

I have friends that I like a lot.

I have family that I love a lot.

But I don't wanna be a burden on anyone.

I think it comes from knowing that Abu didn't want me and Baj to live with the family. He wanted to leave us in Pakistan when we were small, or go live with Dad, but Ammi always put her foot down and said no. Maybe that's why I think, *what if other people feel like that too?*

I know Was and Shibz hang with different, older boys now. I think some of them drink and smoke and stuff (not Was and Shibz). I wouldn't fit in with them. Especially now I'm religious and I always wear a topi. They wouldn't feel comfortable with me even being there.

But . . . I do wish I had the confidence to just ask Shibz to come town with me, because he's got wicked dress sense and style, he's tall and everything fits him nicely. I would ask him his opinion on the clothes that I bought. But I feel embarrassed.

I remember last Eid, I think he got a bit annoyed because he told me that he was gonna buy an Adidas tracksuit for it and I thought that was a well cool idea, so I bought one too. I wasn't trying to copy him, but you know, I guess I was tryna be cool like him.

I'm okay, though. I like my own company. I can go to the shops I want to go to and not waste time just doing laps round town like I see some boys doing.

Wednesday 8th September

I walked into Feilden Street Building today for the first day of college. It's a proper ugly building, but it's where Blackburn College house the A-level students. Which is a bit strange. Why house the cleverest kids in the ugliest building? Is it a punishment? How dare you come from Blackburn and try and make something of yourself?

I walked in, through the little reception and left into a corridor. There were loads of people walking about. No one wearing a uniform. Boys wearing jeans, trackies, hoodies; girls wearing jeans, or dresses with tights, shalwar kameezes. Such a variety. I felt like I was in one of those American high schools from TV.

When I got to class the form tutor goes, 'My name is Sandra—'

'Hey, Sandra!' Everyone looked at me. Oh. I thought everyone else was gonna say it too. Plus, I've never used a teacher's first name before; I was excited. She didn't say hi back – rude – she just carried on talking.

Suddenly, I felt a bit nervous, being in new surroundings (there was not a single person in there who I knew, no one from Witton Park or St Barnabas). So I started fiddling with my pen. Taking the lid off and then snapping it back on. Taking the lid off, snapping it back on. Taking the lid off, snapping it back on. Taking the lid off, snapping it back on. Taking the lid off, snapping it back on. Taking the lid off, snappi—

'STOP DOING THAT!'

I stopped. I didn't even realise I was doing it, or how much noise it was making. Before she could say anything else, I was saved by the bell.

I stayed behind. 'I didn't like how you embarrassed me in front of the whole tutor group on my first day in college. You said we were supposed to be treated like adults. Well, that didn't feel like it, Sandra.'

I didn't say that. Instead, I said, 'Sorry, Sandra.'

Sunday 12th September

Little Tany turned four today. He's gotten so big and SO fast! Can't keep up with him. He's a good kid, though. I love him.

Thursday 16th September

'Knock knock.' I really like it when people laugh at my jokes.

'Who's there?' It's honestly the main reason I like maths class.

'An interrupting cow.' I sit next to Farida.

'An interrupting cow—' Who's really clever and explains things to me like differentiation.

'Moooooooo!' But I especially like how she laughs at my dumb jokes.

Farida put her hand over her mouth as she remembered she was in class.

She hit me on the arm two seconds later, as she realised I'd just called her a cow, then I laughed, like, what?

I fancy her a bit. I think. Or is that only because she laughs at my stupid jokes? But Ebrahim laughs at them too and I definitely don't fancy him.

Ebrahim, from Witton Park, I've decided is gonna be my best friend in college. When I told the joke, I could see him grinning. He sits on the other side of Farida.

He's like me. Clever, likes footy and has no idea how to talk to girls.

I do computing with Ebrahim too and I honestly do not understand it at all. Less than I even understand girls. I thought I'd do it because computers are the future, innit. But . . . I have no idea what is going on. I found IT so easy at school, I thought it'd be more like that, but this is proper rock hard.

Sunday 26th September

I went to the Tablighi Jamaat Annual Youth Conference in Leicester today. A coach took us from Blackburn. I didn't know a single person on it, which is not surprising given that I went to madrassa in a different mosque to every other person going.

It was very interesting. There were lectures all day. The one that I remember most was about girls and how you're not meant to be boyfriend and girlfriend with them. How in fact it's better not to interact with girls outside your family at all. And to lower your gaze. Apparently, you're allowed to look at a girl once (obviously, because if you look at someone you can't help that) and then you're not meant to look at her again.

To be honest, I thought that was a bit too much for me. I get the no girlfriend/boyfriend bit (sorry, Farida), but I like being friends with girls. They have a different perspective about things, they're not aggressive and they actually listen to your point of view.

I guess they had a good point about not looking at them too much. I'm sure I used to stare at Fiona too much sometimes in school. That wasn't good.

Anyway, there wasn't a single girl in this entire conference, so it's not something any of us horny boys had to worry about today.

Saturday 2nd October

College gave us all a diary.

Obviously, I already have a diary. Hello.

The college diary is still useful, though. I've put my timetable in it and I use it to put my homework in that I have to do. It would look quite empty if it only had that in it, so I've been using it to record football and other sports results too, which I think will be very useful information for the future.

Tuesday 5th October

When someone passes away, you do a big khatam after forty days to pray for them. It was Baaji's today.

So many people came. Our extended family like Pua Said lot, so Uncle Zafar, Shahid, Sohail, (other) Shabaz, Harun and

Mammu Toheed, and loads of Dad's and Taya's friends too. It was nice seeing everyone again and it always amazes me how much my community bes there for each other when we need them.

Afterwards we family lads were sat in Wadi Ammi's front room. 'How's college going?' Was asked.

'I love it. Wear what I want, eat where I want. I like the freedom.' Well, Shibz clearly likes it more than I do.

'Is good, Was. Obviously very different to school. I like how we call the teachers by their first names.' I was changing the subject without really changing the subject.

'Yeah, that proper surprised me. It'd be like calling Ms Williams ... Wait, what the hell was Ms Williams's name?'

'It was S. Williams, wasn't it?' I remembered.

'Sarah,' Shibz said.

'No ... it doesn't sound right' Was said.

'It definitely was that.' I suddenly remembered. 'She introduced herself as Sarah to my mum once at parent's evening.'

I asked Was how he was getting on with his auto electronics course, which is at Blackburn College but bes at a different site to where me and Shibz do A levels, but before he could answer, all the adults came in: Uncle, Taya, Dad, Mammu Saeed and a couple of others. We got up straight away for them and then there was an awkward moment where we didn't know what to do.

Normally you'd think, just sit on the floor, but there's a random thing with the men on Dad's side of the family. We can't sit on the floor for more than five minutes without our legs aching and having to shift position. Which is bad, because a large part of being Muslim and Asian is sitting on the floor.

Dad explained, 'Your grandad couldn't do it. If you wanna blame anyone, blame him.' Baaji couldn't do it, Dad can't, I can't, Nads can't, Was can't, Muj can't, Shibz can't, Shiry can't and Jaffer can't. None of the girls have a problem! And the men in Pakistan don't either. Proper weird. Obviously, when we have to, like when we're at mosque, we put up with it, but for example when we have family functions and everyone is sat on the floor eating, us lads sit at a table. Proper baisti.

'Shall we go St John's?' Was asked.

We all agreed that was the best thing to do. So me, Shibz, Shiry, Muj and Was went to play 60 seconds.

'I'm not going in nets,' I said to them on the way out. That lasted five minutes.

Tuesday 12th October

There was a coup in Pakistan today! By the army. A coup is when a government is removed from power, but not in an election. Overthrown, basically. The army is in charge of Pakistan now. General Pervez Musharraf. I feel like that's quite crazy, but everyone here is well happy.

Ammi said that Nawaz Sharif is proper corrupt and him and his family steal money from Pakistan. They take the funding or taxes or whatever and hide it in their own bank accounts abroad. Apparently, everyone knows this. Bloody hell. It's crazy that people would still vote for him then, innit?

It's weird how much stuff is well known by everybody, like the Prime Minister of Pakistan being corrupt, the royal family killing Princess Diana and the refs cheating for United, but no one does anything about it!

Abu said that the army should be in charge permanently because only they care about Pakistan and they're not corrupt.

I don't know about any of that, but I wondered what it meant for Mammu Jamil, because he's in the army. Ammi said it won't affect him because he's just a normal soldier, he'll just be doing his normal duties. At least that's good.

I remember when I went to Pakistan in 1995, Mammu Jamil took me to his barracks near Mangla Dam. That was one of the best times I've ever had in Pakistan. Riding on the back of Mammu Jamil's motorbike for about an hour and a half. The scenery was breath-taking. He took me around Mangla Dam, which is one of the biggest dams in the world. It was right on the border of Azad Kashmir, which is quite cool.

I had a fun two days messing about in the army barracks, playing games with soldiers, being crap at climbing ropes and being spoilt by everyone. Pakistani people are so generous. I think the less you have the more generous you be.

Then Mammu had to take me back home. On our way back we got stopped by a copper. Police in Pakistan are very corrupt; usually you just give them some money and they leave you alone. But Mammu is in the army and he didn't want to encourage their corruption.

The policeman asked for Mammu's licence. Now, I can't remember if Mammu didn't have his licence with him, or he didn't actually have one. I think it might have been the latter.

So, now the copper's asking for money, but Mammu says he's in the army. The copper tells him to prove it, but Mammu didn't have his army card with him. Ah. Shit.

The copper asked who I was. Mammu said something I couldn't understand, at which point the copper let us go.

I asked Mammu what he said to the copper that made him let us go.

Mammu, the absolute joker, told the copper that I was the son of the lieutenant general who is in charge of the entire barracks! Hahahaha.

I asked him who that was, and he explained to me that it was Lieutenant General Perv—

OH MY GOD!

IT WAS PERVEZ MUSHARRAF!

OH MY GOD!

I WAS THE SON OF THE FUTURE LEADER OF PAKISTAN FOR THIRTY SECONDS!

HAHAHAHA!

Mammu Jamil is actually crazy for that!

Anyway, I did a dua for Pakistan and my new 'dad' after namaaz today. I hope this coup is good for Pakistan and they become a less corrupt and stronger country. InshAllah.

Friday 29th October

Saeeda turned eleven today.

Wait . . .

That means she goes to high school next year! Oh my days, that is mental!

That makes me feel well old! In my head, she's still a small child. I mean she still is, but a high-school child?

Damn. It's just occurred to me: I'm going to uni in less than two years!

Friday 5th November

I love it when I learn something new about Islam. That happened today. I was in the college prayer room with Ebrahim, where we go every day for Zuhr* and Asr* namaaz. There were some brothers praying, but I'd never seen anyone pray like that in my life. They never lifted their hands, their hands just stayed by their side the whole time, and then they went into ruku* and prayed the rest of the namaaz like we do.

I was gonna say something to them, because I thought, someone needs to teach them how to pray properly, like I was taught over the summer, but then I thought better of it. There must be a reason that they're praying like that. When they left, I asked Ebrahim if he saw what I saw, and what the heck?

Ebrahim explained to me that they were Malikis, they follow Imam Malik.

Sorry, what now?

He fully explained to me that in Islam there were four big imams who created four separate schools of thought. They're all right, they just have slight differences between them. But you're only supposed to follow one of them.

Which one was I?

Apparently, I'm a Hanafi and we follow Imam Abu Hanifa. The other two imams were Imam Shafi'i and Imam Hanbal.

The four schools of thought recognise each other and always debate (nicely) about rulings and stuff. After that, I had loads of questions. Ebrahim told me some more stuff:

So, I'm a Muslim. A Sunni Muslim, but within Sunni, I'm a Barelvi, and separate to that I'm a Hanafi too.

The Sunni Muslims who go on jamaat and stuff who I've been hanging around with, they're Sunni, but within Sunni, they're Deobandi.

What the heck, man?!

Why does no one explain these things to me?

I asked Baji Rosey later if this was all true and she told me it was, and I asked why no one had told me earlier and she explained that mosque teaching is very lazy and there's lots of stuff, basics and interesting things, that they don't teach us because they just wanna do the bare minimum and send us home. Damn. What else don't I know?

Good job I didn't get too big for my boots and 'correct' those guys. Important lesson for me there. Just because someone is doing something different to me, doesn't mean they're wrong, I may just not be aware of all the information. It's important not to judge and jump to conclusions.

I normally don't have patience. Good job I used what little I do have today.

Wednesday 10th November

Even though it's probably haram, I still like listening to songs.

I can't afford to buy music from HMV, so I've spent a lot of time recording songs from the radio that I like. This year some of my favourite songs that I've heard have been:

1. My Name Is
2. Still DRE
3. The Way I Am
4. Hate Me Now
5. Hard Knock Life
6. Sweet Like Chocolate
7. Mambo No. 5
8. That Don't Impress Me Much
9. Flat Beat
10. ... Baby One More Time
11. It's Like That
12. No Scrubs

I basically like rap, R&B, dance and pop music.

I remember once I got into an argument with Lee in graphics class because he was saying that indie music was the best and I thought it was weird that he was listening to Bollywood, but he explained that indie music is Oasis and Blur and Cornershop. Which confused me even more, because Cornershop are Indian.

And we got into an argument because I think that stuff (not including Cornershop) is proper boring and he got pissed off and said *no, that's actually proper music*, which didn't make any sense to me because music is music – what's proper or not proper about it? But I know I'm definitely not into indie or rock or heavy metal or anything like that. Urgh.

Also ... I don't know HOW other kids listen to music and work.

I've tried it and I find it impossible. So many of my classmates say that they listen to music, it helps them concentrate. Hassim and Shibz say that's how they always work at home. I can't do it.

I've tried different types of music: Tupac, Dr. Dre, Eminem, Freed From Desire. Even slow stuff like R. Kelly or Sixpence None the Richer, or the Corrs. None of it works. If I'm listening to the Corrs, I'm just thinking of Andrea Corr. How is that supposed to help with my homework?

Nope, the only way I can concentrate is in silence. Just me, the natural sounds of the attic and roof and the sound of my pen on paper, or the hum of my computer and the keyboard being tapped away.

Maybe I'm the weird one, but as Eminem would say ... *it's just the way I am.*

Tuesday 16th November

Today was the prize-giving evening at Witton Park, which is basically a night where the school celebrates the Year 11s who left last term.

It was so good to see everyone. I hadn't seen Hassim since my last exam. I'd missed him. I asked how he was doing. He was good, and then I asked about Clitheroe Royal Grammar School and he was telling me that he proper loves it. He asked me about Blackburn College and I told him that I liked it and I was doing really well. Lies.

I said hi to so many people: Mushy, Chucky, Haider, Kelloggs, Golly, Karolia, Quiet Yasin (I think he said hi back), Imran, Junaid, Buxy, Kalpesh, Ebrahim (ironically, because I'd just seen him a few hours before in maths class in college), Lee, Christian, Jack, Halima, Faiza, Deela, Fiona, Laura, Rebecca, Asma, Amina etc. Not Tommy.

It was nice to see my teachers for one last time too. I finally thanked Ms Williams and apologised for being a pain in her butt.

She smiled, wished me good luck and told me to make sure I study hard for my A levels. For a second, I wanted to tell her how hard I was finding it in college and that I was getting bad marks on my tests. I wanted to know if she had any advice. But I didn't want her to worry about me, so I kept it to myself.

It wasn't a very fancy event. Students went up in groups to get certificates and awards for different things:

- 100% Attendance over Five Years (which I thought was a biased award, because no way an Asian could win that: we always take two or three days off for Eid. Even Deela and Kalpesh take a day off for Diwali as well.)
- Most Improved
- Subject Awards

I didn't get any of them. But I did go up with the group that achieved five or more GCSEs at grades A*–C, to collect a certificate of merit. And that's the one that matters in the end. What grades I got. Not which teachers liked me or couldn't cope with me. That's not gonna be on my CV in the future, is it?

When I collected the certificate from Mrs Livesy I looked up and I could see Ammi sat quite far back with the other parents, beaming. That made me really happy.

It got really interesting when Buxy got his certificate – he made a little speech, which we weren't supposed to do! He goes:

'Thanks a lot to everyone, but especially the teachers that didn't believe in me. This is for you.'

Woah! The whole hall started chatting, wondering which teachers he was talking about.

At the end there were two special awards. One was the Governor's Award and the other was the Headteacher's Prize.

Amina won the Governors' Award and Karolia won the Headteacher's Prize.

The headteacher, Mr Gosling, even pointed out that two Asians won the main awards, and that Witton was a school where everyone was equal.*

Hmmmm.

I don't know about that, but I was really happy for them both, especially Karolia. He deserves it, he's really clever and always tries hard. And he's fun to play football with. He's proper shit, even shitter than me, but he goes in nets, where he's decent. But he thinks he's Schmeichel and always shouts at his team when he concedes a goal. It always makes me laugh. I hope he goes on to do good things at St Mary's.

I came home and put my certificate in my National Record of Achievement.

Saturday 20th November

I did another shift at my (non-paid) job today.

Basically, Ammi has put me to work from a very young age. I mean, why hire a babysitter when there's a ten-year-old in the house to look after his little brother and sister, right?

This happened regularly. And then when I was twelve, little Tany came along. So, it was little brothers and sister.

This was when Baj was in Pakistan, so it was just me. At least now she's here.

Sometimes Ammi and Abu go away for hours, and I don't know where they've gone or when they'll be back. They just leave me in charge. By 'in charge', I mean just making sure Saeeda and Zaheer and Tanveer don't die.

Sometimes I end up fighting with Saeeda and then I have to

---

* Today, the school's motto is 'Succeeding Together', and according to its Equality and Diversity policy, the ethos is 'a culture of social inclusion where all students and staff are valued equally'.

spend two hours pleading with her not to grass me up to Ammi and Abu when they come back. Which sometimes means letting her play with my Kinder Surprise Smurfs collection.

What made it worse is sometimes I would have to babysit other people's kids as well!

Ammi's best friend in Edmundson Street was Aunty Sam. I like Aunty Sam, she's really jolly and smiley and always kind to me. She has four kids, though, all girls. I didn't even think that it was possible.* How can you have four kids and they all be the same sex? That's well tight. You wanna mix it up a bit.

Anyway, sometimes I have to babysit Aisha, Mariam, Zohra and Henna too. ON TOP OF SAEEDA, ZAHEER AND TANY!

Aisha's the oldest and is Saeeda's age, and I don't really know about the rest.

Is too much. I mean, they're nice girls, fair enough, but how's that fair on me? At least if the Butts (that's their surname, how funny is that? I call every kid Nicky Butt, but they don't get it) had a kid my age, that would be fair on me, I could play games with them or summat, but no.

It's the most hard when Ammi doesn't come back when she says she will.

Like today, she said she was coming back at 6 p.m. Thirty minutes go past, fair enough, could be traffic.

An hour, where are they? I need to do my homework.

Two hours, okay, they need to come home now, there's no Farley's Rusks left and I don't have milk in my tits to feed Tauqeer. Anyone would panic!

This one time, a couple of years ago, I got so bored I pranked 999: 'Hello, what's the emergency?'

---

* Aunty Sam then went on to have three boys in a row ... and then ANOTHER girl. So the girls took it 5–3.

'Your mum!' Hahahahah! Within ten seconds . . . *Ring-ring* . . .

Huh? I picked up the phone and it was the same operator! Shit! He goes: 'You think you're big and you're clever, yeah? Crank calling 999. Well, we know where you live, 57 Edmundson Street, Blackburn, and the police are coming round and they're gonna arrest you for wasting our time and put you in jail!' And then he hung up.

I shit myself! Allah di kasam, I forced Saeeda and Zaheer to lie flat on their stomachs in the living room, in case the police came, so we could pretend no one was home. I even told them: if the doorbell rings, DON'T answer it, some bad goreh are coming for us! That's well bad, innit?

Today, eight o'clock came and went, and they still weren't home. I gave up on them . . . Kasam . . . 100 per cent, I just thought, well, they're dead.

That was it. They're gone.

I guess . . . I guess . . . Me and Baj are in charge now? Chalo . . . Big responsibility, that, with three young kids. I'll have to mourn later. Probably have to leave college. Get a job. But is okay. The small kids have to come first. I wonder how many benefits me and Baj can get as kids who looks after kids.

And just as I'd thought of the whole story in my head, lo and behold, there's a key in the door. Our faces light up: Ammi and Abu are home!

And I did think THANK GOD! Well, thank God Ammi's alive, at least.

But a small part of me, like 5 per cent, thought, you know what? I could've done it.

Saturday 27th November

When I came downstairs to go to work, Saeeda asked me to take her to the library. I think she forgot that I was working. I asked her to ask Abu.

While I was eating, I noticed Baj looking at a bunch of forms at the dining table.

'What are those?'

'Forms I have to fill in for Uneeb's visa.' Ah cool!

'When's he coming?' Stupid question.

'When I fill out the forms, send them off, they process them and say yes.' Sounds complicated.

I could hear shouting coming from the other room.

'What's Uneeb doing anyway? Do you miss him?'

Baj rolled her eyes. Oh yeah, we don't ask personal questions in this family. 'He's just working at the depot, where Mammu Saeed used to work.'

'Nice.'

Saeeda came in. She looked a bit upset. 'Abu said he won't take me.' I looked at Baj; she understood and said:

'Don't worry, I'll take you. I need to go to do some photocopying anyway.'

Saeeda smiled.

We need some more joy in this house.

Friday 3rd December

We got cable today!

The joy!

Oh yeaaaaaaaaah!

I was fighting for the control with Saeeda and Zaheer. I lost. Because I won. Basically, I made them cry, so I had to give them the control so they wouldn't grass on me.

After sitting through an hour of *Pokémon*, Ammi sent them upstairs. My turn!

So many channels, so little time! First thing I watched was *WWF Raw is War* on Sky Sports. Man … wrestling has changed! I used to love it back in the day. Everyone's favourite was either Hulk Hogan or Ultimate Warrior. One or the other. You had to choose. I loved the Ultimate Warrior! Him and Bret Hart were my favourites.

Tonight was the first time I'd seen wrestling for five years! Last time I watched it was with Shibz, Shiry and Muj … *Wrestlemania IX*, when Yokozuna cheated to beat Bret Hart, but then Hulk Hogan came out and destroyed Yokozuna in ten seconds!

What I watched tonight was … er … very different!

There was no Hulk Hogan, or Ultimate Warrior, or Bret Hart, or Yokozuna. What there was, though, was … The Rock. Oh my God.

He's so cool and funny! I've only seen one episode, but he's definitely my favourite. He was proper just taking the piss out of this other wrestler, I was fully laughing my ass off.

Also, it's full of loads of really sexy half-naked girls now. Trish Stratus. Bloody hell. I almost thought it was too rude, but then I thought … well … the guys are all just wearing kacheh anyway, so in this case they're wearing even less than the girls! So, fair enough, I guess that's some sort of equality, in a way.

Thursday 9th December

I plucked up the confidence.

'Shall we go read namaaz?' I'd walked into the fourth-floor common room with Ebrahim. I saw Shibz on a table with Sheraz, Atiq and Yaqoob.

I was a bit nervous to ask. Today is the first roza and now that

I'm a bit more religious and wear a topi all the time, I feel like I have to show some responsibility, so I should ask people to come pray, but also, I didn't want people thinking that I'm judgemental or forcing them to do anything.

From my perspective, I was only reminding them. I wasn't trying to shove anything down anyone's throat. You're supposed to pray five times a day anyway, but we should try even harder in Ramazan.

'Yeah, man, come on. Get up, guys.' Yes Shibz!

Sometimes things are just easier if you ask. I realise that I make some things into a really big deal in my head, but when you just say it out loud the worst thing never happens. Actually, good things can happen.

'Do you know where the prayer room is?' Yaqoob asked.

'Yeah it's—'

'It doesn't matter if you know where the prayer room is!'

Oh my God. He just done me with one of The Rock's catch-phrases. Baist.

On the way to the prayer room I was saying to Shibz and Ebrahim that it seems like more kids in college are fasting than in school.

'Do you remember inside-out?' Shibz asked.

'Oh yeah.' Ebrahim remembered. 'That was silly.'

In school, every year, some kids would do 'home and away' or 'inside-out', which means at home they tell their family they're fasting, but in school they'd eat and smoke or whatever and then go back home and eat iftari* with their family as if they'd been fasting all day. How daft is that?

'If you're not gonna fast, don't fast,' I said.

'Them boys always thought they were so cool, innit?' Shibz was obviously annoyed at them as well.

'It's like they were acting rebellious. Rebelling against who, but?

Allah watches everything, he knows you weren't fasting, even if you tricked your family! Idiots.' I was on one today.

'Plus, the fasts in December and January are SO short! It's not that hard to not eat lunch, and not have a snack or smoke for eight hours.' Ebrahim was right.

When we got to the prayer room, I was so happy that it was busier than usual. Obviously, we weren't the only ones who thought we should take Ramazan as an opportunity to connect more with Allah.

SubhanAllah.

Friday 17th December

Jason Wilcox left Rovers today to join Leeds. That's it. The end of an era.

He was the last player left in our squad who won the Premier League in 1995. Four and a half years later, we're a completely different, new team who are thirteenth in Division One. A valuable lesson, though. Nothing lasts for ever. The good times don't, and I suppose the bad times won't either.

Still feels fuckin' shit, though.

Saturday 25th December

Another Christmas Day in Ramazan. As usual we didn't celebrate it, but as usual Ammi made us an especially nice dinner for iftari.

The films were SO much better than last year! This Christmas I recorded: *James and the Giant Peach*, *Jumanji*, *Balto*, *Matilda* and *Mission: Impossible*.

Plus, I watched *Pinocchio*, *Ace Ventura: Pet Detective*, *The Goonies* and *The Pagemaster*.

I love *Ace Ventura*! ALRIGHTY, THEN! I used to be able to

do the whole of the dialogue in the scene where they go to Roger Podacter's flat after his murder. *Loser. Loser. Lahu-zahur.* I always used to act out the whole scene for Was, it used to make him proper laugh.

I miss seeing Was (and Hassim) every day.

I love Ebrahim and hanging out with him at college, but he's more sensible than we are. He laughs when I do stupid things but he doesn't join in with the stupid things, I think that's the difference.

Tuesday 28th December

I'm doing my first ever i'tikaaf!

I agreed with Al-Asr that I can do it there, and I planned it with Mum. Every day after tarawee, so around 9 p.m., she's gonna send Zaheer to the masjid with my dinner and some snacks and fruit and stuff. And I can give him any laundry or anything to take back with him. I'm gonna take cereal and milk for breakfast; that'll be the easiest thing to do, I think.

It's ten days and I'm gonna pray as much as I can and I'm definitely gonna read a full Qur'an and try and learn as much new stuff as possible. Hopefully it'll be a bit fun too. Other people will be on i'tikaaf as well. It'll be like jamaat, but we're just in one mosque instead of travelling around.

Thursday 30th December

I've been on i'tikaaf for two days so far. It's been really good. I've been praying and reading a lot. I also played a bit of footy, with rolled-up socks, with some of the other brothers in one of the rooms, that was a good laugh.

We're having some really interesting discussions. There's a brother here called Waqas and he's only young (about twenty-two) but he's got a proper beard and he's been telling us a lot about the end of the world and the signs of Judgement Day. It's really interesting and quite scary.

I was especially interested in the details about al-Mahdi. He's a special man that will unify Muslims. Pai Waqas was saying that if al-Mahdi comes forward in our lifetimes, we have to be ready to drop everything and go to him and pledge our allegiance. Even just talking about it got me really excited. I hope he comes in my lifetime. That'd be amazing.

Al-Mahdi will eventually fight alongside Hazrat Isa* (Peace Be Upon Him) who will return and kill the Dajjal*.

He was talking to us about jihad as well, and how it's important to be ready to fight against injustice, like what happened in Bosnia and what's happening in Chechnya right now. Too right. You can't let Muslim brothers and sisters suffer oppression like that.

I was gonna ask Pai Waqas when he was gonna go, but instead I made the point that obviously in jihad you're not allowed to kill innocent men or women, or any child. He agreed with me and said, 'Yeah, there are strict rules in jihad to make sure that you don't become the oppressor.'

We were on the same page. Phew!

I'm definitely gonna learn a lot from him.

Friday 31st December

Today is the last day of the working week, month, year, decade, century and millennium!

I will never ever see this evening again. I mean, sure, that's true of every single evening ever, it's how time works . . . but still! It feels special to me.

This week I'm on my first-ever i'tikaaf, this month I got back into wrestling, this year I passed my GCSEs, this decade my team won the Premier League, this century England beat Germany and the Nazis in World War II with Baaji's help, and this millennium Saladin captured Jerusalem from the Crusaders. It's been eventful!

It could get even more eventful in about fifteen minutes. There's something called the Millennium Bug. The Y2K problem. Apparently, computers might stop working when the date flicks to 01/01/2000, because computers only recognise 19 or something, so they'll think it's the year 1900. No thank you. I don't want to be a Victorian chimney sweep. Something like that, anyway. I should've paid more attention.

Worst-case scenario: planes could fall out of the sky, watches might stop working and power stations could have a meltdown! Crazy. I mean, the news thinks that it won't happen ... but imagine if it does! Especially with hearing about all the end-of-the-world stuff from Pai Waqas.

Anyway, I'm exactly where I want to be. In the mosque. Thanking my Creator for my blessings and letting me live through this moment. It's just coming up to midnight ...

Update: It's after midnight!

The planes didn't fall out of the sky, my watch still tells the right time and the electricity is on. There was no Millennium Bug.

False alarm.

2000

2000

Saturday 1st January

It's the year 2000!!!

It feels weird to even write that.

Every year, when I go to school for the first few weeks I write the wrong year. Last year when I went back to school, I kept writing 07/01/1998̶9̶. But now, if I make that mistake, I'll have to change ~~1999~~ to 2000. Proper have to make sure I concentrate when I'm writing dates now.

It is crazy to think, though. The only important date I know from a thousand years ago is 1066, the Battle of Hastings. I wonder if anything important will happen this century that they'll be talking about in the year 3000.

Thursday 6th January

Today was the last day of i'tikaaf. I had a good, peaceful time. I've learnt a lot, such as the events leading up to the end of the world, and also that I want to grow a proper beard.

I wasn't sure about having a beard at first . . . but it's grown on me. I've never shaved (my face), so I'll have a lovely virgin beard, inshAllah.

I've seen people leave i'tikaaf, but I've never experienced

leaving i'tikaaf. Till today. It was really nice. I looked at my fellow i'tikaaf crew and I suggested that we do a big hug. It was actually quite funny. When we were in the middle of the group hug I was thinking, chill out, Terry, you're not war veterans who've just come back from Bosnia or summat. I made myself laugh.

I stepped out of Al-Asr and walked down the stone steps and across the car park to the gate, and to my surprise Ammi, Baj, Saeeda and Zaheer were waiting for me!

'MUBARAK!'

They all hugged me, and Ammi give me a big muppi*.

'Paijan, bend down,' Zaheer said. I did as I was told and he put a haar* on me, and when I got up Saeeda was standing there with a box of mitai. Awww.

It felt nice that my family appreciated what I was doing. I knew they did, because when we got home I opened the box of mitai and it only had my favourites in it: gulab jaman and ras gulay. I made sure that I offered them to everyone else first, even Abu, before I took one (or three) for myself. That's good Islamic etiquette.

What a lovely way to finish Ramazan off and celebrate Eid Eve. No one's ever used the term Eid Eve before. I think I just invented it!

Friday 7th January

Eid Mubarak!

Today was the first time ever I didn't do Eid with my normal mosque. That was strange. It meant it was the first time my family did Eid on a different day to everyone else in the family. Shibz and Was lot still had a roza today. As did all my friends in the New Bank area. Let me tell you, it made for a very boring Eid!

It's a shame that people do Eid on different days in the UK. I actually think it's dumb. Basically, the Deobandi mosques follow

Saudi Arabia's calendar, so when Saudi say they've seen the moon, those mosques (which include Al-Asr) do their events then.

The Barelvi mosques (Lancaster Place, Randal Street etc.) say we shouldn't do that and that we should follow the nearest Muslim country's calendar. For us in England, that is Morocco. So, when Morocco say they've seen the moon, we do our events with them.

I don't understand why the different mosque organisations in the UK just don't contact the Royal Observatory or British National Space Centre, or even the big head from *GamesMaster* (he knows everything), and ask them when there's a new moon in the UK! That's scientific and unbiased.

Man, I'm so clever.

Saturday 8th January

Sometimes you get Eid gifts from unexpected places. I was at Dad's in the evening, where all the boys were chilling after eating at Randal Street.

It was really fun at Dad's because Man United were playing in the Club World Championship, which was a special FIFA tournament for all the best teams from each continent. It was a bit controversial because it meant that Man United didn't play in this season's FA Cup. It was the first time an English team hasn't played in the FA Cup ever! But then it was proper full baisti for them because they got twatted! Haha.

Dad, Nads, Was and Muj support United and me, Shibz and Shiry were supporting Vasco da Gama, a Brazilian team. Now that Rovers are shit, no one can give me grief about football, but I can still dish it out to the United fans because they take it SO seriously.

Today was so funny.

Muj was shouting 'FUCKIN' HELL, MAN! IT'S A FUCKIN'

JOKE, MAMS.* I'M TELLING YA, GET GARY, PUT HIM IN A CANNON WITH PHIL AND FIRE BOTH OF 'EM INTO THE SUN! FUCK OFF!'

Poor Muj. Me, Shibaz and Shiry were laughing so much. At half time Vasco were winning 3–0! THREE–NIL! Muj couldn't handle it so he just left. He takes it so serious.

About 8ish, Was said he was heading out.

'Where you going?' I asked. I was just curious.

'Manchester. Cruising on Wimmy Road.'

'What's Wimmy Road?' I asked

Shiry looked unimpressed, 'Wimslow Road, Terry, man. It's where it all happens on Eid.' Shibz knew too. Why am I always the last to get this information?

'All right. Yeah, Wilmslow Road in Manchester. What happens there?'

'Basically, apne lads and girls jump in the car of their one mate who's got their licence and we all gather there. It's a proper laugh,' Was explained to me.

'People hire out cars, there bes some proper sick motors. Kasam.' Shibz was excited about it.

'Right. And what happens?' I was still confused.

'What do you mean?'

'So, is there like an event?'

'No, yaraa. That's it. People cruise up and down, bangin' out tunes, chilling and having a mad laugh.'

'So Asian boys and girls from all over the country will go to Manchester and drive down Wimmy Road, I assume slowly, because there must be loads of traffic. What happens when they get to the end of the road?'

'They turn around and go back. They basically do laps.'

---

* Mams is what Muj calls my dad, short for mammu.

'So ... It's like a haram tawaf*?'

'Shut up, man. Trust me, if you go there you'll see is a proper laugh.'

'Okay. If you say so, Was.'

'There's no space in the car, though. Sorry, Terry.'

I hadn't asked.

Friday 14th January

Today was my first-ever A-level exam.

Maths: Pure 1.

I've worked hard for this exam. I think it went okay. The revising in i'tikaaf paid off ... I finally got my head around differentiation.

I need AAB or ABB in three out of my four A levels. I think I've got my best chance in getting an A in maths. I'm finding biology and chemistry quite tricky, and computing I do not understand at all!

InshAllah I get a good mark in this exam.

Monday 24th January

Life is so embarrassing.

In biology I got paired up with Hafeezah. 'Okay ... so, what's this bit, Terry?'

She's this really sweet girl.

'The matrix space?'

With a very pretty face. Too pretty, I think. Like unreasonably.

'No ...'

It holds the most amazing hazel eyes and ...

'Inner membrane?'

'No, not inner membrane ...'

'Space?'

She has this er ... ~~big~~ distracting chest area.

'Space. Exactly. See, you do know it.'

I definitely don't fancy her. I don't do that now. Oh yeah, shit. Lower your gaze.

'You look tired. Are you all right?'

Oh my God, I am tired! I was up all night watching the Royal Rumble. Can you believe The Rock won? And that bit when Triple H threw Cactus Jack all over the thumbtacks? Ufft!

'Yeah, no. Yeah, I'm good. Thanks.'

'Okay.'

Silence. Was I supposed to say something?

'Do you er ... wanna test me?'

Yes, I did.

'Oh yeah. Course. Yeah.'

Am I a bad Muslim?

Wednesday 2nd February

Wasim Akram took his four-hundredth one-day international wicket today! He's the record holder. I can't imagine being the best in the world at something, or a world record holder.

Hmm ... I wonder actually, what I could be best at in the world?

- Most times forgotten how many rakats he's read during namaaz?
- Most goals scored by someone who is always picked last?
- Most girls fancied without ever having a girlfriend?

What must it feel like to actually be Muhammad Ali or Ronaldo or Stephen Hendry or Michael Schumacher or Steffi Graf or Stephen Hawking? The pressure they must be under every day must be crazy. I would feel sorry for them, but then I'd rather be under a lot of pressure in my own mansion than sharing one bathroom with seven other people!

It's not something I'll ever have to worry about. Kids from Blackburn don't become the best in the world at stuff.

ACTUALLY, THAT'S A LIE! Carl Fogarty: he's from Blackburn and he's the best motorbike racer in the world! Hmmm ... maybe I will break a world record or be the best at something one day ...

Friday 4th February

Abu went to Pakistan today to see his mum and dad. I went to the airport with Zaheer and Uncle to drop him off. Even though I did that, I'm so glad he's gone. I'll feel much more comfortable at home and won't need to tiptoe about.

Wednesday 9th February

I've been applying for jobs. I have no money, except for the £10 a week pocket money Ammi gives me. Which is good: it's double what I got when I first started getting pocket money nearly two years ago. If my pocket money doubles every two years, then by the time I'm thirty, Mum will have to give me a £1000 a week. Hahahaha.

But with that £10, I have to buy my lunch every day and any treats outside of college. Basically, I'm skint, innit.* So I've been going around handing in my CV EVERYWHERE!

Kasam, I think I looked too desperate when I gave my CV in McDonald's. The guy could probably see the Filet-O-Fish and fries in my eyes, like in cartoons.

And the cinema manager looked at me like I'd come to record

---

* These were pre-Education Maintenance Allowance (EMA) days.

and pirate the film. He said they don't take CVs. I said, 'How do you apply for a job then?'

Kasam, he goes, 'You don't.' But he said the *you* in a way like YOU, Terry, don't. I left the CV on the ticketing desk anyway. Saves me the job of throwing it away.

I even went to the Ice Arena. I was so embarrassed when I gave them my CV. I don't even know if an Asian person's ever even been inside that building before me today. They looked well confused.

I stopped at Woolworths, C&A, Debenhams, JJB Sports, Next, Burton, River Island, Tesco, Boots, Sports Direct, WH Smith, HSBC even.

So far, no luck.

Until this week, when QS Fashion, a wholesale clothes shop in Cherry Tree, called home and said I had an interview. That interview is today.

I remember I did some interview training at school, so I know they're gonna ask me about my experience (I don't have any, except for the pharmacy. Ooh, I fold and put away my own clothes ... sometimes); they're gonna ask me why I want the job (I NEED MONEY); and they're gonna ask me why I'm the best person for the job (Am I? I don't know who else has applied).

I'll blag it.

Update: I did not get the job.

Friday 18th February

I thought college and being more religious would mature me, but it really hasn't. At all. The internet hasn't helped! The internet is this new thing you get on your computer through a phone line. It's basically like a big library with all the world's information in it. People can also put their own opinions in there and you can find all the world's music and videos. Plus, you can send messages to each other as quickly as I can snap my finger, through electronic mail.

I created my email account: terryiscool@hotmail.com. Password: terryiscool.

Basically, I am spending way too much time on the internet. When I'm not learning about Islam, I'm looking at wrestling websites for the latest rumours, or at conspiracy theories such as evolution is fake, or at pictures of Catherine Zeta Jones.

And there's chatrooms where you can talk to anyone in the whole world and you can just pretend to be anyone you want because they can't see you. A/S/L, that's what they ask you.

Age/Sex/Location? Twenty-three/no thank you, it's haram (haha)/Dubai.

If I'm not wasting my time on the internet, I'm doing stupid antics around college. And today's might come back to bite me, because it involved the computer room.

So, at dinnertime today I went to use the computer room on the ground floor. I was about to take my card out to swipe in through the gate (I always think that's weird, like they're a FBI operation and they don't want anyone from outside stealing their secrets). But before I could get my card out I saw Yaqoob on a computer. He didn't see me, but. I like Yaqoob, he's a Whalley Ranger and he knows Was really well. And, like us, he's got a big personality and likes to talk.

Ever since Ramazan, me and Yaqoob have been having a contest to see who can do the best impression of The Rock. I don't know what came over me, but I had the sudden urge, there and then, to show him who the real People's Champion is.

I climbed onto the little electronic gate, I posed like The Rock does on his entrance when he gets to the ropes – one fist in the air, the other hand by my side, my face pointed up, and I yelled:

'IF YA SMELLLLLLLLLLLLLLLLLLLLLLLLLLLLLLLLLLLLLLLLL......'

The WHOLE computer room turned around to look at me, including the supervisor (who has NO sense of humour), but I had my eyes fixed on Yaqoob. When his eyes met mine, I stared at him, then said: 'WHAT THE ROCK...' dramatic pause... I looked up and closed my eyes like The Rock does...

'IS COOKING!'

Then I put my arm down and looked at Yaqoob again, and tried my best to do the people's eyebrow (lifting only one eyebrow). I've been practising it for weeks and I think when it mattered I proper smashed it! Because Yaqoob stood up from his computer and clapped. A proper round of applause. A couple of other very confused students joined in. I'm pretty sure they had no idea what was going on.

Think about it from their perspective: they're on a computer, possibly doing some important coursework, it's quiet and then an Asian lad, with a thin moustache, bumfluff on his chin and a mosque hat climbs onto the little entrance gate and starts yelling something about a rock smelling some cooking. And then another Asian boy gives him a standing ovation. What?!

Well, I know how one person in the room felt about it at least:

'GET OUT!' the supervisor screamed.

I climbed down from the gate and I said in a calm, quiet voice, 'Sorry, what did you say?'

And I promise you, he goes: 'I said, GE—'

'IT DOESN'T MATTER WHAT YOU SAID!'

Got him.

Stunned silence.

I'm pretty sure Yaqoob died at that point.

I'm not 100 per cent sure because I didn't stick around to watch, but I think his janaza* will be confirmed for tomorrow.

I was very proud of myself until I realised ... I don't have the internet at home. Shit.

Tuesday 29th February

It's the 29th of February! A leap year.

On the internet (I've found a second computer room in the college building) it said that this is the day that women are allowed to propose to men!

I can confirm that Hafeezah/Farida/Carrie-Ann have not proposed to me.

Nor in fact has anyone else. Which is fine, because I'm way too young to get married anyway. So, thanks ladies, but no thanks.

Thursday 2nd March

I GOT A B!

I got my result for my first A-level exam, Maths: Pure 1. I was so happy, I got 76 per cent, which I think should be an A. But whatever! I'm actually really happy. If I can push that to an A, that'd be awesome. Then I can try and get an A or B in chemistry and a B in biology.

I beat Ebrahim. He only got a C and he's doing further maths! Farida beat us both, though: she got an A.

'I'm gonna copy you next exam, bro,' I told her. She giggled.

Paul said well done and keep it up. That made me happy. He's my favourite teacher in college.

I might drop computing. I literally sit in class and it might as well be in French. I mean, if it was in German it would at least be a little bit helpful.

I think I've actually forgotten most of my German already. Shit, man. I got an A in that and it's only been nine months. In the time it takes to have a baby I've said goodbye to a language I spent five years learning and which was one of my best and favourite subjects at school.

What's the point? I can go to uni and say I have an A in German, but apart from *Wie heißt du?*, I know nothing.

It's almost as if exams are not the best way to measure how clever we are.

Wednesday 15th March

Lee Bowyer and Jonathan Woodgate, the Leeds United players, got charged today for an attack on a Pakistani boy on a night out.

Proper bastards, if they did it. 1) they're athletes, so obviously stronger than normal people and are role models for kids who look up to footballers. And 2) how can anyone be racist now, in this day and age, after everything that happened with Stephen Lawrence and how much that was in the news?*

Whenever someone gets attacked in the street, it always reminds me of Pai Shehzad's murder, which is always just a horrible feeling.

Horrible daft kuteh* kameeneh.

Thursday 16th March

Eid Mubarak!

Again, Eid fell on a different day to my cousins and friends, so we celebrated on our own. Mum made some nice food and I went to the shop with Saeeda and Zaheer and Tanveer and we got lots of sweets which we ate together. It's nice hanging out with my family, obviously, but it was even more boring than Eid in Pakistan!

---

* In December 2001, Jonathan Woodgate was cleared of GBH, but found guilty of affray. Lee Bowyer was acquitted

Friday 17th March

Second day of Eid today. I was really excited about seeing everyone, but Shibz and Shiry and Was had made their own plans with their friends, so I didn't have anyone to hang out with.

It would've been two really boring days in a row for Eid, which has never happened before! But it turned out to be one of my favourites, actually. Last week, D, who is Aunty Zaida's* son, lent us all his *Star Wars* videos. I like D a lot, he's older than me, probably about twenty-five, really tall and big, and he's really friendly and always calls me Junior, which I like. I think because I don't have a big brother, I look up to D.

I was saying hi to him on my way home last week and for some reason we started talking about films and I asked him what his favourite film is.

'*Star Wars*,' he said, and I laughed. And then he glared at me like I just swore at his mum. I stopped laughing.

He went inside and came back with three videos.

'There you go, Junior. Watch these and then we'll see who's laughing.'

Star Wars Episode IV: A New Hope, *Star Wars Episode V: The Empire Strikes Back* and *Star Wars Episode VI: Return of the Jedi*. I was a bit confused and said, 'Okay, but if you want me to watch these, I want to watch the first three films first. Where's 1 to 3?'

D laughed. He explained these were the first three films released. And that, funnily enough, the prequel, Episode 1, came out last year and Episodes 2 and 3 are coming out in the future.

Hang on … this guy, George Lucas, made films in 1977, 1980 and 1983, but because he knew he also wanted to tell the story that came before the one that he was actually telling at the time,

---

* Mum's friend who used to live a few doors up from us on Hickory Street back in the day, and who we reconnected with when we moved to Leamington Road.

he was smart enough to call them Episodes 4–6, so that he could release Episodes 1–3 sixteen years later?!

That's actually crazy.

I have no idea what I'm gonna be doing sixteen years from now. Well, some idea. I'll be a doctor, with a big house, nice Merc, fit wife and two or three kids.

But I don't know what I'll actually be doing, though!

Anyway, me, Baji Rosey, Saeeda, Zaheer and Tanveer watched *Star Wars Episode IV: A New Hope*. Wow. D was right. It was flippin' wicked! Where has this been my whole life? Then we watched *The Empire Strikes Back*. THAT WAS EVEN BETTER! And what the hell, Darth Vader is Luke's dad?! NOOOOOO! And Han's been kidnapped by the bounty hunter? We were tired, but we had to find out what happened next, so we actually watched *Return of the Jedi* there and then.

And ...

The best trilogy ever! Kasam. Even though I didn't really like the Ewoks, I loved how it all ended and that Leia and Luke are brother and sister (even though they kissed in the film before ... URGH!) and that Darth Vader became a goodie.

Apparently, Episodes 1–3 are about how Darth Vader became Darth Vader. I can't wait to watch them!

Wednesday 29th March

It's Zaheer's seventh birthday today!

He (we) got a PlayStation! With two pads, two memory cards and *Crash Bandicoot 2*, *Tomb Raider III* and *FIFA 99*.

It was so much fun. We spent all evening playing *Crash Bandicoot 2*. I loved it. It reminded me so much of *Sonic 2*, which is my favourite game ever!

When the kids went to bed, I played a bit of *FIFA 99* ... and while I was playing Baj was telling me that Pai Uneeb's finally got his visa! That's good news. That means he's gonna come and live with us in England. Finally.

'No,' she said.

'What do you mean?'

'I'm moving out. Me and Uneeb are gonna go live in the Edmundson Street house.'

I pressed pause on the game. I was doing shit anyway.

'Oh, right.' I couldn't hide my sadness.

'It's all right, you can come visit and you can stay over whenever you want.'

'Yeah. Okay. No, it makes sense. Obviously. It's just. Yeah, it's really happening now, isn't it?'

'Yeah.'

We sat in silence for a few awkward seconds. I wanted to say, I'll miss you . . .

'All right, I'm gonna get back to this game then . . .'

She nodded. 'Yeah. Yeah. Just wanted to let you know.'

'Thanks. And let me know when you need help with moving your stuff and all that.'

I was so sad that I didn't even care that I lost.

Thursday 30th March

'Oi! Guess what?' Hussain had some big news he wanted to share as he sat down next to me at the back of our chemistry class.

'You got heels for your birthday?' Neelam is proper tight! She said that because Hussain's short.

I like Neelam and Hussain. I sit next to them in chemistry. They're funny and like to mess about like me. Hussain is actually one of the most confident guys I know, and that's something for someone who's shorter than me and has a surname for a first name. And Neelam is such a weirdo! She wears a hijab and always comes out with proper hilarious and random things.

'Very funny. No. Apparently today is National Cleavage Day!'

That was not what I expected Hussain to say. So random and so haram!

'Looks like Carrie-Ann's celebrating.' Me and Hussain both looked to where Neelam's eyes were looking.

I pushed her. 'Why did you make me look?'

'Oh, come on, Tez, a topi doesn't make you blind,' Hussain said.

I looked away. Annoyingly, my eyes went to Hafeezah. I don't think she knows about National Cleavage Day. Unfortunately.

Taubah, I have to learn to control my nafs* better.

Friday 7th April

Today I went to Lancaster University for the Higher Education Conference.

Lancaster Uni is supposed to be a really good uni, but it's this big campus in the middle of nowhere and looks SO boring. I'm glad they don't do medicine. I would hate to come here.

The conference was really good, but. It was basically a big university fair, where all the universities in the country came and you could talk to people from them.

I'd already done some research by Asking Jeeves. I know I don't want to go to London and I'm not so dumb to think of applying to Oxford or Cambridge. I'm focusing on unis up north that do medicine. My preferences, in order, are:

Leeds	AAB
Liverpool	ABB/AAB
Manchester	AAB
Sheffield	ABB

And then:

I also have Nottingham as a back-up option because they accept ABB, so if I do less well this year in my exams, I'll apply there instead of Leicester.

All the people at every single desk I went to were really nice and polite. I got loads of prospectuses and freebies like pens and badges and stuff. Some of the desks had free sweets too. I made a mental note of that. Thank you, Sheffield!

I asked them all for advice about applying for medicine, and they all said the same thing. Obviously, I need to get the grades, but I need to be able to stand out. I need to pay a lot of attention to my personal statement and make sure I do lots of extracurricular activities and work experience, so I'm more than just a clever person who can do exams. Basically, they don't want boring bastards. Uh-oh. I'm gonna have to sort that out! I mean, I know I'm not a boring bastard, but I can't put that I got to Warp Room 5 in *Crash Bandicoot 2* in two hours on my personal statement. They're gonna need something more.

Goreh are well lucky, they get to go on really exciting trips and holidays or even take a gap year. We can't do that.

'You wanna go somewhere? Go Pakistan,' I imagine is what Taya or Dad would say. I couldn't even go to Preston two years ago. Haha.

Saturday 8th April

Aww man. Today was the BEST!

After playing footy at St Silas with Shibz and Shiry we walked back to mine. I was telling them about Zaheer's PlayStation and that we could play *FIFA 99* on it.

'Dibs on Arsenal.' Shiry supports Arsenal now.

I opened the door to the living room to let Ammi know I was home and that Shibz and Shiry were here—

'SURPRISE!'

Oh damn!

A SURPRISE party. Kasam I had the biggest smile.

Everyone started singing 'Happy birthday to you . . . ' I went so red, I turned around to Shibz and Shiry who were singing their heads off and laughing. They knew!

I could see Ammi beaming. She was holding Tauqeer and pointing at me as if to get him to join in. Zaheer and Saeeda were belting it out and Tanveer was giving it a good go as well. Baj, Poupoh, Uncle and Jaffer, Baji Shanaz, Mammu Saeed and baby Zara and Safa were there too.

After I got over the shock, I looked down at the cake and it was a huge Rovers shirt. I'm telling you, flippin' massive! Easily the best cake I've had in years and years and a million times better than the cake I had in Pakistan for my sixteenth birthday last year. Sorry, Mammu Abbas!

This year it had seventeen candles on it and I was so proud that I blew them all out in one go. I actually felt so much pressure with so much people watching. But especially in front of Shibz and Shiry.

Ammi gave me £150. I gasped. Everyone else gasped too. 'Ammi, that's too much.'

'It's for driving lessons,' she said.

'Oh wow.' I got a bit emotional.

I LOVE HER SO MUCH!

'So you can take your mum Tesco shopping, Terry.' Poupoh made everyone laugh. Humour proper runs in our family.

I looked at Baj, who was smiling, and I thought, I'm so lucky to have such a wicked family (when Abu's not here)!

I'm so sad she's moving out.

Tuesday 11th April

Pai Uneeb arrived from Pakistan today. I went to the airport with Baji Rosey and Dad to pick him up.

I love it when someone from Pakistan comes to England for the first time. I proper study their face and reactions, because everything here is so different.

Pai Uneeb is a bit shy and reserved, so when I asked him what he thought about England when we got home, he just said, 'Very nice.'

But I bet he must've been thinking, *woah dude!*

The houses are different, the roads are different, we have big shopping centres, big, tall buildings. No farm animals, no open courtyards. I'm sure he'll get used to it and will be fine.

It's nice to have a big brother now.

Welcome to England and to the family, Pai Uneeb.

Wednesday 12th April

I had my first-ever driving lesson today!

Pai Ansar, my driving instructor, came to college to pick me up at 3 p.m. He's a cool guy, Pai Ansar,* he's a family friend, so I thought it'd be good to go with him. Plus, I like that he's got a big beard too, it means he's religious. But he's chilled out and he jokes around a lot. I think we're gonna get on.

He drove us to an industrial estate. And then told me to get out and made me sit in the driver's seat. Eeeeeek!

He explained to me all the different things in the car. Gear stick, handbrake, the three pedals, accelerator/brake/clutch. The

---

* Allah rest his soul. Pai Ansar sadly passed away a few years later from cancer. He was only thirty-six. That's younger than I am now. May Allah grant him the highest station in Paradise. Ameen.

mirrors and when I'm supposed to look in them, and my blind spot, just over my right shoulder.

In my head I was thinking, I know some of this already from riding a motorcycle, but I'm gonna use my feet now, instead of my hands.

So, it was time to start.

Gear is in neutral. Switch the engine on. Clutch down. Put it in first gear. Put the indicator on. Put the handbrake down. Look in the mirrors. Check my blind spot. Lift the clutch slowly. Start to press the accelerator. Move the steering wheel. And—

I stalled.

Shit.

I stalled the next two times as well.

I didn't stall the motorbike once! Ever.

This is like football all over again. Why am I so shit with my feet?

Fourth time lucky. I did it. I was driving.

I got up to third gear, driving 25mph, practising braking. Putting the gear back in neutral, then back in first and setting off again. Working out my biting point. It was hard, but I did it! I drove a car!

I wanna pass within twenty or twenty-five lessons, because Was said that you shouldn't really have more than that, otherwise you're a shit driver. Plus, is £12 a lesson, that's well expensive! I told Pai Ansar that. He said, 'We'll see.' We will see, Pai Ansar!

Wednesday 26th April

D got the new *Star Wars* on video and so he lent me that today. It was so sweet how excited everyone was for it. What's nice is that me, Baj, Saeeda and Zaheer, we have very similar taste in films. We love Disney cartoons and action and sci-fi films. Baj and me love horror as well, but also good films like *The Shawshank Redemption* and *Kuch Kuch Hota Hai* too.

We all sat in our places. I sit in the corner of the settee that is right in front of the TV. That's my place. First, though, I had to remove Saeeda: 'Er ... get out of my place, Saeeda.'

'Aww, you always sit here, Paijan,' she whined (as she moved).

'Yes, cos that's my place.'*

Next to me is Zaheer, next to him is Saeeda and then Baj in the other corner.

Tany was sat on the floor in front of us and we told Mum to put Tauqeer to bed: 'Ammi, we don't want the movie to be disturbed with baby cries.'

It was Pai Uneeb's first big movie night with us. He was sat on the other settee, perpendicular to ours, but against the back wall, where the view of the TV isn't the best.

BUT ... he hasn't seen the first three *Star Wars* films and he doesn't understand that much English yet anyway. Plus, I don't think he cares.

Anyway, so ... we watched *Star Wars Episode I: The Phantom Menace*.

The second the little boy came on the screen, Saeeda said, 'Who's that?'

'Shhh. I don't know. I'm watching it with you.'

Actually, I did know. He was a young Darth Vader, but I thought Saeeda should figure that out on her own.

When the film finished, I could tell that Zaheer and Saeeda loved it.

I looked at Baj ...

'It wasn't that good, was it?'

'No. It really wasn't.'

'What you talking about? It was wicked!' Saeeda wasn't having it.

I'm not sure who's worse, Jar Jar Binks or the Ewoks.

I'll still definitely watch the next one, but.

---

* This still happens today. I'm thirty-eight, she's thirty-two!

Saturday 29th April

I got a call this week from the big JJB near Asda. I got an interview! This is only my second interview since I went round begging every company in Blackburn to hire me.

I really want this one. The interview was with the manager, Karen. I actually remember her from when I went to drop my CV off. I gave it to a worker behind the customer service till who passed it to a woman (Karen). She looked at it, then looked at me and smiled and I smiled back. As soon as I recognised her, I felt a bit more relaxed. But I still had bullshit answers.

'So why do you want to work for JJB Sports, Tehzeeb?'

'I love sports and I love sports clothes and equipment. I also love interacting with people, so this is the perfect job for me, really.'

You know lying is gunnah, yeah? Shut up, brain.

It seemed to go okay. Karen said she'll let me know.

Monday 1st May

AAAAAAARRGGHHHH! I GOT THE JOB! YAHOOOO!

Friday 5th May

Today was a mixed day of good and shit.

Good: I had my JJB Sports induction today. I got my uniform: a top, some jogging bottoms and a jumper. Darren showed me around everywhere, including the staff room. I'd never been behind the main floor on a shop before, so that was really exciting! Darren kept laughing at how excited I was. He showed me the different areas of the shop and how they work. Clothes (the most boring area), trainers (Nike, Adidas, Reebok, K-Swiss uffffft!), equipment (so many footballs!), plus the storeroom in the back, where there's hundreds and hundreds of trainers. It's so cool. I can't wait to get started!

Shit: Abu came back from Pakistan today.

Thursday 11th May

I took another step on my journey to becoming a proper man today. A working man.

I finished college at 3.30 and then walked to JJB. My shift was 4 p.m.–7 p.m. I had my uniform in my bag and when I got there I asked Darren where I could change.

He laughed, 'In one of the changing rooms of course.'

Oh yeah! Haha.

I got changed and put my bag in the staff room. Then I went and started my first shift. I'll be honest, it was pretty boring.

I was working in the tracksuit section and I had to make sure all the clothes were on the right racks, in the right order (small at the front, XXL at the back) and that there was enough of each size. If not, I would have to go to the back, look through all the crates of clothes, find the right one, unpack it and hang it up where it belongs.

It reminded me of the boring pharmacy. Are all jobs like this? Just going to the back, grabbing stuff and putting it on shelves and racks? Very boring, but I made £9 doing that. Not bad.

After work, I went to Bangor Community Hall for Nazira's birthday party. Nazira's this Bengali girl from college, she's really nice. I see her in the common room quite a lot. She invited us all to come. Shibz said he was going, so I went along with him. He told me is probably best if I don't wear my topi because it's a party, it doesn't look right. I agreed with him.

I wore my favourite Adidas tracksuit and Reeboks, which I got changed into after work.

I asked Ebrahim to come. Three times. But he said no, it's not his thing. 'It's not exactly my thing either, Ibby. Come on?' He wouldn't budge.

Hussain was there, though, which was nice. And Hafeezah. Which was *nice*. It was a really fun party. I thought about it and, actually, I think it's the first-ever party that I've been to that's not with my family since I was in primary school. There was a lot of food and after a bit all the girls started dancing. I was stood with the boys on the side, looking proper awkward. Some of the girls tried to get the boys to dance, but we refused like our lives depended on it. I wish Hafeezah asked me to dance. Obviously, I would've said no. But can you imagine if she asked me?! Well I can, that's why I'm writing it.

I did talk to her, one time by the sweets table. 'Are you having fun?'

'Yeah, it's great isn't it? Here, try this.' She passed me a chocolate Rice Krispie cake.

'Thanks.'

'Are you gonna dance?' I nearly choked on a Rice Krisp.

'No!'

'Chill. I was only asking.'

'Oh yeah, I kn—' Oh, she's gone.

Wait, did she ask me to dance? No. Did she? DID SHE?

I could tell that, secretly, one or two of the boys wanted to dance. I tried egging Hussain on to dance. I could tell he was proper tempted. He was proper moving his shoulders about. But none of us dared. No one wanted to risk baisti.

I'm glad I got invited, it was a proper mad laugh. When I went home, I prayed Isha* and asked for forgiveness for the sins I did tonight. The music I tapped my foot to and for looking at Hafeezah … more than once.

Tuesday 16th May

Today was the University of Manchester open day. There was a free bus from college, so I signed up.

What a brilliant day. I can't wait to get to uni. We got shown around by current students. Around the library (it's SO big) and around the halls of residence and students' bedrooms and common rooms and computer rooms and the medical labs and lecture halls and student union. It looks like so much fun. Most of the students I saw looked really happy. Chilling with their friends, books in their arms, wearing T-shirts that said things like Peace and Love. Everyone looked so cool. Not because they were trying to be cool, just because they were being themselves. At least that's what it looked like to me.

I want that. I want to be happy. Studying medicine at a place like Manchester Uni will make me proper happy.

Thursday 18th May

It's Ammi's thirty-seventh birthday today!

HAPPY BIRTHDAY MUM!

I bought her a really nice brooch from Debenhams. Because I love her so much and she did such a nice birthday for me last month and because I have a job now.

Wednesday 31st May

I'm getting a pay rise at work! From £3 to £3.20 an hour. Not because I'm good, but by law the national minimum wage has gone up for everyone. If I was twenty-two, I'd be getting £3.60 an hour! But then if I was twenty-two and still working at JJB something would've gone wrong. Unless it was a part-time job at uni. But can you juggle a part-time job with doing medicine? Probably not.

Basically, without sounding like a snob, I don't want to be working at JJB Sports when I'm twenty-two. (Maybe if it's a summer job. But even then, I hope I'll have graduated to Argos at least!)

Monday 12th June

Just watched England's first game of Euro 2000. We lost 3–2 to Portugal. Luckily nothing important is happening tomorrow that I should have been paying attention to instead—

Oh no, wait.

I HAVE TWO EXAMS.

Fuck you ~~Portu~~ – wait, it's not their fault. Fuck you, England!

Tuesday 13th June

I had my Stats 1 and Stats 2 maths exams today. I really need As. I think they went okay. I did revise hard for them. But there's also been a lot going on recently, hasn't there? With my new job, Abu being back home, which isn't easy, Euro 2000. So much.

I cannot afford to take my eye of the ball now.

Muhammad Ali, the legend, once said, 'I hated every minute of training, but I said, "Don't quit. Suffer now and live the rest of your life as a champion."'

That's like me with these A levels. I hate them. But don't quit: suffer now and live the rest of my life as a doctor.

Saturday 17th June

SHEARER!

You might not be at Blackburn Rovers any more, but I fuckin' love you, man!

What a goal. He scored a diving header and we beat Germany

1–0! Take that! That's revenge for when they beat us on penalties four years ago in Euro 96.

Next game is Romania, that should be easy enough, and then we can concentrate on the quarter-finals.

It's gonna be a good summer.

Tuesday 20th June

'I'm gonna have to drop computing, kasam,' I said, slouching as I put the burger in my mouth in Tasty Spot. I was at lunch with Ebrahim, Hussain and Neelam. Taking a break from our ~~torture~~ exams.

'Drop it then, man. Just concentrate on your other exams.' Hussain made it sound well simple.

'You never know, Terry. You might surprise yourself.' Ebrahim, reassuring as ever.

'I think you failed it.'

'Fuck you, Neelam. No one asked you, man.' Ebrahim and Hussain started laughing.

'Do you think England will win today?' She's the only girl I know into footy.

'They have to. Otherwise they're out.' Actually, Ebrahim, we only need a draw, is what I would have said if my mouth wasn't full of a delicious cheeseburger and I wasn't distracted by how much I love how they toast the teacake in takeaways, and it has those little seeds on it. The teacakes mum gets from Tesco don't be nowhere near as nice as this.

Chalo, summat to look forward to now. England's last group game before the quarter-finals.

Update: WHAT THE HELL?!

We lost. We're out. For goodness sake, man! We were drawing, which was fine. That's all we needed. And then Phil FUCKING Neville gave away a penalty in the last minute and we lost.

Wednesday 21st June

I had my last exam of the year today. Chemistry.

I don't know what's wrong with me. At school, I used to be so good at this. Head down, revise and get the grades I need. I never ever found it that hard.

I found today's exam hard. I don't think I'm revising hard enough. Or maybe my revision technique is really bad.

The worst thing is, I've lost all my confidence to ask for help. I should've asked Hussain or Neelam or Ebrahim or Farida or Hafeezah to be my study buddy. Probably not the last two, actually. Am I too proud? Arrogant? Lazy? Distracted? Scared?

I wish I wish I wish I'd gone to Clitheroe instead.

I hope it's not all too late.

Monday 26th June

I saw on the internet today that scientists around the world have mapped the genetic code of humans. They're saying it's one of the most significant scientific landmarks of all time, and they're comparing it to inventing the wheel or splitting the atom.

I mean, splitting the atom, fair enough, I get that, but how can you compare *anything* to inventing the wheel? I mean ... come on, before wheels people had to lift wheelbarrows ... sorry, what am I saying? It couldn't even be called a *wheel*barrow – before that it was just a barrow! And then a hero came along and literally INVENTED A WHEEL! It doesn't get more useful than that.

That's something everyone can use, from a baby playing with a toy car to a grandad in a wheelchair. Most everyday people are hardly gonna make use of a written version of their genetic code, are they? It'd be like tryna read the Matrix. Not everyone is Neo, innit. It's impossible for most people.

Good job, scientists, that's top and hopefully somehow useful to me when I'm a doctor, but making comparisons is not the thing you lot are best at.

Friday 30th June

Today was a really fun day at college! Probably the most fun day I've had since I came here. It's only taken a year!

It was Challenge of Management Day, which was an all-day workshop where all students from the college got put in different teams and practised key skills of management in a pretend business.

I was on a team with people I didn't know, but we worked really well together. At one point we had to pitch a new product to a board of investors (people who put money in a business). We could use our imaginations and design whatever we wanted. I had the idea to design a CD that has all your revision notes on it, and when you play it at night and fall asleep, all the information gets subconsciously stored in your brain so that you remember it all for an exam.

I got the idea from *The Matrix*. God, that film is amazing! But that bit where the computer guy just uploads stuff into Neo, then he knows the stuff straight away. I loved that.

That film really made me think about what I would change about myself. If I could design my ideal self, I would be:

- Taller. Like six foot at least
- Slimmer. A thirty-inch waist.
- Size 10 feet.
- More muscly, with a six pack and bigger wrists and arms.
- Less hairy on my body and legs. Why are my legs so hairy?
- No more hair in my pits or groin area, so I don't have to worry about the admin of shaving those bits.

- Also, perfect-length fingernails all the time (basically they never grow beyond that), again to save the time of cutting them.

Yeah, so just a few things. Oh, I would be really tough as well, so no one would mess with me, and fast. Oh, and I can do the splits. Yeah, I think that's about it.

Anyway ... the board of investors loved our idea, so my team won that round.

It made me realise that I can't wait to open my own practice one day and be a businessman as well as a doctor, like Hassim predicted.

I wonder how Hassim's doing at Clitheroe. I miss him. I should ring him.

Anyway, the actual best thing about today? I got a certificate! A sweet, sweet certificate. Oh, how I've missed them. I used to get around about five certificates every term at Witton, and now this is the first one I've had in a year. It felt so good. Even though it was nothing to do with my A levels and probably won't help me overall really. Still. It felt SO good.

Sunday 2nd July

France won Euro 2000.

I think life is really unfair. In the last fifteen months, Rovers have been relegated, Pakistan got to the final of the Cricket World Cup as the best team but then got thrashed, and England embarrassed themselves by getting knocked out of the group stage in this tournament.

Imagine you're a French Manchester United fan. Your national team wins the World Cup and the Euros on the trot, and United win the treble after winning the league nearly every year anyway.

Please, Allah ... share out the glory a little bit. At the very least, let Rovers get promoted this season. It's too much baisti playing in Division One.

Was goes to me: 'Division One? Does Teletext even go that far down?'

Please!

Monday 3rd July

I hate this place.

I was walking around college thinking it's really quiet. Even in the classes there was hardly anyone in them.

And then I found out that there was a trip today to Alton Towers. No one told me. The first I heard about it was today.

I didn't cry.

Tuesday 4th July

Today was better! We played University Challenge at college.

There were four people in each team, and Sandra picked me to be in our tutor group's team. Not that there were that many volunteers!

There were eight teams, so it was a quarter-final straight away. Damn ... What an exciting match. We were drawing, with time running out. The quizmaster goes, 'Your starter for 10: Who wrote the fairy tale "The Ugly Duckling"?'

I KNOW THIS!

BUZZ

'Hans Christian Andersen?'

'Correct! Your bonus questio—'

AAAAARRRRGH!

Laura, their star player, buzzed in just before I did! NOOOOO!

Literally twenty seconds later, the time was up. We lost! By one question, which I knew the answer to!

I didn't feel too bad. Two hours later, Laura's team (well, Laura really) won the whole competition. They won the final by 150 points!!!

I felt like we were England and we had to play Brazil in the first round, and they were there for the taking but we just couldn't quite do it, and as the tournament went on their star player, Laura (Ronaldo), got better and better. I heard she's going to Oxford. That makes sense. I'm not even sure what she's doing in this college, to be honest. She's better than this.

My favourite part of the quiz, though, was when one of Laura's teammates, Harry, from my biology class, complained that he buzzed in before me and I shouted:

'KNOW YOUR ROLE AND SHUT YOUR MOUTH!' (One of The Rock's famous catchphrases.)

Everyone laughed. I enjoyed that feeling again.

Thursday 6th July

I got kicked out of home today.

I GOT KICKED OUT OF HOME.

Abu, the fuckin' bully, kicked me out when Ammi wasn't home.

I'd come back home from college to get changed to go out and play footy. As I was leaving, I walked past the front room, the door was open.

And he goes, 'Eh . . .'

He didn't even say my name.

'Eh . . .'

'Jee, Abu?' (I wish I never gave him that respect then. He doesn't deserve it.)

'*Aaj tee baad tu is kaar nah rai'sakda*': From today, you can't stay in this house.

'Heh?'

'*Aaj tee baad tu is kaar nah rai'sakda. Kidreh aur ja keh reh*': From today, you can't stay in this house. Stay somewhere else.

I was shocked.

Why? Why, man? What have I done? Why today? How's today different to yesterday, or the day before or any other day? I haven't done anything wrong. This has just come out of nowhere. Please.

'Fuck off.' It was the only thing I could think to say. And I ran out.

Truth be told, I was a bit scared that he might try and hit me because I swore at him. I was shaking. I didn't know what to do.

When I got to St Silas, I saw Shibz and told him what happened. He looked proper pissed off! He said that he's gonna grab Shiry and they can go kick fuck out of him. Part of me wants that more than anything! But I thought of Ammi. I said no, we can't do that.

So we played our game of cricket instead.

I took all my anger out on this one ball. I hit it so clean and hard it went sailing out of St Silas. 6 and out.

Afterwards, I asked Shibz to come home with me, so I could collect some things and go stay with Baji Rosey. Abu wasn't in. And everyone said hello like everything was normal. He hadn't even told Ammi.

WHAT A FUCKING BASTARD!

When I told Ammi, she didn't say anything, but just immediately burst into tears. I started crying too. I hate seeing Ammi cry. It always hurts too much.

I went upstairs and packed a couple of bags for now. I went into Ammi's room and kissed Tauqeer on the cheek. Then I went downstairs and gave Saeeda, Zaheer and Tanveer a big hug and a kiss.

They didn't know what was going on, which broke my heart.

'Where are you going, Paijan?'

'I'm just gonna go stay with Baji Rosey for a little while, Saeeda. Nothing to worry about.'

I gave Ammi a big hug and then me and Shibz left.

He walked me to Baji's, which was nice of him, because the bags would've been too heavy to carry all by myself. I'm so glad he's here. It's good to have people with you when you're feeling down or going through a hard time. The people who care about you will always be there for you. You just need to ask them for help.

I got to Baji's. Ammi had already rung her to explain everything. We didn't have to say anything to each other. We just shared a look and we both understood. We've been through so much in life together already. This is just one more thing.

I thanked Shibz, who left after having some Ribena, and then I went upstairs and unpacked in my new/old bedroom.

I'm really sad.

I feel sorry for myself. And I especially feel sorry for Ammi. The position he's put her in.

I hate him so much.

I can't even begin to imagine the fight Ammi had with him today.

Today, I did cry. A lot.

Friday 7th July

It was the last day of college today. I was in a daze the whole day. How could I concentrate?

I looked around my classes and thought, I wonder if any of you lot got thrown out of home yesterday by an abusive stepdad? No, probably not.

I've heard stories of goreh being thrown out of their houses by their mum and dad, but I would never have thought it could happen to me. The only other apna I know who's been thrown out of their house is Pervaiz. But he was an actual smackhead, who stole money from his mum and used it for drugs and stuff.

One thing I did see today, when I was on the internet in the computer room, was that Tony Blair's son was arrested yesterday for disorderly behaviour! That's crazy. The Prime Minister's son got arrested! I love this country. No way in Pakistan would the police ever arrest the Prime Minister's son, or now, I guess, General Musharraf's son (oh wait … that's me! Hahahahaha!!!).

I bet Tony Blair doesn't kick his son out of home, though.

It's also Pai Uneeb's birthday today, so that was a nice distraction. Baji ordered some pizzas, we cut a cake and then watched *East is East*. What a film! *Bastard bitch!* I was crying with laughter!

But … I didn't like how the half-caste kids were all okay-looking, but they made the full Pakistani girls at the end really ugly. I didn't like the message that sent. But otherwise, what a funny film!

I'm so glad we've got stuff like this and *Goodness Gracious Me* now. Hopefully there'll be even more Asian comedians and actors coming forward. Especially, it would be wicked if Pakistani Muslim actors played Pakistani Muslims, because at the moment I think everyone is Indian Hindu or Sikh. Pakistanis are well funny. So, hopefully, when I grow up there'll be some British Pakistani comedians and actors. InshAllah.

Friday 21st July

Aww shit, man. I've been begging Baj all summer for her, me and Pai Uneeb to go to Blackpool Pleasure Beach. Today we put the news on, and it said that a boy died after falling off the Space Invader ride at Blackpool Pleasure Beach!

Shit. That's well sad. His poor family.

Fuck that.

We'll go Alton Towers instead.

Wednesday 2nd August

I passed my theory test today! Yay! Take that, A levels!

Only just, though . . . I got 30/35. The pass mark is 30/35. Eeeeek.

To be fair, that's 86 per cent. That's an A at A level. Probably should be an A*! I think I could've gotten 100 per cent. But I didn't take it that seriously, and to be fair it's hard to take a test seriously where one of the questions is:

You are at the scene of a collision and someone is suffering from shock. What should you do?

I mean, you could never have seen a car in your life and understand that 'offer them a cigarette' is never the appropriate thing to do at the scene of an accident!

Anyway, I passed, that's the point. One step closer to becoming a driver. I've had sixteen lessons so far. I want to pass within the next nine. InshAllah.

Monday 7th August

We got the internet today!

Thanks, Baji. Ammi never let me have the internet. I couldn't quite explain what it was in a way that would make her think it's useful. 'If you want information, read a book.' She didn't get it at all. Bless.

I went to Ammi's to pick my computer up. It was the first time I'd been since . . . you know.

I rang ahead to make sure he wasn't there. Saeeda was well happy to see me and I was so happy to see her. Ammi made sure that I stayed and ate. To be honest, I didn't want to, because I was nervous in case he came home, but then I smelt that it was spinach and I thought, if he comes home I'll do a Popeye and just knock him out. Haha. After food (God I've missed Ammi's food. No offence, Baj!) I played PlayStation with Zaheer and

Tany, which was fun. Tauqeer still recognised me too, so that was
wicked as well. I asked Ammi if she was okay and she said yeah.
But if she wasn't, I don't think she'd tell me. I know she's sad that
I'm not at home. But . . .

Anyway, I picked up the computer and brought it down to
Edmundson Street, plugged everything in and set up the dial-up
modem. It makes this crazy noise when you're connecting to the
internet. Beeps and gargles . . . like the computer's clearing its
throat. It's so weird AND loud! Not like in college.

 Also, it's definitely slower than college internet too, and
because it uses the phone line, if you're on the internet you can't
use the phone!

 Apart from all of that, I'm so happy! I feel like I'm living in
the future.

Wednesday 9th August

I bought the new Rovers top today. It's so sexy. It fits really nicely;
I feel muscly because it's a tight fit. Haha. It's made by Kappa and
I'm so proud that it has the Time Computers logo on it!

 My old Rovers top, the one we won the league in, was sponsored by McEwan's Lager, and I wore it because it's my team, innit,
but I didn't like that it was sponsored by alcohol. What if you supported Rovers but didn't wanna wear an alcohol company's name
on your shirt? Then you're left out, innit? I think they shouldn't
have alcohol or gambling sponsors on shirts. It's haram.

Friday 11th August

Today should have been such a nice evening. Instead, I'm left feeling like crap again, man. I knew he was home today, but Ammi
said it'd be okay.

It's baby Tauqeer's second birthday, the little cutie pie. Me, Baj and Pai Uneeb turned up at the house. I knocked on the door and he answered it.

Kasam, the second he saw us his expression turned from one that was smiling to someone who was forced to smell rat's piss. I mean, we're right here. At least he could pretend or something. You've kicked me out the house, what more do you want? It's like he wants us to know that he hates us. Fine. I hate him too.

At least my brothers and sister were happy to see me! Big hugs from everyone. It was all fine, if not a little bit awkward because of the tension coming from him. That is, until it was time to give the presents. As I stepped forward to give mine to Tauqeer, he goes to me:

'It's okay. Keep your presents. We don't want them.'

I didn't know what to say, but Baji goes:

'Don't play with them then.'

I had to stop myself from laughing. She was always braver than me. But I added, 'Yeah, they're not for you.'

I looked at Ammi, who just looked so shocked. She said, 'Taqueer's brother and sister will give him whatever present they like. No one will stop them.'

Tauqeer, who is too small to understand, opened my present. It was a nice Pikachu soft toy and he gave it a big hug. Ha. What you gonna do now? Snatch toys out of a baby's hand? Even he can't be that stupid and evil.

I was so angry, though. He's saying this right in front of Saeeda, Zaheer and Tanveer. What must they be thinking? Whoever he is or isn't to me, they're still my little brothers and sisters and I'll never think anything different. I hope he doesn't make 'em think any different about me and Baj.

I fear the worst, man.

Sunday 13th August

Besides everything that's going on, it's actually been a really nice summer.

I spend my days playing cricket in St Silas with the Maliks, Shibz, Pats and other boys from the area. We usually play about five games a day. Ten overs each, or until the whole team is out (which is usually what happens first).

It's actually quite a hard ground to play on. 1) There's a sideways slope. 2) It's small. If you hit it out of the ground (or on top of the side Portakabin and it gets stuck) you're out. And 3) the actual wickets are small and some of the bowlers are really fast with a taped ball. It takes a lot of skill to bat well in this ground.

There's some good players: Nisar (Malik), Nazir, Deemy, Faisal, Jameel (he's well fast), Ditta, Rizzy, and Shibz is a good bowler.

And then players like me, who are usually last pick, and who bat last and hardly ever bowl! So basically football all over again.

At least three times a day I try and convince my friends to come with me to the masjid to pray. Either Zuhr, Asr or Maghrib ... but it usually falls on deaf ears. Sometimes I find it hard to be motivated to go and pray. It would be a lot easier to do it if at least one of my friends was up for it too.

In the evenings I chill at the Maliks with Shibz and Pats and some others. We've started our own football fantasy league. But ours is different because we're playing with every single top-flight league in Europe! Turkish, Lithuanian, whatever. We use the internet to find the most obscure top scorers of random divisions. It's well funny.

The other thing is, only one person can have a player. So, if someone gets Michael Owen, no one else can have him! It's proper competitive and the amount of arguments is so funny. At the start of the season we do a draw out of a hat for each position and that person gets to pick who they want.

While everyone was concentrating on big names like Owen, Shearer, Rivaldo, Raúl, Shevchenko, I was looking at the internet to find proper random players from random leagues.

I got this one midfielder called Vermant, who plays for Club Brugge in Belgium. Thing is, he's a midfielder, but he scores loads of goals! They were well pissed off when they researched him themselves. Hahahaha.

We're such geeks. No wonder none of us have girlfriends.

Then when I go home at night I sit on the computer on the crazy internet, and then I get up the next day and do it all again!

Oh, and three times a week I go work at JJB Sports. I'm enjoying it more now. They've moved me to trainers. I love looking at all the trainers that I can't afford! If I had the money, I'd love to buy some Reebok Classics and Nike Cortez's.

But I'm saving my money for uni.

Thursday 17th August

Shit man. Shit. Shit.

I got my modular results for my A levels today.

- Biology: C (to go along with my D from the first module).
- Chemistry: D (to go along with my B from the first module).
- Maths Stats 1: B.
- Maths Stats 2: C.
- Computing: 42 per cent (a pass, but it doesn't count towards my final grade, it was just an internal assessment).

This is an emergency now. I'm gonna drop computing. I don't enjoy it, I don't understand it and I'm shit at it. No fucking about next year. Head down. I basically have to get all As from now on. Enough is enough!

Saturday 19th August

RIP Jack Walker. The hero of Blackburn.

I had to go watch Rovers today. To pay my tribute to Uncle Jack.

Even though you're not really meant to pray for non-Muslims, I did a little dua for Uncle Jack last night.

I even went on my own, because as usual I had no one to go with because no one supports Rovers. Everyone else is a glory-hunter supporting United or Liverpool or (now) Arsenal. I don't respect that at all. You're not from there. Why do you support them?

I didn't mind being on my own, though. I sat in the Jack Walker Stand. The view from here is absolutely amazing. I love coming to Ewood Park. I wish I could afford to come more.

Uncle Jack bought Blackburn Rovers in 1991 and four years later we were the champions of England. Talk about passion and vision. Even our ground used to be proper shit and run-down before Jack Walker took over. Then he built three proper big stands, the Jack Walker Stand, Darwen End and Blackburn End, and then one stand which they did up a bit, but it's not as developed as the others, the Riverside Stand.

The best thing about Ewood Park is the pitch. It's lush. Like a carpet. We always won the awards for best pitch in the Premier League. It's cool that Uncle Jack actually spent money on making the whole club modern. It wasn't just about spending money on transfers, but making sure the club is ready for the twenty-first century.

The team proper let him down today, though. Such a boring game. 0–0 against Crewe! Who the fuck are Crewe, man?!

We have to get promoted this season to say thank you to his legacy and to move forward.

Thursday 24th August

Ay ay ay! Pai Uneeb's face is too funny on roller coasters! Hahahahaha.

He doesn't scream like me and Baj do, he just screws up his face and closes his eyes. Probably praying to Allah.

I said to Baj last night, 'Has Pai Uneeb ever been on any rides?'

She goes, 'No. Where would he have been on rides like Alton Towers in Pakistan?'

Fair.

'So what's he gonna do tomorrow, when we go on the rides? Hold our bags?'

'As if! I'm gonna drag him on with us!'

And she did!

I said to him after Oblivion, '*Maza ayeh?*': Enjoy that?

He said, '*Ufft taubah!*': Ufft. Repent! Which to be fair could've meant yes or no.

I remember in the morning when we were queuing for the first ride of the day, Nemesis, he couldn't understand why we would come all this way for a queue. Then when we turned a corner and he could see the roller coaster whizz past and go upside down, his face went proper white.

'This is why!'

But he did go on all of them: Oblivion, Nemesis, Rubber Dinghy Rapids, Ripsaw, Corkscrew, Black Hole, Log Flume and Energizer, so he must've enjoyed them on some level! I gotta give him credit for that.

Some of the queues were well long. But it was okay. We had brought loads of sweets with us and we got some ice cream and had a nice picnic in the grounds there. It's actually a really nice park.

I needed today. It took my mind off everything.

Thanks, Baji and Pai Uneeb.

Monday 28th August

I remembered what all of the unis said at that big open day in Lancaster. I need work experience and have to have stuff in my personal statement to stand out.

So today I started work experience for a week at Johnson Street Pharmacy. Where I did my work experience in Year 10.

Urgh.

But also, thank you, Uncle Professor.

Wednesday 30th August

OH MY GOD!

When I got home from the pharmacy, Baj came rushing out of the living room with her big childcare textbook, and before I'd even taken my shoes off she goes, 'Terry! You'll never guess what's just happened!'

'Have Rovers signed Ronaldo? Are you going on *Who Wants to Be a Millionaire*? Are you having a baby?'

'No. Idiot. He's left!'

'WHAT?!'

'Ammi told him to leave and he's gone.'

We both screamed and jumped up and down and hugged each other like she'd actually just won the million pounds on *Who Wants to Be a Millionaire*? It felt even better than that.

I put my shoes straight back on.

'Where are you going?' Baj goes.

'Ammi's!'

I floated up Addison Street and Adelaide Terrace, before going left on Granville Road and then right onto Ammi's street. I excitedly opened the door and went in: the house was busy. Mammu Saeed and Baji Shanaz were there. But I ignored them all. I saw Ammi in the middle of the front room. I walked straight over to her and gave her a massive hug.

'Are you okay?' She nodded. Thank you, Allah.

I didn't really want to ask her what happened in front of everyone. So I let her have some air and space.

I've dreamed of this moment for so long, and now it's finally happened. Good riddance.

Friday 1st September

Today was a double good day! I finished work experience (thank you again, Uncle Professor).

And . . .

I moved back home! Yay!

There's no need for me to stay away now. It's gonna be a good year this.

Tuesday 5th September

Today's the first day back at college. The first day of the year that I work the hardest I've ever worked and kill my A levels.

I told Ammi to make sure that I work hard and to treat me just like she did when I was at school. Be proper strict with me. Less TV and less going out to play footy and stuff. She's ready to crack the whip.

InshAllah.

Sunday 10th September

He's come back home.

FUCK.

Monday 11th September

I've had to leave home again.

Back to Baji's in Edmundson Street. Déjà vu.

Pai Uneeb and Baji ordered pizza because they know it's my favourite. It made me feel 5 per cent better. So now I'm feeling 5 per cent good.

Tuesday 12th September

It was little Tany's fifth birthday today. I got him a football. I gave it to Mum to give to him, because I didn't wanna come inside the house.

I can tell all this is breaking Ammi's heart. But what am I supposed to do? I'm just a kid (kinda) myself.

Wednesday 13th September

I started volunteering in an old people's home today.

It's basically a big house on the corner of Preston New Road and Saunders Road. I can't believe I've never noticed it before. It's really sad. A lot of the old people there have dementia or Alzheimer's or something or other.

This one buddah, bless him. He got proper dressed up for work. I asked where he was going.

'I'm off ta factory, sonny Jim. Here, you remind me of a lad I was in Monte Cassino with, fighting the Krauts. Iqbal, do you know him?'

I looked at one of the nurses. She told me that you just have to hold his hand, take him out of the room, back in and then he forgets about it. So I did that. I sat him down. And he was just quiet.

'Do you need anything, Roy?'

He didn't answer. So after a bit I just left him to it. I was wondering if he ever met Baaji, maybe. But then I have no idea where Baaji was stationed in World War II. And now I can't ask him.

I was speaking to this one buddie* and she said that her

children never come to visit her. I didn't know what to say, man. I held her hand and she started crying. Then I started crying.

It's gonna be hard, volunteering here. Kasam. Oh, by the way, they were all goreh. Not a single apna or black person was in there. I don't understand how their kids can just leave their parents in a home and expect other people to look after them. I'm never gonna do that. Never in a million trillion years.

Baaji was really ill, but he lived at home with Dad right till he died. Obviously, if they're in hospital that's different. But putting them in a home ... It doesn't feel right, man.

Friday 15th September

I had to hand in my UCAS application form to Sandra today, for her to look over. I am officially applying for medicine. I've spent weeks going over my personal statement. Why I wanna be a doctor, my different work experiences and why I would be suited to it. I even used the word 'thus' in it! Take that, Shakespeare! How can they say no?

I looked at Ebrahim's. It was really good. He's applying to do maths. He proper loves it. I said to him, you coulda just wrote 'I'm a big nerd who loves perving on numbers' and with your grades they'll accept you. He laughed me off. In Pure Maths 1, I beat him, I got B and he got C. But ever since then, summat clicked for him and he's gotten As in every maths and further maths exam since. Including the Pure 1 resit.

That's what I need this year. For it to click for me.

Saturday 16th September

The 2000 Olympics in Sydney started yesterday. The opening ceremony was well cool. This Aboriginal woman called Cathy Freeman lit the flame. It was proper special, because in Australia they're proper racist to Aboriginals, even though they were there first, before white people came, took over and killed loads of them. Basically, the same thing they did to Red Indians in America. And with black people in Africa, making them slaves.

Proper evil shit.

I love the Olympics! I always learn about new sporting heroes I never knew about.

Like today, for example, I learnt about Ian Thorpe. He's seventeen (my exact age) and he broke two WORLD RECORDS today and won two gold medals! WOW!

Ian Thorpe is doing that, while I can't even get one single A in any A-level exam.

Sunday 17th September

I was sat in my room last night, listening to this song '7 Days' by this new guy called Craig David and trying to figure out how to play Minesweeper, minding my own business, when Baj came in. 'We're going to a wedding tomorrow.' Okay, cool.

'Put the clothes you want downstairs and I'll iron them.'

'Cool.'

'Mum said you have to go early in case they need any help.'

'Oh really? Are Shibz lot going?'

'Yeah.'

'All right. Well, okay then.' I didn't even ask whose wedding it was. It actually doesn't matter.

Fifteen hours later I was stood in Rizwan Masjid in Audley. And as Ammi had predicted, I got to work. Even though I have no idea who I was about to put this shift in for. At least I was with Shiry and Shibz, amongst twenty other guys.

We set up four long rows of tables. And for each row forty

chairs, nineteen on each side and two at the end. On each row, we put four strips of table cover rolls. Then in front of each seat we placed one big plate (for rice), one small plate (for dessert), one bowl (for saalan), knife, fork, spoon, a cup and a tissue. All disposable, obviously. Then on each table four bowls of salad, four little bowls of raita and chutney and four two-litre bottles of drink.

At this point, the guests began arriving. The first 160 grabbed a seat, so we started serving them.

There was a system. Two people per row. They communicate to the people going to and from the kitchen what their row needs and then the guys going to and from the kitchen tell the kitchen what they want, the kitchen passes it to them and then they pass it on to the guys working their row.

I was working the row furthest from the kitchen with Shiry.

The first pass is easy: the roast chicken legs came out in trays and we put the trays on the table. Then we had to keep an eye on the trays, and as soon as one is 70 per cent empty you take it off the table and send it to the back for a refill. Same with the raita.

Me and Shiry were very good at anticipating and making sure the people eating were never waiting for food. This is not our first tombi*.

Food is THE most important thing at an Asian wedding. The guests like a nice stage and a nice hall and they like looking at the flashy hired cars and all that stuff, but if the food isn't tip-top – warm, on time, lots of it and tasty – then the wedding is shit. No ifs, no buts.

So there's a lot of pressure on us servers. For all the preparation the families have done for the wedding, the success of it rests on our shoulders. Strangers.

Once the roast is done, time for the main course. Pilau rice, gosht* saalan, saag and chapattis. Now it gets tricky, because you have to juggle four different things and the three rows in front of you, making sure nothing runs out for your row.

Me and Shiry worked top together. No one on our row had anything to complain about, except for the stains on their white shirts. But we can't feed them as well. That's their responsibility.

After we've cleared mains, the miteh* chawal come out. That's not too bad.

At this point, people start getting up and making way for the next 160 people eagerly waiting to sit down, but before they can, we have to clear up.

Shiry grabbed a black bin bag from the side of the stage, then I cleared up the disposable plates and cutlery, throwing them in the bag along with the empty bottles of Coke and 7-Up.

Once that's done, and all the guests had cleared our row, Shiry went to one end of the table, I went to the other, we scrunched our ends up and then rolled the paper till we met in the middle. We then put that in the black bag, and that was one sitting done!

There's paper already down for the next sitting, as we'd laid down four at the beginning, but we now have to re-lay our row with plates, cutlery, salad, raita and drinks, at which point the 160 people that had been waiting on the sides, like the hungry hyenas in *The Lion King*, sit down.

'CLANG!' Shouts!

Oh shit ... Shibz's partner dropped a whole saalan on a guy's lap! Shit! He's ruined that guy's clothes. Hopefully he's not burned. The saalan is piping when it comes out the kitchen.

The guy yelled out a couple of words in frustration, but then very quickly calmed down. Lucky. I looked at Shiry. 'Imagine if he did that to an aunty!'

'She'd have twatted him, man!' He's not wrong.

The women and girls are a lot more demanding and mean than the men, let me tell you. It's probably their revenge for cooking and serving their dads, husbands, brothers and sons for the rest of the year. Fair enough!

And repeat and repeat. First 320 men and boys, then 320

women and girls. Shibz goes, 'Why do Asian ladies dress like Christmas trees at weddings?' and me and Shiry couldn't stop laughing. I looked at one aunty, dressed in a green shalwar kameez with loads of sequins on it, her finest jewellery and mehndi on her hands and arms, and I could see exactly what he meant.

It was such a tiring day.

Eventually, once the last row of guests had cleared, it was our turn to eat. Right at the end. Who serves the servers? Answer: the servers. Who else? We took it in turn to serve each other.

That meal tasted wicked, let me tell you that.

I got to talking to one of the bride's brothers. He asked me how I know the groom. I said, 'I have no idea,' and just carried on eating.

But that's how we do in our community, innit. If people need help, you step up.

Thursday 28th September

Really bad violence has kicked off in Jerusalem between Palestine and Israel. Basically, this horrible Israeli politician called Ariel Sharon visited our Holy Sites, which angered the Palestinians, because he was responsible for a massacre that happened to Palestinian refugees a few years ago. Proper rubbing salt into the wound that, innit?

Taubah though, man. The violence was really bad and loads of people have been killed and injured. Mainly Palestinians. The news said it's the second intifada (uprising) by the Palestinians because they want their rights and land back from Israel. May Allah help them succeed and make it easy on them.

Sunday 1st October

The Olympics finished today. There were twenty-eight different sports and three hundred events, wow! It was proper amazing, man. I hope one day they have it here; I would love to go.*

Great Britain did all right. We came tenth in the medal table with eleven golds, and also a silver medal from a guy called Ian Peel, FROM BLACKBURN, for shooting! That's so cool. As long as he doesn't go around shooting people in Blackburn, that is.

The best moment, though, was Cathy Freeman winning gold. She was the Aboriginal woman who lit the torch right at the beginning, at the opening ceremony. I LOVED what she wore. Everyone in athletics wears shorts and a vest. Men and women. Cathy Freeman wore a full body suit that even covered her hair. She looked so cool, like a superhero! You could tell before the race how much pressure there was on her. She's the home favourite, but also she's doing it for her people. The Aboriginal people. When she won, she didn't smile, she just looked relieved and emotional, and to be honest, it made me emotional. She did that for her country and for her people! That's how I would feel if I was in the Olympics. Obviously, I would be competing for Britain, but I'm Muslim and I'm Pakistani. I'm all those things. I think goreh don't understand that sometimes. That we have to represent all those different things all the time. It's not easy.

Bye-bye Olympics. See you in four years.

---

* Not only did I go, I worked on it for three years. If you ever see me, ask me about my story with the military and how I helped save the Olympics.

Monday 9th October

One of my favourite shows on TV at the moment is *Trigger Happy TV*, which is this guy who does pranks on real members of the public. It's SO funny!

I don't have a big telephone, or the access to things that he has in that show, but what I love doing, my *Trigger Happy TV* moment, is messing about with the lifts in college. I don't really like college. But this, almost, makes it worth it.

Sometimes, if I'm in a rush, I get in and press the close button before I press my floor button. This is especially fun when I know someone also wants to get in, but they're a little bit behind me. What makes it worse/funnier, is that I shout, 'I'm pressing the hold button,' so they don't think to press the button on the outside. By the time they get to the lift doors, they're shut and it's too late to open the lift from the outside. Mwahahahaha.

Other times, when the lift is full and I can't get in, I keep pressing the lift-open button on the outside. You stand on the side opposite to where the button is . . . you have to wait till the lift doors are almost closed . . . then you sprint to the lift button, press it, sprint back . . . and so when the doors open you're in the exact same spot as you were when the lift door closed . . . so it can't be me! Ufft . . . the swearing some people come out with! Five times is my record, before people got out of the lift and decided to use the stairs instead. 'Ooh, a space for me. Thank you.' Although that becomes suspicious when the lift then works first time.

My favourite, though, is when you're in a packed lift, people are in a hurry to get to lesson and you yourself press the lift-open button from INSIDE the lift. That's a dangerous one. Because you have to pretend that someone is doing it from the outside and you have to get really angry about it.

'WHAT THE FUCK, MAN?! WHO'S MESSING ABOUT

WITH THE LIFT BUTTON? WE'RE ALL GETTING LATE FOR LESSON ... IT'S NOT FUNNY!'

And everyone goes:

'YEAH!'

And then you press the lift-close button, but at just the last moment you press the lift-open button and repeat the process. This one requires balls and the ability to keep a straight face ... which I can!

Because I'm wearing a topi and look religious, no one ever suspects me ... Mwahahahaha!

No, but I do pray for forgiveness to Allah later in the evening, in case I actually upset anyone. And for lying, which technically, even though it's for a prank, I was doing.

Friday 13th October

It's true: Friday the 13th is definitely unlucky for me!

'Go on, I bet you I won't flinch.' I was at the pharmacy outside the Maliks' and I told Kes I'm not scared of the ball, and he half-spoke and half-mimed the words:

'If I kick from here, you will be scare.'

'No I won't.' And I stood like a scarecrow.

BOOF!

The lunatic booted the ball straight into my face! Luckily for me I did flinch, because I turned my face. If I stayed facing straight on, he probably would've broken my nose!

'ARGH! You moth—' He ran.

'AHAHAHAHAHAHAHA!' Pats, Nisar, Zak, Nasir, Chyna and Shibz were bent over laughing. I thought about chasing Kes to lamp him ... but he's much faster than me, so the humiliation of not catching him would've added to the baisti of getting the ball smashed in my face. No one needs double baisti. And if I did catch him, I wouldn't have lamped him ... let's be honest. It hurt, but luckily nothing's broken, just my pride.

Also, three horrible things, all in the Middle East:

1. This ship called the USS *Cole* got bombed. It was a suicide attack. They're saying seventeen people died and thirty-nine got injured.
2. A plane has been hijacked! It was supposed to be going from Saudi Arabia to London, but now Allah knows. InshAllah everyone on board is safe and no one gets hurt!
3. There's still really bad fighting between Palestine and Israel.

One good thing that happened, though, is that I watched *South Park: The Movie*. Ay ay ay ay ay. It is THE FUNNIEST thing I have ever watched in my life. Kasam. The jokes they get away with in that. Uncle Fucker!

Sunday 15th October

Good news! No one got hurt in that hijacking. It was actually a mad story.

The plane got hijacked by these two Saudi guys, because they wanted more rights for Saudi citizens. The plane was meant to go from Jeddah to London, but they made it go to Baghdad instead. The passengers didn't even know the plane had been hijacked till after they landed! How crazy is that?! Luckily everyone was safe, and the hijackers got arrested.

Bad news: no change in Saudi Arabia. They still ruled by the corrupt, awful royal family.

But, inshAllah, no more bombings or hijackings or wars in the

Middle East please! It'd be nice to just have peace there in this new millennium

Thursday 19th October

Raja Videos is my favourite shop. It's on the corner of Addison Street and Devonport Road, and is basically quite a small corner shop. But I love going in there.

Firstly, they have all the different types of chocolates, crisps, sweets (rosy apples and cola cubes and acid drops etc.) and drinks you could want.

But ... they're also a video shop. So they have all the latest Hollywood and Bollywood films on tape, and now DVDs too. At the front of the shop there's a catalogue with all the films they have, and along the sides of the walls there's shelves covered in the films. I love looking at them.

Then, behind the counter, there's the back room with ALL the films. There's hundreds, maybe even over a thousand! I like the guys who run it as well, they're a dad and son team, Uncle Raja and Azmat. They're always really friendly and let me take my time when I want to choose a film.

Today, I chose *Gladiator*. I've heard really good things about it and they finally had a copy for me. £2.50 for new films for one night. They write down every single film that has gone out by hand in their register. And it's been the same system since we first moved here ten years ago: Name / Address / Film / Fee paid? / Out / In.

I hope they're here for ever!*

Update: I WAS ENTERTAINED!

---

* In fact, they're still going in 2021. Although I don't know what their business model is now given the advent of streaming. They're still called Raja Videos, though.

Sunday 22nd October

As part of getting more experience to help with my medical school application, I start work experience tomorrow at Brookhouse Medical Centre for half-term week.

It's this doctor's surgery in an area with a big ethnic minority community, so it should be interesting to see how they handle that sort of responsibility.

Friday 27th October

'And what if you lose the notes, Jo? Do you just give the doctor someone else's?' Joanne, the receptionist, looked at me like I must be joking.

It's my last day of work experience. It's been so interesting.

'Tehzeeb, without us there is no doctor.' She closed the filing cabinet and gave the notes to a nurse.

'I think one of the main things I've realised is how much everyone who's not a doctor does.'

'Exactly. We have to make sure all the records are properly sorted out and filed correctly. It's not exciting work, but if we get it wrong, it's a matter of a life and death, isn't it?'

'Yeah, man. Also, how come the nurses do everything, Jo?'

'Basically, a doctor tells you what's wrong with you, but 75 per cent of the time a nurse can actually treat you or take your blood or – *uhum* – other samples. Nurses do a lot but get like 10 per cent of the credit. And pay.'

When I be a doctor, I'm definitely gonna be really nice to the receptionists and nurses. Without them, a doctor's job would be a million times more hard!

Sunday 29th October

It's proper shit and stressful when you fall out with your friends.

We were playing footy in Sacred Hearts. Me and Pats were on opposite teams and I kept teasing him.

'Ooh, another shit shot by Pattu there!'

I was just taking the mick. Then suddenly, in the middle of the game, he comes at me, 'What the fuck's your problem, you speccy four-eyed twat?' And he pushed me.

'Woah, man.'

Shiry, Zak and Nisar came running over and grabbed him, and got him to cut it out before things could get any worse (for me).

'Go on, say summat else. Go on.'

'I was just messing about, man.'

'No, go on, you're so clever, always taking the piss out of my dad as well.'

That's not fair. I really like Pats's dad, he's a top guy and he's one of the people I always pray with in mosque. I thought we just always have a bit of banter with each other, but obviously it's annoyed Pats. I didn't even realise.

'Leave it, Pats, man. Come on.' Shiry had a firm grip on him.

'No. I want him to say summat. Okay, then I'll say summat. Shall I take the piss out of your dad? Which one?'

Woah.

I just walked off.

'What the fuck, Pats, man?! That was well out of order.' I could hear Shiry shouting at him as I climbed the gates and got out of there. No one ever talks about that with me, because they know it's too sensitive a subject. And I didn't want him to see me tearing up. I didn't cry. I probably would've if I had to stay there, though.

I went out of the alley, turned right and walked up to Ammi's. It was Saeeda's twelfth birthday today, which I couldn't even enjoy properly because I couldn't stop thinking about what Pats said to me.

On my way back to Edmundson Street, I plucked up the courage and knocked on his door. I knew he wouldn't just start fighting me there. We're friends and he would've calmed down. I hoped.

He opened the door.

'Salaam,' I said

'WalaikumSalaam*.'

'Can we talk?'

'Yeah. Go on.'

I told him I was sorry if I'd offended him about his dad, 'But it wasn't nice what you said, man, it made me feel really small. Especially in front of everyone.' He agreed and he said sorry too.

'Okay. Friends?' I put my hand out. He took it.

'Friends.'

I'm glad I sorted that out straight away. It's best to sort any disagreements out with your friends, swallow your pride and try and move forward. I don't like holding on to bad feelings. Plus, if I didn't, then the next time I saw him in front of the rest of the boys, it'd be well awkward, innit. And it's hard to have a mature conversation with anyone in front of other people.

No, I'm glad we sorted it out.

Wednesday 8th November

Big drama in America! Big drama!

The American election was yesterday, and it was between Al Gore (goodie) and George W. Bush (baddie). Apparently, it's really close and it's going to a recount. They're saying that Bush is winning by summat like three hundred votes! But in a country the size of America, where a hundred million people vote, three hundred is nothing!!!

They haven't declared a winner yet and Al Gore wants a

recount in Florida. That's the key ... whoever wins Florida, wins the election.

Come on, Gore!

Thursday 9th November

My stepdad got jumped by some goreh last night. They nicked his money from his taxi and twatted him.

Obviously, it's bad that racist goreh are twatting Asian taxi drivers. I can't imagine how hard their job is, going into areas where you don't know what might happen ... but ... but ... it's him, innit, and so ... is it bad that I'm secretly a bit happy?

Tuesday 14th November

I probably shouldn't have laughed at him last week. What goes around comes around.

I was just walking back to Edmundson Street, it was late at night, about 10.45. Another late night, chatting shit at the Maliks with them, Shibz, Pats etc.

I've gone along Preston New Road and turned right and I'm coming down Addison Street. I was literally forty-five seconds away from home, about halfway down Addison Street, when a ginger woman stopped me. I've seen her around; she always looks really busy, walking here and there. Today's the first time I really noticed her. She's not old, but she looks ... I dunno ... tired?

'Hiya.'

'Hi.'

'I really need your help, please.' She waves me over to cross the road and go to her side. I hesitated. Don't talk to strangers and all that, innit.

'Please. It won't take a second. I really need your help please. Just inside here. It's an emergency.'

She looked really scared and desperate.

I was still hesitating, but for some reason ... kindness of my heart ... I said okay, and reluctantly followed her inside. She closed the front door behind us. Uh-oh. I was feeling really uneasy. She goes ...

'I'll give you a blowjob. Fiver.'

Er ... what?

'Er ... what?'

'I'll give you a blowjob. Fiver.'

I started backing off.

'Er ... no thank you, I'm not interested in that.'

And the reason I said that is because I wasn't interested in that.

'Okay, a pound then?'

That ... What? I wasn't haggling, but I got that down quick! Maybe I learnt more from watching Naani Ammi in Pakistan than I thought.

I explained as succinctly as possible that it wasn't the price that's the issue here, 'No thank you, I'm just not interested in that.' She looked disappointed. And then asked if she could have 20p.

'Please.'

I felt really sorry for her at this point. What must she be going through in life to offer blowjobs to a kid for £1. I got my wallet out to see what change I had; she took her opportunity and snatched a note! I tried to snatch it back but she started screaming! 'TONY! TONY! HELP! HELP ME!'

I legged it. As quick as my legs could carry me. I ran out of the room, through the little corridor, opened the front door and ran down Addison Street, turned left and there was my house on the right corner. I got to the front door, fumbled with the key, got it in the lock, turned it and fell inside. I said hi to Baj as quickly as I could and ran straight upstairs.

Good news: I still have my wallet.

Bad news: I lost £10, and as I ran down the street I noticed a car. I caught eyes with the driver and it was Fidge, a guy that I work in JJB with! Shit.

Saturday 18th November

'Oi, Romeo. I need to talk to you.'

Oh crap. Fidge. I knew he'd seen me running out of that woman's house.

'Listen,' he was whispering, 'what were you doing, coming out of a prozzie's house the other night?'

A prostitute! That's the word I was looking for. 'Prostitute?'

'Yeah. I saw you, running down the street from that crackhead's house.'

That's why she looked so 'tired'! Crackhead! Of course. How silly of me to miss the signs. I'm not gonna lie, I was panicking a bit. But I explained to him the full story, and he couldn't stop laughing at how naive I was.

'Wait, she offered you a blowjob for 20p?'

'No, no. She offered me a blowjob for £1. But when I said no, that's when she asked for 20p, so I gave her 20p then legged it.' He didn't need to know that on top of everything else I'd been mugged.

'Kasam, don't tell anyone, yeah?'

'All right, 20p.' And annoyingly he kept calling me 20p all day: 'Oi, 20p! Can you lend me a hand please?'

I think that's gonna stick for a while. He's not gonna tell anyone else, though. He's a good guy, Fidge. Fun to work with and he's the only other Asian guy in this entire store, so ... obviously, we're friends.

Wednesday 22nd November

Teachers are FUCKING ridiculous.

I got thrown out of maths today. Seventeen years old. In college. Thrown out of class like I'm a child. Stupid Gordon.

There's this thing in maths that he was trying to get us to learn, the 'all sin cos tan' rule. The abbreviation is ASTC.

And Gordon said the classic way of remembering the rule is 'All Students Take Calculus'. But because he's Scottish, he said he would like us to remember it as 'All Scottish Tea Cups'.

And then I said (because I'm incapable of keeping my mouth shut), 'What about "All Scottish Teams are Crap"?'

The whole class cracked up.

'Get out.'

Everyone stopped laughing. He was serious. 'Come and see me at the end of the lesson.' I left the room.

Afterwards, he told me off for being a racist.

HAHAHAHAHAHA!

It's a joke about an acronym and also, SCOTTISH TEAMS ARE FUCKING SHIT, BRO!

Joke's on him, anyway. That's 100 per cent how I'm remembering it and how I'm gonna teach it to anyone who ever asks.

Saturday 25th November

I ... I don't know how to write this.

Shahid died today.

Inna lillahi wa'inna elaihi ra'ji'oun: Surely we belong to Allah and to Him shall we return.

Monday 27th November

It was Shahid's janaza today. It was at Chester Street mosque.

What makes today especially hard is that it's the first day of Ramazan. What a horrible way to start it off. I normally love the first day of fasting. I didn't enjoy today. At all. I'm still finding it hard to process, to be honest. He was twenty-three! There was nothing wrong with him.

Baji Rosey told me that Baji Siema told her: Shahid and the family were hanging out at their house on Friday night and ordered a takeaway. The food arrived, they sat down to eat and suddenly Shahid collapsed. No warning. It just happened.

I cannot begin to imagine how scary that was.

Taubah.

They tried to wake him, but couldn't, so they called the ambulance. The ambulance arrived and the paramedics took him straight away. They tried to resuscitate him . . . but it didn't work. He was gone.

Just like that.

Like . . . Like a candle in the wind.

It was a brain aneurysm and usually there's no symptoms for an aneurysm. Anyone could have one at any time. That's so scary. I'm so gutted that something like that happened to someone as nice and kind as Shahid.

I feel so sorry for his family, his three brothers (Sohail, Shabaz, Harun), two sisters (Siema and Halima) and mum (Pua Said) and dad (Uncle Zafar).

Twenty-three years old. His whole life ahead of him. They say that Allah calls those he loves the most early. That's some solace, I guess. He must've loved Shahid (and Shehzad). A lot.

We buried him at Pleasington cemetery. It was the first time I'd ever been there. Up to now, anyone in the community that's passed away has been taken to Pakistan to be buried. But I actually think it makes more sense to bury a loved one here, where the majority of their family are.

It was very emotional committing Shahid to the ground and laying the dirt on to his white shroud.

Kasam. This life is just . . . you can just never know what is around the corner.

Tell the people you love that you love them. Ask anyone you may have wronged for forgiveness. And live your life to the best you can. Enjoy yourself, while keeping away from haram, man. I pray for my brother Shahid, that his afterlife is a good one. You will be missed.

I pray that Allah forgives you, Shahid, for any sins you may have committed, major/minor, big/small, knowing/unknowing.

May your grave be illuminated, and it be an abode of ease for you. And may Allah grant you, Shahid, the highest station of Paradise.

Ameen.

Monday 11th December

England beat Pakistan in cricket!

We lost the series 1–0. Jeeves tells me that's the first time since 1982 that Pakistan have lost to England in a Test series. This is the first time in my life … but, worse than that, the first time since 1962 that England won in Pakistan! I can't catch a break in sports, man.

Tuesday 12th December

Yesterday Pakistan lost. Today it was announced that Bush won the American election. After a full month of fighting in court, he ended up winning anyway.

I hope he doesn't start a war like his dad did!

Wednesday 13th December

Urrrrrrrrrrrrrrrrrrrrrrrrrrrrrgh!

Thirty-five driving lessons and I failed my driving test. I got eleven minors, but I made two major mistakes. The first major was a proper piss-take, man. The examiner pressed the brake and everything. 'But the guy's only got one foot on the zebra crossing, man, we could've made it!' But I didn't say that.

As soon as he pressed the brake, I knew it was over. That's a serious fault right there. Then I made a mistake in my reverse park, but to be honest I wasn't fully concentrating. By then I knew I'd failed already.

Pai Ansar said not to worry about it, but when I told him what happened, he looked at me like it was my fault. 'Come on. We could've made it!'

Everyone says that the best drivers pass second time. I used to think only losers said that . . . but now, completely coincidentally, all of a sudden, you know what? It makes sense. I guess I'll just be amongst the best drivers then.

I do wanna pass before I go uni, though.

Sunday 17th December

At least the week finished on a high! We beat our main rivals Burnley 2–0 . . . at their ground!

I was so happy. This is our derby. Our Everton v Liverpool or Celtic v Rangers or India v Pakistan.

After the game, Burnley fans, the proper daft bastards, started rioting and smashed up the town centre! Why would you do that? Who smashes up their OWN town centre?! Who's gonna pay for that? They are! Proper dumb. Haha.

The best thing: winning this game against the Dingle scum means we're sixth and in the play-offs. There's a long way to go, but I really wanna get promoted.

I wanna go to uni supporting a Premier League team, man. Also, we're only six points behind Bolton in second, which would get us automatic promotion.

Come on, Rovers, we can do this!

Monday 25th December

It's Christmas Day today.

We only missed Eid being on the same day as Christmas by two days ... SO CLOSE!

This year, on TV I watched: *The Borrowers*, *Walking with Dinosaurs Special*, *The Jungle Book* (so shit compared to the cartoon), *Home Alone 2* and *Big*.

And I also recorded: *Jingle All the Way*, *Independence Day*, *Titanic* (this took up a full cassette!) and *101 Dalmatians*.

Since moving to Edmundson Street, though, and living with Baji, I rent a film from Raja Videos nearly every day. At least three or four times a week. I've seen so many films this year!

It's bad, though. I mean, it's fine in the holidays, but sometimes, during term time, I'm up till 2 a.m. watching a film, then I have to go to bed and I find it hard to wake up in the morning for college and I'm a bit late sometimes. I can't really do that for the next six months. It's too important. My entire future rests on me clawing these A levels up.

Tuesday 26th December

The night before Eid is always so stressful. As soon as the day for Eid is confirmed, the barbers jack up their prices. Suddenly a haircut is £5! What a rip off. But you still have to have one, so you have to pay.

That's not even the worst thing, though. The second I walked into Faisal's I knew I'd fucked it. Every seat was full and people were standing. I just stood and started to wait. Eventually, THREE HOURS LATER, I sat in the hot seat.

'How are you, Faisal?'

'Don't ask, bro. You've seen the state of this!' I looked around the shop. It was just as busy as when I walked in.

'What do you want?'

'Number 2 all over please, Faisal.'

It's sunnah* to have the same length hair all over your head (so basically no short back and sides any more).

Faisal asked me if I wanted him to trim my beard too.

'NO! Sorry, no, man. Just shape it up around the sides please.'

I've never shaved my face and I'm really proud of my little growing virgin beard. It's so soft and fluffy. I hope it stays for ever.*

After he'd finished, and I was looking very smart, he took out a reel of sewing thread.

'Uh-oh.'

'It's time,' Faisal replied.

I could hear a murmur behind me: 'Good luck, lad!'

I've heard about threading. It's to remove the fine hairs above your beard line but under your eyes. That cheek area. You don't wanna shave them because they grow back thicker, so you get them threaded. I've heard it's painful, but no words could prepare me for what was about to happen.

'OW!'

Laughter filled the whole barber shop. For a second the pain had made me forget how many people were in there. I just had to be tough. Ow. Ow. Ow. He gets a bit of thread, twists it around the hair and then just pulls it out. FUCK OFF.

My cheeks were red raw.

I hate growing up sometimes.

'*Maza ayeh?*': Enjoy that?

'Yeah, Faisal! Thanks a bunch! Ow.'†

---

* Spoiler: it did not. I eventually trimmed it in April 2002, in Pakistan of all places.

† Sadly, lovely Faisal left us a couple of years ago after a fairly lengthy illness. I miss his barber shop and I miss playing cricket with him. Genuinely, Faisal: thanks a bunch. RIP bro x

Wednesday 27th December

Eid Mubarak!

It wasn't the same this year. The first one since Shahid passed away. I still read Eid namaaz and wore new clothes. But you know, it just wasn't the same.

Third Eid this calendar year, though! That's not gonna happen again for a good while.

2001

Monday 1st January

Happy New Year!

The biggest year of my life. The year I sit my A levels and go to university and set off on my life to be a doctor. InshAllah.

My college diary starts every week off with a quote by a famous person. This week's quote, to start off the new year, is:

'The ink of the scholar is more sacred than the blood of the martyr.' Mohammed.

I would've liked them to have spelt it 'Muhammad' and put '(Peace Be Upon Him)' afterwards, but still, that's really cool, though.

Also, that quote makes me feel a lot better about myself. In the olden days, I would've definitely been a scholar, not a warrior. I'm not a fighter at all. Was can fight, Shibz can fight, Shiry can definitely fight. Loads of boys in college can fight as well.

Like Lateef lot and Haider lot, who fight with each other. Which is awkward for me, because I'm good friends with boys from both gangs. Obviously, Haider from Haider lot, I went to high school with him for five years and I can still hear him singing 'Terry with the Leopardskin Specs On' in my nightmares!

But then, on Lateef's side, there's Anjem, a lad that I was at

St Barnabas with. My favourite memory of him is when we got put in a pair together in Year 6 and had to design a tech product, and he basically, single-handedly, designed and made a football out of cardboard. He designed it in such a way that it was almost a perfect circle. The teacher was really impressed. And Anjem gave me equal amounts of credit, even though it was his idea and he did nearly all the work! He ended up going to Beardwood and I went to Witton, but now we have a couple of the same classes together. He's still that same clever guy, but now he's obsessed with the gym and fighting.

I hate it. All this fighting and gang stuff. What's the point?

I get you have to be able to defend yourself, that's important. But none of 'em are gonna make a living from punching each other, whereas if they used their brains – and they're all really clever – they'd be able to achieve good marks and do summat top. Anyway, I would never say that to them. I would just use Anjem's favourite phrase: *give it death, innit.*

I will say it has its perks, being friends with the boys that can fight, because I might get teased here and there, but no one ever bullies me. Small mercies.

Thursday 18th January

I'm feeling a bit sorry for myself today.

You know when someone just slams a door, right in your face? That's what today felt like.

I went to the staff room to see Sandra, my form tutor, because I had to get her to sign something for me. I knocked on the door and heard a 'come in'. I opened the door and instantly smelt coffee and fags.

So this is what they do, eh?

I walked down a thin corridor, basically a partition between the room and the door. When I got to the end I could see Sandra sat at a table with four other teachers I didn't recognise. She got up to see me and I told her about the form.

'For the pre-med course?'

'Yes, Sandra.'

'Okay. Yes, I see. I'll just have to sign here. Leave it with me and I'll get it back to you on Monday.'

'The deadline to hand it in is tomorrow, Sandra, so if I could get it now that'd be awesome.'

'If you knew the deadline was tomorrow, why didn't you bring it sooner?' I felt like she was biting her lip to say something else. She signed the paper and gave it back to me.

'Thanks, Sandra.' I turned around and went past the partition and into the little corridor to leave, then I overheard her speaking to another teacher.

'Pfft, medicine!' I froze. 'That's never gonna happen.'

You know what, though, I'm gonna prove Sandra wrong! I'm gonna study hard, pass my exams, get into medicine and then rub it in her wrinkly red face.

Thursday 25th January

Really bad news in India today. There was a massive earthquake there, 7.7 on the Richter scale. That's really big. Anything over 7 is really dangerous.

The damage on the news looks horrendous. They think thousands have died. Taubah. May Allah make it easy on them.

I can't even think about it that much, because tomorrow I have my one and only interview for medicine. Liverpool have taken a chance on me.

Friday 26th January

I got up early today. Had a bath, put a suit on. Read Fajr* and made a dua. Ate breakfast and then walked to the train station. I've read so much about every moment of a university application. From doing your research, attending open days and getting extra-curricular experience to applying, doing the interview and then weighing up your offers and making an informed decision.

One of the things that has always stayed with me when reading about these experiences is that the students always talk about talking things through with their parents. Going to university open days with their parents. Their parents driving them to their interview. I feel like I've been on my own throughout all of this. I haven't told anyone how much I've been struggling with my A levels. My concentration. My motivation.

I felt really lonely on that train. Trying to cram in last bits of information in my head.

Why medicine? *I love the idea of carving people up, looking inside and then fixing everything.*

What do you know about Liverpool? *Michael Owen.*

Why should we pick you instead of another student? *I'm desperate, bro.*

I got to Liverpool in good time. I had printed a map out to show me how to get from Liverpool Lime Street station to the University of Liverpool School of Medicine on Ashton Street. So far so good.

I went inside, smiled at the receptionist, who told me where to go, and then I sat and waited.

Fidgeting. Looking one last time over my notes. Thinking how bad it was that I've missed Jumma and would that mean that Allah would punish me with a really hard and bad interview?

'Tehzeeb Ilyas?'

It was time.

The interview was tough.

I answered all the questions they had for me, but I didn't think any of my answers were particularly inspiring or original, or that I came across that confident or charming. I wasn't myself. My nerves got the better of me.

Plus, there were two men and they sat in opposite corners, one at my two o'clock and one at ten o'clock. I know that eye contact is a key part of an interview, but I didn't know who to look at. I was trying to look at both of them, and after a while I felt like I was watching a match of tennis or summat daft.

The interview lasted forty-five minutes, and then I was done.

Outside. All alone again. Wondering if I've done enough, but deep down knowing I haven't.

And then I came home. Alone.

Sunday 28th January

About 20,000 people died in that earthquake in India, 160,000 got injured and 300,000 buildings got destroyed. Bad shit, man. It put my interview at Liverpool in perspective. It could be worse. I could be a failure *and* be living in a pile of rubble.

Wednesday 7th February

I've failed again! I guess I'm not gonna be one of the best drivers who passes second time after all.

It's fine that I didn't pass first time. First the worst, innit. But second the best! That's what I wanted. Needed! Where am I now? Third the royal princess? Fine. Whatever.

But if I don't even pass next time, where does it leave me? Fourth the ghost eating the toast halfway up the lamp post.

Baisti, man.

Thursday 15th February

I pulled a proper shady prank in biology today!

I feel bad about it. Well, I do and I don't.

It's the last day before half term and our biology teacher, Steve, didn't turn up for the morning class. Typical: when I'm on time, the teacher isn't.

Harry, who sits next to me in this class, even tried to sneak in five minutes late and then realised there was no teacher, so strutted in with a big grin on his face.

9.10, still no sign of Steve.

So I suggested to the class that we should all leave, because if we all left, then none of us would get into trouble. Everyone else looked at each other.

'Come on, Harry.' He thought about it for a second.

'Yeah. Fuck it. If he can't be on time, why should we stay?'

And then like sheep everyone else agreed.

So we all got up and left. Like we were striking against Thatcher.

Except ... I went down one flight of stairs, crossed the entire third-floor corridor, came up the stairs back to the fourth floor from the other side, walked back across the fourth-floor corridor and back into the classroom.

Literally three minutes later, Steve walked in.

'Sorry I'm late, I – er ... Hi, Tehzeeb. Er ... Where is everyone?'

'I don't know, sir. I told them all to stay, but Harry said there's a fifteen-minute limit for waiting for teachers, and if the teacher doesn't turn up in that time, you can leave.'

'I'm sure that's not a thing. Is it?'

It's not a thing ... because I literally made that up on the spot. I was well impressed with myself.

'Yeah, I don't think it is. I'll have to have a word with Harry.'

Harry's in trouble, the rest of the class, including lovely Hafeezah, are not. Success.

Now, why was I being Slim Shady on Harry? Because Harry's this rugby kid and we've always got on well – we make each other laugh – but then last week, the painchod goes to me, 'Tez, I've got a joke for you ... How long does it take for an Asian woman to have a shit?'

'I don't know.'

'Nine months.'

And then he burst out laughing.

My face! So, for revenge, this is my prank on him. Steve said I could go, because he can't just teach the lesson to me. Mission accomplished.

Sunday 25th February

'What sort of party is it?' I asked Darren while I was out the back checking to see if we had any size 13 Nike Air Force 1 high tops. It's one of the most expensive trainers we have.

Darren's throwing a house party next Friday night for his birthday and he asked me if I wanna come.

'I dunno, mate, just a house party, innit. Everyone here's comin'. You're comin' aren't ya, Laura?'

'Hell yeah, Dazza!' Darren's eyes lit up.

'She's mental when she's wasted, Terry. You don't wanna miss it ... Laura who cheated on her boyfriend with her workmate at my last party.'

'It wasn't me!' We all cracked up laughing, because Shaggy's 'It Wasn't Me' was playing on the store radio and she said 'it wasn't me' at the same time Shaggy did.

I think that means it was her.

'Oh right, so is there gonna be like alcohol and stuff?' I asked as I grabbed the shoebox I was looking for from one of the shelves.

'Yeah, man. Don't worry about that. More booze than you can handle.' Oh, I think he misunderstood my question.

'I'll think about it, Dazza.'

'Good man.'

'Yeah.' I walked out front to serve my customer knowing full well that there was more chance of these Bigfoot trainers fitting me than there was of me going to Darren's party.

Friday 2nd March

Woah … Something called foot-and-mouth disease is happening, which means there's actual shortages of meat for Qurbani! Apparently, it's really serious. If an animal on a farm gets it, they have to kill every animal on that farm! Damn.

~~Poor animals~~ – that's not right, is it? I mean, it's sad if an animal dies from this disease, but we were gonna kill that animal to eat it anyway. So what does it care?

No, it's the people we should feel sorry for. The farmers who will lose out on all that money because they can't sell the milk or meat. And us lot, who can't get milk or meat for Qurbani. Poor us.

Also, I didn't even know that that many Muslims did Qurbani in England! My family sends money to Pakistan; they sort it all out there. I can't imagine how it works here. Do you ring up an abattoir and say, 'Sacrifice a cow for me, please'? Then what? Do they do it and bring the meat to you, or do you have to wait for three hours and then collect the meat from them? And bring it home in your car? Presumably.

Sounds like a headache, kasam. Who do you distribute the meat to? Who's needy here like that? Obviously, there's beggars on the street, but you can't just give them a bag of meat and think you've done your duty. What they gonna do with that? They can't cook it. They can't sell it. Who's going to buy a bag of meat from a beggar on the street?

I guess those people who normally do Qurbani here will have

to find a way of organising it to be done abroad now. Hopefully it's not too late. Eid's in three days!

Tuesday 6th March

Eid Mubarak!

What an evening. After all the hype from the last couple of Eids, I actually went to Wilmslow Road with Shibz and Was. We went in Was's mate's Golf.

And let me tell you, I do not understand it at all.

Wilmslow Road was chocka. Full of young apne in cars, most of them hired, going up and down at 3mph blasting tunes, beeping their horns, flying Pakistani flags and having a 'good time'.

I could see a lot of lads drinking, which didn't make sense to me. Drinking to celebrate a Muslim festival is like eating a burger to celebrate being a vegetarian. Or sucking a dick to celebrate being a nun. It makes no sense.

I mean ... it was a sight to see, so many apne, so many police as well, not that I saw any trouble really. It was just fun. I actually had fun, but mainly because I was just laughing at everything going on. The funniest part was Haider and his friends and cousins. They were in a car and they were going up and down Wimmy Road blasting this funny rude Yogi Bear song. It was hilarious, because everyone else is tryna be cool and blasting bhangra, or at least Dre or summat, whereas these lot are going:

> I know a bear that you won't know, Yogi, Yogi
> I know a bear that you won't know, Yogi, Yogi Bear.

So, so funny! Everyone was staring at them and they were acting like it was the best tune ever.

I was dying.

It fully turned into a reunion from school because we saw Boojo too!

'Hassim!'

'Terry!' He got out of the passenger side of his cousin's Beemer, such a flex, and we gave each other a big hug! We didn't have that much of a chance to catch up properly, but I found out he has a girlfriend who he met at college, which is nice, and I did get to ask him where he was going after college.

'Manchester to do accounting and finance, man.'

'Nice. Good luck, bro.'

'You still gonna be a brain surgeon?'

I quickly laughed it off.

'Haha. Yeah, of course.' Was I convincing him or myself?

It was really nice to see him, and it sounds like he's doing so good at Clitheroe. I'm really glad and happy about that. He deserves to do good.

The whole night was really fun … but most of the time I was just bewildered by it all. It was nice of Shibz and Was to take me, but I think that'll be my first and last time, thank you. I'm officially retiring from Wimmy Road tamashe*.

Wednesday 7th March

Sandra gave me my student report today. She didn't say, you'll never become a doctor, but she might as well have.

The worst thing is, in the bit where I'm supposed to put my comments, it said: *Absent 06/03*. Well … yeah … it was Eid! You couldn't wait a day till I came back and ask me for my comments then? Apparently not.

The reports all said that I was a decent student who needed to work a bit harder. I didn't really care about that. All that matters now is my grades. My predicted grades are:

Subject	Predicted Grade
Maths	C
Biology	C / B
Chemistry	C

I need ABB to get into Liverpool, who for some reason offered me a place despite my very average interview. Thank you. I've been given a chance.

Ironically, my pre-med teacher, Karen, gave me a glowing report. But it hardly matters, there's no A-level grade for that.

I'm gonna do general studies A level too. Who knows, getting an A or B in that might help me get in.

Friday 9th March

Sometimes I understand why my A-level grades are the way they are. My chemistry class is a fucking doss.

I sit in the back row with Hussain and Neelam. When we're not laughing at our teacher, we're pulling stupid pranks like putting lab equipment into people's jackets or, in my case, water. I filled Neelam's jacket pocket up with water and she didn't even realise when she put it on!

Me and Hussain love ripping into Neelam, but she gives as good as she gets. She's such an interesting character. She's a part-time butcher and also a vegetarian. I have no idea how that works. She also, for reasons beyond my comprehension, has the telephone numbers for all the members of Boyzone and Westlife.

What?

Why?

When?

Where?

Who? Well, no. I know who.

How? Yes. That's the main question. How?

She wouldn't tell us. Initially, I didn't believe her. But then she wrote some of them down in my college diary.

Shane Lynch's home number.

Ronan Keating's home number.

Brian McFadden's home number.

Shane Filan's home number. And then Shane Filan's mobile number for good measure.

I didn't believe her. Who would?

But then, when I got home ... I rang Brian McFadden's home number and an old Irish guy answered the phone. I fully panicked. 'Er ... is this Brian McFadden's house?'

Sigh. 'No, it's his folks' house, he doesn't live here no more.'

'Oh ... tell your son he's a prick!'

And then I hung up.

And then I felt bad. If I have his number, how many other random people must have it and crank call them all the time? Poor McFaddens.*

Anyway ... today, mid-doss, Alan, the chemistry teacher, got so angry and fed up he banged the wall behind him with the outside of his fist, out of frustration and to get our attention. And then ...

Kasam.

The clock fell off the wall and banged him on the head.

KASAM.

Awkward silence.

I don't know how no one laughed. But they didn't. I mean, it did look like it hurt, but it was funny enough to override that. It was the most *You've Been Framed* moment I've ever seen in my

---

* I've actually worked with Brian and we follow each other on Twitter and everything. I'd forgotten about this story until I was writing the book. Sorry, bro!

life. And then . . . my dumb stupid mouth did that thing where it speaks before I can stop it.

'I think it's *time* to pay attention, everyone.'

OH MY GOD.

Hussain looked at me. He didn't say anything, but his facial expression said: *Why?* I didn't have an answer. If I had got thrown out then, I wouldn't have complained.

Fortunately for me, the clock must have concussed Alan, because he just goes: 'Yes. Yes, it is. Thanks, Tehzeeb.'

I wish there was an A level in wittiness.

Sunday 25th March

'Do you like it?'

Please, Allah, let her like it! It's the most I've ever spent on a present.

Ammi said, 'It's beautiful. Thank you.'

'You're not just saying that? I've got the receipt if you want to change it and get something else.'

'No, it's so nice, puttar. We don't have a clock in this room, and it'll look really good on that wall.'

YES! She pointed to the wall opposite us. The main wall of the living room with the chimney breast popping out.

'Look, see how the pendulum swings. Isn't that cool?'

'Yeah. No, it's really nice.'

'Kasam, you're not just saying that, yeah?'

'Puttar, I love it. Thank you.'

'Happy Mother's Day, Ammi.'

£59.99 well spent.

I don't really ask her personal questions, and I'm not sure she'd answer them. I hope she's okay. I admire Ammi so much. I know her marriage is hard, but she always smiles and works hard and makes nice food and makes sure that Saeeda, Zaheer, Tanveer and Tauqeer wear nice clean clothes and eat properly. She's actually my hero. I know it's hard, me not being home, but if me not being there means it's okay for everyone else, then fine.

Thursday 29th March

AAAAAAAAARRRRRRRRGGGGGGGGGHHHHHHHH!!!
    I failed again!
    This was my third driving test. I should've fucking passed today. He failed me on some total bullshit, man. I couldn't even enjoy Zaheer's birthday.
    I bought him *WWF Smackdown* for his PlayStation, which he was really happy about. But I wish I could've given my family some good news.

Friday 30th March

Some sad news from Pakistan today. Baeji Aisha passed away. My great-grandma. Naani Ammi and Uncle's mum. She's such a sweet lady. I always like being around her. It's nice that she lived such a long, mostly healthy and full life. Five kids, twenty-two grandkids, eleven great-grandkids. Pass away with loved ones around you? What more can you ask for in life?
    Uncle, Poupoh, Jaffer, Saddia and Wadi Ammi had already gone to Pakistan last week, because they knew she wasn't well and it was coming up to her time.
    I'm glad Uncle got to see his mum before she passed away. I can't imagine what that feeling would be like, if you didn't get to say goodbye.
    Inna lillahi wa'inna elaihi ra'ji'oun.

Sunday 1st April

Rovers 5, Burnley 0! That is NOT an April Fool's joke.

Hahahaha. Imagine smashing up your own town centre and then three months after you lose 5–0 in the return game.

Fuck off home you daft Dingle bastards! We're going up!

Saturday 7th April

I'm so uncool sometimes. I've never worn headphones and talked to someone at the same time . . . until today.

I was in HMV, listening to new music, Shibz was on the other side of the shop. 'Shibz . . . check this new Eminem track out.'

He came running over well fast, which I thought was a bit keen. But he was laughing, and I realised everyone in the shop was staring at me. He took the headphones off my head. 'You just shouted that at the top of your voice.'

So embarrassing. What I actually said was, 'SHIBZ! CHECK THIS NEW EMINEM TRACK OUT!' Hahahaha.

It was a good song, though. I'll look out for it on the radio so I can record it.

Sunday 8th April

I'm eighteen!

I don't feel any different, to be honest. I didn't have a big party like last year. I'm not really in the mood for a big celebration. Mum gave me £100, which was nice, and Baji and Pai Uneeb gave me £50, which I said was too much! But they wouldn't hear of it.

I always find it well funny how Pakistanis be with money. Someone will give someone some money as a gift (could be a birthday, wedding, birth of a baby etc.) and the other person HAS to say, 'Oh no, this is too much! I couldn't possibly accept this much.'

And then the person giving it has to say, 'Oh no, don't be silly, it's nothing. Please, it's yours.'

And they go round and round a couple more times, until eventually the person keeps what they're given. NEVER in my eighteen years have I ever seen the person receiving say, 'This is too much,' and then the person giving it say, 'Oh, I didn't realise, I'm sorry,' and take some of the money back.

I would LOVE to see that!

Tuesday 24th April

I'm a football manager!

Nasir's entered a team into the summer league, the New Bank Bulls, with his brother Nisar and some mates, and he asked me if I wanted to be the manager. Oh my God. Obviously, yes. Following in my dad's footsteps. Minus the twenty-year widely respected amateur career and coaching certificates.

I met Nasir and his mates – my team – at St John's. Tuesday evenings, 6 p.m., that's when we train. Ten of them showed up (it's a seven-a-side league) on time. I was impressed.

A few of the boys I knew, obviously: Nasir, Nisar, Kes (who I swear is overage, but that's not my problem), Laily, a couple I'd played football with at Sacred Hearts, Steve and Gareth, and then four boys I didn't know, who are friends of Nasir's.

'Right, lads, come over and sit down,' I said.

They all sat on the AstroTurf, in front of me and Zak (Nasir's older brother), who I recruited to be my assistant coach.

'Who's played in a league before?' Nasir, Steve and Gareth put their hands up.

Right. I told them that we're putting this team together to win the league. Then I went over what I expected of them. Basically: commitment, effort and teamwork. 'Understood?'

They nodded. So far, so good.

'Right, get up. Give me two laps of the pitch. Go.'

They all looked at me blankly. 'What?' A tall boy with scruffy hair didn't understand what was happening at all.

'What do you mean, what?'

'What do you mean, two laps?'

'What's your name?'

'Guffy.'

'Right, Guffy, what I mean is run round this pitch twice.'

'But people are watching.'

I looked around. There was a small game going on in one corner of the pitch and there were some people walking along the railings.

I looked at Nasir, who shrugged his shoulders.

'And? People are gonna watch you play your games.'

'Yeah, are you gonna get shy in a game because people's parents are on the side?' Thanks, Zak. Good point.

'No.'

'Then run,' I demanded.

They all started running.

'Oi, Guffy!' I shouted after him.

'What?'

'Three laps for you, please.'

'Hardcore.' Yeah, Zak. Gotta show 'em who's boss.

I remember the first sessions of the season with Dad, there was hardly any ball work. I put them to work, press-ups, sit-ups, six-inches, burpees, drills. They were not happy! Haha. Now I know how my dad felt. The power is nice.

Eventually I let them play a game. And all I can say is, I've got my work cut out. There are some really good players, but they're not a team ... yet.

I'm confident I can get them there, but.

Imagine I win the league as a manager. Haha!

Okay … Terry, stop daydreaming and stay in the moment. You're coaching this team, one session at a time. The league starts at the end of May and then you can take it one game at a time.

Imagine, though!

Wednesday 2nd May

Just over eight weeks to go and then I'm finished with my A levels, and I've got so much to do! Not just revision but work at JJB and coaching New Bank Bulls.

I've got twelve exams. All the modular exams that I've got left for maths, biology and chemistry, three general studies exams, plus six resits. And I have to hand in my pre-med folder.

But I'll be okay. I want it so bad. It'll happen. InshAllah.

But tonight I'm nervous for another reason. Rovers are playing Preston North End. If we win, we're promoted back to the Premier League. Please, Allah, let us win.

Update: YES! YES! YES! We won!

Rovers are back in the Premier League. Back where we belong! God bless Matt Jansen! We're on ninety points! That's more than we got when we won the Premiership, and we're gonna finish second. Crazy.

I'm so, so happy.

Shukr-al-hamdulillah!: Thanks and praise be to God!

Hopefully I can follow in their footsteps and get promoted to medical school. Please!

Monday 7th May

I was on my way to Ammi's for dinner this evening, just minding my own business as I walked up the street, when a police car screeched up and stopped next to me. Two officers flew out the car, a man and a woman. I was thinking, *what the hell?* But before I could even say anything, they were on me.

'We need to ask you some questions,' the man said, and straight away the woman took her handcuffs out.

'I'm gonna put these on you,' she said.

'O-okay.' I was so nervous.

I didn't really know what else to say. I've always been told that when a police officer says to do something, you should do it.

The only experiences I've had with police officers is when PC Chadwick used to come into primary school and be really nice and tell us to stay away from strangers; that time Was shouted 'PIGS!' at them and I got caught; or whenever they chase us out of St Silas for playing footy. I've never had to go through summat like this.

She put the handcuffs on me. Really tight. They hurt, but I didn't say anything.

The man started patting me up and down, like I was at Manchester airport, asking me what was in my pockets. I only had the two things I always have in my pockets. My keys and my wallet. That's it.

'What's your name?'

I didn't think this was a good time to say Shah Rukh Khan.

'Tehzeeb Ilyas.'

'And where do you live, Teazab?'

Tehzeeb.

'A few doors up from here.'

'Right. We've made this stop because we're looking for someone matching your description. Where were you earlier this evening?'

I got well confused. I realised at this moment ... I panic when someone asks me questions like that.

I fully started thinking, *where have I been? Did I do summat? I don't think I've done anything. I finished college, went home, did some revision, and now I'm here. I don't think I committed any crimes along the way. Did I?*

'Where's the knife?'

WHAT?!

'Someone matching your description used a knife to stab a young man this evening. Where is it?'

I was speechless. I had a quick flash of being sent to prison and getting twatted and then making friends with people because I'm clever and funny and then one day, in maybe twenty years' time – I'll be thirty-eight then – I'll dig my way out of there. And then I realised I was just thinking about *The Shawshank Redemption* because I watched it last week. What a top, top film. But now wasn't the time.

'I'll ask you again: where's the knife?'

'I haven't got a knife.'

Then the woman officer goes, 'Yeah? What do you cut your food with at home?'

'Cutlery.'

At this point, a car stopped in the middle of the road and four lads got out.

'OI! WHAT THE FUCK DO YOU THINK YOU'RE DOING, PIGS?!'

I could see Zaheer in the driver's seat. Sam and Granny, older lads from my area, had got out the car and were striding over to us.

If you told me to guess what might be the outcome of this situation when the woman officer put the cuffs on me, never in a million guesses would I have predicted this.

Sam and Granny started arguing with the police about why I

was in cuffs. They were properly angry. The police actually looked intimidated. I would've laughed if I wasn't so confused.

'Why have you got my cousin in cuffs?'

'Why you harassing good lads like Terry? He goes to the mosque and college and goes home.'

'Come harass us, mameh*, we've got drugs in our car. Come on, search us.'

'Waste of time. Proper joeys, the lot of you.'

The officer asked me who Granny was to me. Granny said again, 'He's my cousin.' I felt like it would've been looking a gift horse in the mouth if I said anything else at this point. He's not my cousin. We're not related.

'He's my cousin.' At this point I was more nervous of him than I was of the police.

Thank God neither of them thought to ask me what his name is, because fuck knows. I don't think we'd have got away with Granny.

The woman then uncuffed me! They gave me a form and then left. Sam asked if I was okay and told me, 'Don't take any shit from these fuckin' pigs, Terry lad.'

I said I wouldn't. Which is obviously not true.

Sam and Granny gave me a pat on the shoulder, told me to go home and then they jumped in the car and Zaheer drove off.

WHAT A WEIRD EVENING. Definitely one of the weirdest of my life.

I got arrested!

Well … no. I didn't get arrested. I got stopped and searched, that's what it's called.

It only occurred to me when I got home that they were Pai Shehzad's friends, the ones that were with him the evening he was murdered. They know our families are close. Maybe that's why they looked out for me the way they did? Whatever their reason, thanks lads.

I didn't tell Ammi when I got home. I don't tell anyone anything these days.

Tuesday 8th May

At footy training today, while the lads were doing their two-touch drills – which they're getting much better at because I think they've become a lot less self-conscious about other people staring at them – I was telling Zak the story and he told me that Billy was arrested about a stabbing last night.

That kid looks NOTHING like me! Except that he's Asian too. Fuck the mameh, man.

Sunday 20th May

OUCH! I twisted my ankle really bad.

One thing I learnt today, I'm not gonna grow up to be a stuntman.

We were messing about outside the Maliks' house as usual and Nasser (Pats's older brother) drove past in his white van. He stopped to have a little chat with us, and when he went to leave, for some reason that I cannot explain Zak and I climbed onto the back of his van, clinging on to the top of the door. There was a very thin rim that we gripped on to.

Now, Nasser didn't know we had done this, and he sped off like a madman! I was barely holding on when he took a right corner at stupid speed and I flew off into the wall of Leamington Road church! Ouch. Twisting my ankle.

I hobbled back to my friends and zero sympathy. Zak came back a few minutes later, happy as Larry.

Fortunately for me, I just got a certificate in the basic management and treatment of injury this week in pre-med, so I know what to do with a twisted ankle: keep your weight off it and cry into your pillow.

Friday 25th May

And that's that. Officially the last day of college.

I've still got revision classes and exams, obviously, but yeah, I'm done. And so glad to be done.

I have not enjoyed being here. Yeah, Ebrahim and Hussain and Neelam are wicked and I had a good laugh here and there, but it wasn't the same as school, man. I feel so quiet here and have no confidence. In school, I felt like I was friends with everyone, the cool kids, the gangster kids, the girls, the goreh, everyone. Not Tommy.

But in college, I feel like I'm on the outside looking in. I don't feel part of anyone's group. The guys my age all think about different things: cars, gym, girls. I mean, yeah, I think about girls . . . sometimes . . . but no one wants to go prayer room with me, or talk about who will win King of the Ring next month, or how *From Dusk till Dawn* is the best film ever!

Even football. I support Rovers while everyone else supports United and Liverpool, with the odd Arsenal fan now. If you're not in the Premier League, you might as well be invisible.

I miss hanging out with Was and Hassim. I see Shibz most days still, but we're doing different subjects, with different timetables and different classmates and stuff. He's more mature than me now.

Nope. I definitely won't miss this place.

Bye.

Sunday 27th May

I made my football-management debut today. I even swapped shifts at JJB Sports so I could make it.

Nasir, my captain and star player, basically our Bulls' Michael Jordan, had a free role, but everyone else had clear instructions on their position and role within the team.

It was so strange to stand on the sidelines and actually be in charge. Have lads listen to my instructions, or at least try to. I felt very proud of myself today.

It was a bit of a mess, to be honest, but New Bank Bulls won 2–0. We scored two late goals, but we didn't play as well as I'd have liked. Lots of work to do. Too many players playing as individuals and not contributing to the team. Not that I'm getting carried away, but we won't win the league playing the way we did today.

Most of what I was saying to the boys was things I'd learnt from watching Dad coach. Maybe it's time to break out and be my own man. Have my own ideas, like, I dunno, make them wax some cars and paint my house – no, wait, that's *Karate Kid*.

Then again, Dad has played football nearly his whole life pretty successfully and he has coaching certificates. I'm shit at footy, always last or second-to-last pick and have zero experience in leadership or management.

What to do. What to do.

Monday 28th May

The news said there were really bad riots over the weekend in Oldham. Between Asians and goreh.

But BBC bro, I'm from Witton Park, innit, don't talk to me about race riots, man. Been there, done that. It'll be fine. Trust me.

Sunday 3rd June

I watched this top film called *Good Will Hunting* today. I can't believe how serious Robin Williams was. From *Mrs Doubtfire* to that. What an amazing actor.

It was really emotional. At the end the clever kid was talking to Robin Williams's professor character, and the professor talks to the kid about the abuse the kid suffered.

'It's not your fault.'
He kept saying it.
'It's not your fault.'
He kept saying it.
'It's not your fault.'
He kept saying it.
'It's not your fault.'
He said it so much it felt like he was talking to me.
And I started crying.
He's right.
It's not my fault.

Thursday 7th June

It's the general election today.

The first one that I'm allowed to vote in.

Some Muslims think it's haram to vote. I heard this guy in town talking to a group of people. He was really passionate, and I could tell he was convincing a lot of people. I wanted to argue with him, but I chickened out in the end. He was basically saying, you shouldn't take part in a democracy because then the country doesn't follow God's law.

I don't think that's right or fair. Our circumstances here in the UK are different and so we should take part in civil processes, otherwise how can we make things better or easier for ourselves?

Some people think in a very black-and-white way, which I don't think is helpful. In my experience, most things are actually quite complicated. Even the Qur'an says, *Oh People of the Book, don't go extreme in your religion* (Surah An-Nisa': 171) and the Prophet (Peace Be Upon Him) said we should always follow the middle way and *never be extreme regarding religion. Many nations have been destroyed before you only because of extremism in religion* (Nisaai; Ibn Majah).

I really like that about Islam. That we should consider both sides, not be too extreme in our activities, even when it comes to worshipping Allah.

I think people who start saying this is haram and that's haram need to chill out. If learned scholars aren't saying that something is haram, then who are you, a guy smoking a cigarette on the corner who reads one namaaz a week, to start giving fatwas out?

Having said that ... I didn't vote.

Haha. After all that.

I didn't think there was any point. Labour are definitely gonna win and Jack Straw is definitely gonna win in Blackburn, plus no one I know who's my age voted, so you know, it's not cool, innit.

Friday 8th June

Labour won! As I predicted.

Proper thrashed 'em, just like in '97.

Jack Straw, Blackburn's MP, won, and also he's now the new Foreign Secretary! How cool is that? The Blackburn guy is in charge of the international affairs of the UK.

Well, I think it's cool anyway. From Home Secretary to Foreign Secretary. What's next? Prime Minister? Kasam, could you imagine, but? Half of Whalley Range know him, and he becomes Prime Minister. There'll be fireworks here, bro. I hope they do as well in the next four, five years as they have done in the last four.

Sunday 24th June

Er ... there were more riots between apne and goreh this weekend. This time in Burnley. That's very close to home.

To be fair, they just love smashing up their own town anyway. The government and police should just leave them to it.

Friday 29th June

Well, that is that. I had my last exam today. A levels done.

I came out of the exam hall and asked Hussain,

'How'd you reckon that went?'

'It was all right, man. Anyway, it's done now. What will be will be.'

He's right. All I can do now is wait.

We went to Oasis to grab some lunch. I got my usual (cheeseburger meal with chilli and garlic sauce all over) and sat down opposite him.

'Do you reckon you did your best?' I asked.

'What do you mean, Terry?'

'I mean, I wanna say I tried my best. But if I'm honest with myself, I don't know if I did.'

'Are you still going on about the exams? Chill out, man. It's done. Enjoy your summer. Have you got any plans?'

'Just chilling at home. I want it, though, Hussain. I want it so badly. But I just can't concentrate on schoolwork any more like I used to be able to. You know?'

'Well, that sounds good, man. It'll be good to chill. I've got a holiday booked with my boys, we're going to . . .'

Ironically, I zoned him out. There's been too many distractions in my life. Football, cricket, New Bank Bulls, job, films and TV, the internet, my stupid wandering daydreaming and fantasies.

Hussain's right, though.

What will be will be.

It's Allah's will.

Saturday 30th June

I don't know whether I'm a top manager or the team is just amazing – or a bit of both – but we are strolling this league.

Today was our sixth game of the season. We won the first game, drew the second, and then have won every game since.

We were doing so well – 6–0 up at half time – I told the players to ease off a bit. Obviously, I said well done too.

Midway through the second half, after we went 8–0 up and I took Nasir off, my mind wandered . . .

I can't remember the last time I saw a ladybird, you know. I used to see them all the time. They were the one insect I liked picking up and I didn't mind being on me. But I cannot for the life of me remember the last time I saw one—

9–0. 'Well done, lads!'

Or a bee, actually. When was the last time I saw a bumblebee? Not wasps, I still see them, the little painchods. Are there less ladybirds and bees now than when I was growing up? Does that even make sense? I think—

10–0. 'Okay, no more goals, lads,' I shouted from the side. The other team's manager gave me a dirty look. A bit rude. I'm saving your lads from embarrassment here. My lot could score fifteen if I let them. Trust me, you don't want that. They print the results in the *Citizen* newspaper every week, it's there for ever then. Ungrateful guy.

I am interested in finding out more about the mystery of the ladybirds and the bees.

Monday 2nd July

A certificate got delivered home: ASDAN's Universities Award for Personal and Social Competence.

To be honest, I have no idea what it means. I think that's been part of the problem. I've been doing everything I can do to get into medicine: research, applications, practice interviews, work experience, pre-med, extra little courses, extracurricular activities. Basically, everything . . . everything except working hard for my A levels.

Everything I was so good at in school I've reversed.

~~I feel really shit abo~~

I don't wanna jump the gun, actually.

You never know, the results might surprise me!

Thursday 5th July

Oh my God!!! Amazing news!!! Baji's pregnant!!!

I'm gonna be a mammu!

Allah-hu-Akbar! Alhamdulillah! SubhanAllah! MashAllah! JazakAllah!

Saturday 7th July

Bechara* Tim Henman, man.

I wouldn't know what I'd do if I was him.

He lost in the semi-finals at Wimbledon again. His third time!

At least the previous two times he lost to the best player in the world, Pete Sampras. But this time he lost to Goran Ivanisevic, who used to be wicked, but this time he wasn't even seeded. He had a wildcard. They basically said to him, *Oi Goran, bro, are you free June/July? Come and play some tennis in London, innit.* And he went, *Yeah, safe. I'll give 'em death, innit.* And now he's in the final!

He's beaten both our home favourites, Rusedski and Henman. What a villain! Haha.

This was Henman's best chance too. Agassi and Sampras are both out. Actually, Henman beat the guy Sampras lost to, even though Sampras always beats Henman. It's a weird world, innit. Sampras was chasing the record to win five Wimbledons in a row and some random Swiss boy I've never heard of called Roger Federer beat him.

Anyway, what was especially tight was that rain kept stopping play. And when rain stopped play last night, Henman was proper thrashing Goran. He'd actually just won the third set 6–0! But today, when they started again, he couldn't capture that same form.

Poor guy. I can't imagine that kinda pressure where the whole country is just disappointed in you. I hope he wins it at some point. Or at least one of the other Grand Slams. He's twenty-six, but, so probably too old now.

Monday 9th July

Goran Ivanisevic won Wimbledon! It was so emotional, man. Well, he was so emotional, and you couldn't help be happy for him. He lost two finals before and he's been injured a bit and he just thought he'd enter Wimbledon and see what happens and he ended up winning it!

He's the first-ever wildcard and the lowest-ranked player to ever win Wimbledon. History-maker. It's always cool seeing people like Ali, Jordan, Schumacher, Zidane, Hendry, Sampras win, but when someone like Ivanisevic wins and you see how much it means to him, there's something about that that is even more special.

Like when Rovers won the Premier League, or when Pakistan won the Cricket World Cup. It's romantic. Something I know almost nothing about . . . but I still feel it inside.

Tuesday 10th July

Shit, man. There've been more race riots. This time in Bradford. That's Oldham, Burnley and Bradford. Blackburn next?

I'm actually paying attention now. It's the same thing as it was at Witton. Young Asian and goreh lads not getting on. Tension. A couple of fights and next thing you know, full-scale havoc.

The news said that one Asian guy got stabbed on Saturday and that's what triggered it. I mean, fair enough. If one of our friends got stabbed by a racist, you better believe that we'd be rioting.

Goreh youths attacked Asian-owned businesses, stabbed a boy and even attacked the police. If that's happening, obviously apne are gonna retaliate, innit. I'm not saying we innocent, and we have some people who do bad things as well, but in this case it looks like we were tryna defend ourselves and our community. Sounds almost like jihad to me. You have to defend yourself. It's literally our religion.

I hope shit calms down, though. Can't be having this ALL summer.

Wednesday 11th July

I was really worried today.

We were playing footy, when Rizzy came to the fence at St Silas and told everyone to get ready. The BNP are coming to Blackburn today. We have to fight.

Everyone went home to get their cricket bats. I went to Ammi's and got Zaheer's cricket bat. I told him that I'd bring it back in one piece, though I couldn't be sure.

'Are you okay, Tahir?' I swear Ammi's got a sixth sense. I said yeah and left.

About twenty of us waited on New Bank with bats this evening. Me, Shibz, Shiry, Nasir, Nisar, Zak, Big Riz, Saki, Rizzy, Nads, Was, Manny, Yahya and a few other boys.

It went dark. No one came.

Rizzy said he'll call us if anything happened.

I was so grateful today that I don't have a mobile phone.

Thursday 19th July

I committed a crime today. Not a bad one. Well, I guess it is if you're Mr Patel.

We were playing free kicks against Patel's shop with the shutters down. After hours of practising shooting against Hadi over the last five years, I'm really good at free kicks.

I tried to experiment with one, by going for loads of power. Basically, hitting it through my laces. Power I got. The problem was I got too much lift too.

Nisar was in nets; it went straight over his head and smashed the nice shiny PATEL'S SHOP sign, cracking it and leaving a massive dent right across where it says SHOP. It was so destroyed that a couple of pieces of the sign even fell on Nisar. Leaving the words PATEL'S S***. Which ... shouldn't have ... but did ... make us all laugh. And then we looked at each other and ran.

Monday 23rd July

Sometimes Pats can be a mad guy. Kasam. Like today. We all went into Patel's, picking out crisps and chocolate, trying to act cool. Pats took his stuff to the till and asked Patel's daughter what happened to the sign. We tried so hard not to laugh. She looked at him with narrowed eyes and asked him if he knew what happened. Obviously, he said he had no idea. She accused him of lying and he said to her, 'If you don't believe me, I'll shag your mum,' and walked out.

I mean. I've never been so speechless in my life.

She didn't know what to say. The rest of us didn't know what to say. We were all flabbergasted.

Me and Nasir have been pranking Pats all summer. It's been so much fun. We do this thing where one of us will duck right behind him and the other pushes him over. It's childish, yes. But when you get someone twice in the space of thirty seconds, it's incredible.

Today was the best, though. I was helping Pats practise headers. I would throw the ball high in the air; he'd let it come down and then head it back to me. We were in the middle of the road, just outside the Maliks' house, and I would throw the ball in such a way that for Pats to get underneath it he would have to take a tiny step back every time. I kept doing it. He'd take a step back. And then one more. And then one more.

Until eventually he took a step back and tripped over the kerb behind him.

Genius.

Anyway, some might say, why the hell were you in Patel's after breaking their shop sign? To which I'd say, listen, first of all, I love that shop, it's been there as long as I can remember. Secondly, we needed to coolly suss out what they were thinking and see if they were on to us – I mean, sure, we didn't have to all turn up to their shop at once and ask what happened to their sign in such a smirky way. That makes it fairly obvious that we're guilty, especially given the fact the Maliks live LITERALLY diagonally across the road. Thirdly, and most importantly, where else am I meant to get a chocolate and crisp from?

After Pats made his scene, it was very awkward. I stepped forward first and paid for my Time Out and Skips. Very quietly. I mean, one of the benefits of wearing a topi and having a little beard is that no one suspects *you* of being the one who smashed their shop sign to pieces.

Tuesday 31st July

Okay, today wasn't me!

The lads were chilling in the Maliks' when we heard a smash

from outside. We ran out and Muj was there with Chyna. Muj was panicking. He'd kicked the football and it smashed an upstairs window of the grocery shop across the road from the Maliks', on the opposite side to Patel's.

I told him to calm down, there was no one around. It's late. We'll just deny it.

Then Zak made a good point. Even though the ball didn't go through the whole window, they'll know it was us because we're always playing football out here.

Shit. Good point.

Before we could stop him, Chyna had found a brick in the alley, and he lobbed it through the window. He might be shit at almost everything, but he has a wicked aim. He completely smashed the window, literally put a brick through it.

'WHAT THE FUCK ARE YOU DOING?'

'What? Now they'll think someone smashed their window with a brick. They'll never think it was us.'

'WELL—'

Actually, we couldn't really argue with his logic.

We looked at each other and all ran in different directions.

Wednesday 1st August

We've got an actual nemesis.

She's called Trish. We call her Trish Stratus, but that's only because Trish Stratus (from WWF) is the only other Trish we know. This Trish looks nothing like Trish Stratus.

Every time we play football or cricket these days in St Silas she marches out and tells us to stop or she'll call the police.

But there's nowhere else for us to play. I've said before, the problem in our area is that there's nowhere to play football. And we have tried everywhere:

- On Lancaster Place, literally on the street, using people's front-garden fences and bushes as nets. Can't do that now, too many parked cars. I mean, we tried, but we kept hitting the cars, setting off their alarms, and we'd get chased by some uncles.
- In the alley maze that connects Lancaster Place and Granville Road. Can't do that now, we're too big and it's too narrow.
- Sacred Hearts. It's okay, but too small for a proper game.
- Corporation Park. The grass is uneven and the slant is annoying.
- Hargreaves. Again, fine when we were small, but a bit too small now.
- In front of the pharmacy. If someone parks their car there, we can't play.
- In front of Patel's. Well, we all know why we have to keep away from there for a while.

We've tried to explain it to her so many times. Where should we go? Would she rather we were outside smoking and dealing drugs or summat? We're just some boys who want to play sport.

She says she doesn't like it because of the noise. If it's too noisy, go to your garden, or the back of your house. It's a free world and it's not like we're playing at night when she's trying to sleep or anything.

I mean, technically we're not supposed to be in St Silas, hence her threats of calling the police.

We've tried ignoring her, but it doesn't work. She calls the police and then we have to run and that's the end of the game.

Chyna suggested that we brick her house. All right, Vinnie Jones, you've already bricked one window this week, let's not make it a habit.

I don't know if she's racist or what, but she's a proper nuisance.

Sunday 5th August

My coaching career is going pretty good, even though I can't always be at the actual game because of work. When that happens, Zak deputises and runs the game, and then gives me a full analysis of what happened.

I think Nasir prefers it when his brother is in charge, because when I am I always take him off at half time because the team is always more than five goals up.

We're having a really good season. They won one game 13–0. Ridiculous. Played 10, won 8, drew 2, lost 0.

Today, though (I've swapped shifts so I can be there), we're playing the second-place team, Whalley Range. Not to be confused with Dad's team, Whalley Range Tigers. These lot are completely different.

Although imagine playing against Dad. Coach dad v coach son. Epic!

Anyway, this Whalley Range are also very good. They're one of the two teams we drew earlier in the season. They're only two points behind us, so it's crucial we don't lose today, because whoever wins will most likely win the league.

Update: We're gonna win the league! Yes!

We won. 3–1. Get in!

It was 1–1 at half time, but I gave such a sick team talk. I told them, 'Boys, we're better than they are, but do you want it more than them? Because if you do, go out there and show 'em.'

And they did.

The deadly duo, Nisar and Nasir, got 2 and 1.

Thursday 9th August

Oh my God, this lady, man!

At least we pranked her today. Dad had come to play footy with us at St Silas and Trish must've seen that there was a grown-up with us. She came out of her house and across the street, shouting at us as usual.

Dad asked, 'What the hell is this?', and we quickly explained to him who she was and how she gets mad at us every day.

Trish started climbing over the fence and was saying, 'I want to talk to you, sir.' Clearly directed at Dad.

Now, Dad has two options at this point:

1) Run. Probably not a great option, to be fair.

2) Explain to her, adult to adult, why she is wrong and that she should stop bullying us.

Dad did neither of these things. Dad went for a third option that I didn't realise was on the table.

Trish stopped right in front of Dad and goes, 'Right, who are you to these lads here?'

Dad looks at me and goes, '*Innu aakh minu ingraizy kauny anvdee.*'

WHAT?

Some warning would've been nice, Dad!

I closed my mouth and then said, 'He doesn't speak English, Trish.'

'Really. Okay, well—'

So now I have to do a back-and-forth between Dad and Trish, Dad giving his answers in Punjabi, me translating for Trish, Trish giving her answer to me in English, me then translating that into Punjabi for Dad, EVEN THOUGH I KNOW THAT DAD KNOWS WHAT TRISH IS SAYING.

Also, I swear Trish knew we were bullshitting, but there was no way she could prove it.

She eventually left and so did we, and how we laughed. Because . . . it was well funny!

Saturday 11th August

Sometimes things happen that are so perfect, you can't make them up. And if you told other people, they wouldn't believe you.

Today was Blackburn mela* in Corpy Park. It was a lot of fun: there were singers and musicians, big crowds of lads and girls dancing, loads of food stalls and the weather was really nice.

But it's not really the sort of thing me and my boys, Shibz, Maliks, Pats etc., are into.

So what we decided to do instead was egg the innocent people in the crowd having a good time. Because that is the sort of thing we're into.

Nasir stole a tray of eggs from his house and came and met us. The action was at the bottom of the field, where there was a big stage and hundreds of apne having a great time. We stood at the top of the slope and started lobbing eggs. Nisar has the best aim of us all and I probably have the worst. I threw one egg, but we all had to duck and hide and pretend we were doing something else because it didn't travel very far. Like a baby crow trying to fly off a roof in Pakistan.

Got away with it, though.

We must have thrown about twelve or fifteen eggs altogether, with no idea who they landed on. If anyone.

After the egging, we walked down towards where the action was to soak up the atmosphere. This guy walked past us. He had egg stains on his head and all down his top.

We all looked at each other, flabbergasted.

Out of all the people that we could've randomly hit with an egg at Blackburn mela, we hit . . . the one GORA that was there! FUCK SAKE.

This poor bastard probably got dragged out by his Asian mates to come have a dance and chat up some Asian birds, and he gets smacked in the face by our egg. He probably thought it was a racist attack because he's white.

I swear I didn't see any evidence that anyone else had been egged. Only him.

Pats goes, 'Yo bro, what happened?'

This guy can't let shit go! He always has to give an ungle*.

'Some bastards egged me, man!'

I mean, what else was he gonna say?

Did we laugh after he left?

Yes, we did. More than ever in our life.

Sunday 12th August

I got to watch my first-favourite team versus my second-favourite team today! Rovers v Barcelona! At Ewood Park! This might never happen again in my lifetime.

Me, the Maliks, Shibz all went to watch. The tickets were only £10, because it was a pre-season friendly. Even better, we won 3–2! I couldn't believe it. Mark Hughes, the legend, scored near the end.

I was gutted that Rivaldo wasn't playing, but still I got to see BARCELONA and Overmars, Cocu, Xavi, Saviola and Kluivert in Blackburn! What a top weekend.

Thursday 16th August

I woke up today with a clear head and accepted what will be will be. Allah is the best of planners. Hussain is right.

I had a bath, got changed, had breakfast and walked to Blackburn College. I went to reception and asked for my envelope. This nice gori gave it to me and goes, 'Good luck, love, I hope it's what you need.'

'Thank you. Fingers crossed.'

I left Feilden Street Building and sat on a bench in the college gardens. There was no point delaying it. Waiting wouldn't change what was inside.

I opened the envelope and saw my A-level results:

Maths	D
Chemistry	D
Biology	D
General Studies	D

Not even close.

I could just imagine my thirteen-year-old self looking at me and shouting 'BAIIIIIIIIST!!!'

The dream is well and truly shattered.

I looked in the envelope to make sure there was nothing else in there. Like, as if these were joke results and there'd be another paper with my actual results on them. Nope. These are my A levels.

Four Ds.

As clear-headed as I was going to college, my brain was that much muddled up when I got home. I mean, I knew, but my brain can be such an optimist sometimes. Almost delusional: *It's okay. Maybe they'll make an exception for you*, I thought.

I got home and went straight upstairs, so I could avoid Baj.

I rang Liverpool. From the second I picked the phone up to dial the number to the second I hung up, I felt stupid the entire time. Of course they weren't gonna let me in to study medicine with four Ds. I mean, who gets a D in general studies?!

It's not like I even have a good excuse. Ooooh, I stayed up late every night to watch every movie that ever came out and spent 90 per cent of my revision time staring at my notes daydreaming about being a doctor.

I failed.

I'm not going to become a doctor.

AAAAAAARRRRRRRRRGGGGGGGGHHHHHHHH!!!!!

*

Update: I've just had a long cry.

Because … to be honest, with these grades I'm not sure I'm even going to go to university.

Ammi hid her disappointment very well, which I was very grateful for. I mean, on one level she must understand that the upheaval that's been happening at home did not help.

I don't know what I'm gonna do next … Maybe it is my destiny to work at JJB Sports after all?

Friday 17th August

I stopped feeling sorry for myself today. I've had my cry. Good.

What's happened has happened and I can't change that.

I went on the internet and went on the UCAS website, where they've got a list of all the courses that are available through clearing. I crossed my fingers and looked to see if there were any for medicine. There were not. Obviously. It's massively over-subscribed. I looked for any physiotherapy courses. There were a few. Yes!

I rang University of Birmingham. They said no.

I rang University of Liverpool. They said no.

I rang … eight different unis. They all said no. Not with four Ds.

I was getting quite upset now. I started panicking. I can't do physiotherapy either.

I went back on to UCAS to see what science courses were available. There was a biomedical science course at Manchester Metropolitan University. That sounded okay. I rang them up and they said they couldn't take me on that degree with my grades, but they would consider me for a colour chemistry course. What the fuck is colour chemistry?!

The lady explained to me what it is, but to be honest I wasn't really listening. I asked her if I could think about it and she said I should let her know by Monday dinnertime.

Then I found another biomedical science course. This time at

Lancaster Uni. Urgh. I really didn't wanna go there, but unless I end up going somewhere really far like Sunderland, which I don't wanna do, I don't have much of a choice.

I rang Lancaster. They told me that their biomedical science course was already full up. Thank God! But . . .

'We do have a space left on the almost identical biochemistry course.'

'Oh. When do I need to let you know by?'

'Monday lunchtime, please.'

'Thank you. I will do.'

Okay. Now I have two offers.

Manchester Met to do BSc colour chemistry, or Lancaster to do BSc biochemistry.

Decisions. Decisions. I have to get this one right. I messed up the Clitheroe Royal Grammar School one. I can't do that again.

Monday 20th August

After doing a lot of research all weekend, talking to my mates and doing istikhara*, I decided that I'm going to . . .

Lancaster University!

Wednesday 22nd August

The more I read about Lancaster Uni the more excited I get! I think I judged it too early; it looks like an amazing place. Plus, they're a top-ten uni. Bloody hell. I failed my A levels and fully fluked it into one of the best universities in the country.

Allah works in such mysterious ways.

Instead of falling downwards, I've fallen upwards! *Alhamdulillah.*

Saturday 25th August

'I'm going to Huddersfield, man. They accepted me to do law.'

'Awesome, man. Mubarakah!' Shibz didn't do that great in his A levels either, but I'm so happy he's managed to find a place to keep his dream of becoming a lawyer alive. We were sat in the Maliks' front room as usual, talking about what we were doing next.

'Where are you going, Zak?' Zak smashed his A levels. I didn't even realise how clever he was. He went to Beardwood High School and we've never really spoken about grades and stuff like that.

'University of Manchester to do physics.'

'Damn, man! That's top.' I was genuinely impressed.

Mr Four As Ebrahim is doing maths at Manchester, Hussain is off to Sheffield and Neelam's going to UCLan.

I'm glad we're all going somewhere, even if for some of us it might not be our first choice.

'Have you heard?' Nasir interrupted as he came rushing in.

'No, what?'

'Aaliyah's died, man. Plane crash.'

Holy moly! That's so sad, man. It really made me realise even more that we should never take our friends or loved ones for granted at any age.

Sunday 26th August

We won the league! Comfortably.

I'm a championship-winning manager!

It was the last game of the season for the New Bank Bulls today. We won. Again. 8–0. I didn't take Nasir off at half time today. I put him in goal instead, so that our keeper could play up front and score. Which he did. That meant that every single one of my players scored this season.

Played 14, won 12, drew 2. Scored God knows, conceded a lot less.

The thing that I'm really proud of is that we're the only team in the league that is mixed. Every other team is either all Asian, or all white. We've got two goreh in our squad. Steven and Gareth. My defenders.

Okay, yes, we've also got two overage players in the team, Kes and Nisar. But whatever.

We didn't get the trophy today, there's a presentation ceremony in a few weeks and we'll get it then. I can't wait.

Tuesday 28th August

I'm so heartbroken.

Baji had a miscarriage yesterday. She lost her baby.

I know she was finding it hard being pregnant, obviously it's not something I will ever be able to understand, but I was hoping it was just a phase in the pregnancy and that after a while she'd be okay. Unfortunately, that didn't happen.

I went to the hospital and Ammi, Pai Uneeb and Poupoh were already there. I just ignored everyone and went straight to Baj and gave her a big hug. We embraced for a long time and we cried and cried and cried.

Ya, Allah, please protect my sister first and foremost, she's been through so much in her life already. Please ease her pains and tribulations. And, if it is the best thing for her, please give her the gift of children in the future.

Ameen.

Wednesday 29th August

I went with Pai Uneeb and Mammu Saeed to Pleasington cemetery to bury the dead . . . foetus – I'm not sure what the right term is.

We buried it in a tiny box, it was like the size of a shoebox. It was really surreal.

There was no funeral because it wasn't developed enough to qualify for one. But we stayed for a while and read some prayers. I squeezed Pai Uneeb's shoulders when he started crying.

Friday 31st August

We called a truce with Trish today.

She was pissing us off, and clearly we were pissing her off. I mean, she cried last week. We started becoming more and more verbally abusive, which is wrong, but also, why is she such a grass, but?

Today, when she came out again (she doesn't give up, I'll give her that) we were about to launch at her when Nazir stopped us and started talking to her. Nazir is the cleverest kid in our whole area; actually, probably the cleverest guy around our age I know (he is studying medicine). He was calm and talked to her properly. He suggested that she writes to the council and Jack Straw about the lack of playing facilities in our area.

Instead of directing all her rage towards us, she should 'direct it at the people who've neglected to provide young people with adequate facilities'.

At one point, Trish said the reason why she hates us playing here so much is because it's too noisy for her to play the piano. And then Nazir said, 'Bit of an oxymoron that, isn't it? That you want us to be quiet, so you can be noisy?'

She didn't have anything to say to that. I looked at Shibz and we didn't say anything, but I'm sure he was thinking exactly what

I was thinking: *what the fuck is an oxymoron?* I didn't ask Nazir afterwards. I didn't want him to think I'm not clever.

To be honest, when he was talking the rest of us were standing there in awe. I was a bit jealous, actually. I used to be this confident and clever at school. What happened? He said what we were all thinking, but none of us knew how to express. It was really inspiring.

She thought about everything we (Nazir) said to her and said that we were right and she would write to the council.*

Wow.

Talking does resolve things.

Saturday 1st September

I heard the funniest insult I've ever heard in my life today. Even funnier than mouldy sheep. We were playing football at Sacred Hearts playground – we thought we'd give Trish a little break after our truce – and Kes went in hard to a tackle with Farooq and they got into an argument, and Kes said to Farooq, 'Your dad drink beer.'

Incredible.

Stopped Farooq dead in his tracks. What do you say to that?

Now, Kes is partially deaf, so he can't speak clearly, which I think made the insult even funnier. It definitely added a layer on top of what was already a killer insult.

I mean, saying to a Muslim boy, your dad drinks beer. That is low!

We couldn't stop laughing.

---

* And she did. The football cage at Corporation Park, opposite QEGS, is because of her campaign for the council to provide us with playing facilities. She also started coaching kids' football too. It's a funny world, and it turns out Trish wasn't racist at all. If you're reading this: Hey, Trish.

Tuesday 4th September

About two weeks ago, before she went to hospital, Baj was obsessed with this book I'd never heard of. I asked her what it was, and she was really excited about it: 'It's about this orphan who goes to a special school for wizards and witches and—'

No thank you. That is not for me. She tried convincing me.

'It's really good! He has these two best friends and they get up to all sorts of adventures and—'

Look, I was obsessed with the Secret Seven and the Famous Five and Roald Dahl and *The Lion, the Witch and the Wardrobe* and Point Horror and Asterix and Obelix and *Where's Wally?* when I was a bit younger and used to go the library twice a month.

But, truth is, since leaving school and especially since leaving Ammi's, I haven't done that much reading. Nowhere near as much as I used to. I've become too obsessed with TV, films and the internet.

So if I am gonna start reading again, I'm gonna make sure I read really good stuff, like the sort of stuff that Mrs Place used to make us read for English.

I heard that George Orwell is supposed to be good, *1984* and *Animal Farm*. And *Lord of the Flies*. And *Lord of the Rings*. And *The Hobbit*. They're the sort books I need to read now.

Not a kid's book about a bloody ten-year-old wizard.

She got the books off Jaffer, which to be honest convinced me even more that it wasn't for me. Jaffer's thirteen. It makes sense that he's reading them. Why is Baj, a twenty-year-old, reading them?

Then she said, '. . . and Shiry loves it too.'

Huh?

Well . . . That changes things.

If my hammer-wielding, hard-as-nails cousin is into this *Harry Potter*, then . . . maybe it's worth a go?

That was two weeks ago.

And . . .

I've just finished the fourth book! And I'm gutted that the next book isn't out yet! Honestly. I know it's a kid's series. But. It's. Wicked.

And there's a film coming out later this year. I'll 100 per cent be going to watch that.

Wednesday 5th September

I'm so excited about Lancaster.

I have to choose what college to go to. I guess it's a bit like which house you want to go into in *Harry Potter*.

Hahahaha! Allah. I'm obsessed.

I have a choice between nine colleges and I've put Furness College as my first choice. I looked at Bowland, but it apparently has the highest suicide rate in the university, which apparently has the highest suicide rate in the country. I saw that on the internet. I don't know if that's urban myth, but I don't wanna be in the college where you can jump off a tower. I've seen way too many horror films for that. I mean, what if they're not jumping? What if they're being pushed?!*

The main reason I chose Furness is because it's right next to the science lecture theatre. So it's the least amount of walking to class. Honestly, I've become SO lazy.

I also made a really important phone call today. I had to ring Lancashire County Council so that they would pay my tuition fees because I'm poor ('from a low-income background'). It's £1075 a year! There's no way I can afford that. Luckily, they said yeah!

Yay!

I've applied for a student loan as well. That'll be £4000 a year,

---

* They weren't.

from which I have to pay my rent and all my food and living costs, books and travel and everything. I've still got my JJB job on weekends, but I'm not sure how long I'm gonna do that for because I'll be rich when my student loan comes.

Monday 10th September

I went to visit Lancaster Uni with Shibz and Zak today. I had to go and register, get assigned my college and sort my accommodation out.

We walked around the place; I actually like that it's one big campus with everything on site. Makes it feel like an American college, or a boarding school.

Loads of apne from Blackburn end up at Lancaster, or one of the Manchester or Liverpool unis, or Uni of Central Lancashire (Preston) or Edge Hill College, and they always commute. They go to uni in the morning and come home in the evening, like school or college.

I don't understand that. I'm so excited to have the full uni experience. I want to see what it's like living away from home and experiencing new things with new people.

I guess for me it's also a fresh start. Hopefully, I can start being my old self again. The people I'll be here with don't know who I am or what my history is. They don't know that I was thrown out of home, that I failed my A levels, that I'm shit at footy. All they'll see is what I show them.

I looked around Furness. The porter who showed me around told me it didn't look like much (he was right) but that 'it's the people that make a place, not the bricks and mortar'. Those were probably some of the wisest words I've heard in a long time.

I think about the times I've had the most fun, it's always been because of the people I'm with rather than the thing I'm doing.

Except Alton Towers. I would happily ride Oblivion on my own, all day.

Tuesday 11th September

!!

Wednesday 12th September

Okay, so I need to say what happened yesterday, from my perspective.

It was the second road trip in a row with Zak and Shibz. Shibz needed to go Huddersfield Uni to register. I'd never been to Huddersfield in my life. It looked pretty boring, to be honest. The only thing I really remember about it is that to get into town you had to go via this big circular road, like a giant ring, and I thought that was quite cool. I'd never seen something like that before. Like the town was in the middle of a maze.

Shibz managed to register and then we walked around a couple of blocks of student accommodation, which looked pretty nice. They were en suite, which I think is just the coolest thing in the world. Especially because they have cleaners who come and clean for you. It was really expensive, though. £75 a week. Taubah.

But he didn't really have much of a choice. Going through clearing meant that everyone else had already chosen where they wanted to live.

We got some lunch, chilled out for a bit and then we left Huddersfield around 4ish. On our way back, just like on the way there, we were listening to some sick tunes. Dre, Tupac, Biggie, as well as some Metz N Trix and RDB.

This is not relevant to the story, but Metz N Trix are hilarious. They're these two Asian rappers who always rap on bhangra songs. And I honestly can't tell if they're proper shit, or proper sick. The songs are always bangers, but their lyrics are mental: *Lamborghini diabolo . . . ipsy dipsy lala po.* I mean, what even is that?

Anyway, about halfway back, it must have been about 5ish, Zak went to change the CD and so the radio came on.

It was the news.

The presenter said something about a plane going into a building.

None of us really clocked it. I actually laughed it off. I thought the news guy meant like those small crop-duster planes.

Oh, how wrong I was.

We put on *The Chronic 2001* and blasted it full volume all the way home.

We got home around 5.30 and we parked up outside the Maliks' house.

The street was full of people. A bit unusual at this time of day, to be honest. I saw Nisar and he asked us straight away:

'Have you seen? Have you seen?'

Seen what, man?

He dragged us inside in front of the TV and that's when I saw it.

A ... a plane ... no ... two planes (jumbo jets) crashed into two skyscrapers (the Twin Towers) in New York.

And then ... about half an hour later, the skyscrapers collapsed. They just fell down like their legs buckled after being chinned. It was like something out of a film.

The news said that thousands of people have died.

FUCKING HELL.

I watched the news for about fifteen minutes. I was shocked.

I came out and everyone was talking about it. I've never seen New Bank this busy on a random Tuesday evening. Everyone wanted to discuss it. I walked across the road to Patel's and must've popped in and out of half a dozen conversations.

A mixture of confusion.

'Who could have done this?'

Excitement.

'Must be on purpose, right? It can't be an accident?'

Speculation.

'The news was saying it might be jihadis.'

Explanation.

'Well, what do you expect? If you go meddling around the world, then those things come back to haunt you, innit.'

And, from one or two people, justification.

'Serves 'em right.'

I got into an argument with Uncle Walid. He was saying it was good what happened. Which I was a bit shocked about, to be honest. I said to him, 'Uncle, you can't say that. Whatever America has or hasn't done, you can't just go and kill innocent people for revenge like this.'

'What about the innocent people that America kill?'

'Right? So these people are just as bad as that, then? How are they any better?'

The one question that entered my mind straight away was: *what happens next?*

There's no way America takes this sort of baisti lying down. Somewhere is gonna get caned in the next few months. And I bet it'll be a Muslim country.

On the news they been putting the blame on Al-Qaeda and Osama bin Laden. Saying that it's Islamic terrorists who did this. If this was so-called jihadis, then people will blame all Muslims. That's what happens. I HATE that they're dragging Islam's name into this. Islam does not teach this. EVERYTHING I've read about jihad says you can't kill innocent people, it's very clear.

If it is bin Laden's lot, then he's a fuckin' scumbag that's made it ten times harder for all of us. I really, really pray and hope it's not.

There's gonna be no winners from this attack. Only losers. It is not gonna be good for anyone. Innocent people have died, more innocent people will die now and there'll be more racism against Muslims, making even more division between people.

I've already seen it.

When I left New Bank and went to Ammi's for Tany's birthday (happy birthday, Tany), I bumped into Steve, a kid I'd coached all summer, my star defender for New Bank Bulls, my second-best player, one of the two goreh on my team.

He didn't say hello, he just asked if I was Muslim. I said yeah.

'Go fuck yourself, you bastard!' And then he ran off.

It made me so sad . . . Who's gonna play in defence next season?

Friday 14th September

I knew it.

It didn't take a genius to work out that America's gonna take big-time revenge on whoever they think did these attacks.

People can be so fuckin' short-sighted, man. Yeah, it's nice for a bully to get smacked around, or even hurt really badly. But if he comes back with a gun and shoots you and your family in the face, is that a victory? Especially when, really, you didn't even smack the bully, you hurt (well, killed) lots of innocent people that live with the bully.

People need to start seeing further than the end of their noses, man. I know for Pakistanis that's hard, because our noses are massive, but have some common sense. Please.

Plus, as I wrote before, it's AGAINST our religion to kill innocent people. I double-checked, just in case I was the idiot. So, whatever we think about America, it was haram. Full stop.

I'm mad now, because it's been three days and America has already passed a law, called the Authorization for Use of Military Force Against Terrorists, which lets the President attack and bomb whoever they think carried out the attack.

May Allah keep safe the innocent people of Afghanistan and any country that faces America's wrath in the coming months.

*

Oh, I saw Steve again on the way to Ammi's. He apologised for what he said to me on Tuesday. I told him not to use that sort of language again. He agreed and said sorry. We shook hands. He told me that his dad explained to him about how America killed loads of people around the world and goes around bullying other countries, and how they've got army bases in Muslim countries, so it's no wonder that people want revenge on them.

I nodded, without really agreeing with him. I told him I was glad he was thinking differently.

I shook his hand and whispered to him, 'You're back in the team.'

I thought it was so interesting how even goreh have that thinking, that America sort of had it coming.

Tuesday 19th September

There's some other shit happening now!

Something called anthrax.

The news was saying that some crazy guy/terrorist/supervillain^ is posting anthrax, which is basically a bioweapon, to news media offices and to politicians.

Shit, man.

It's only been a week since 9/11 and America are already chatting all sorts of crazy shit about revenge and stuff. They wanna bomb Afghanistan to get this Osama bin Laden guy and Al-Qaeda. They don't need more excuses to go around bombing stuff.

We should send Nazir to see the President. He'd explain it to him proper, that if he starts bombing a country and innocent people die, it'll create more bin Ladens, not less. But then he'll probably say summat about an oxymoron and Bush will think that Nazir's insulting him, because he's even more dumb than I am.

How crazy is it that some guy's just posting a bioweapon,

though? Here's your telephone bill, a postcard from your poupoh and a death powder, all in the same delivery. Blows my mind.

I hope they catch the guys quickly, before they do even more damage.

I just realised . . .

I, a young Muslim man, am starting a degree in biochemistry, one month after 9/11 and three weeks after a biochemical attack on America.

SHIT.

^ Please don't be Muslim!

Thursday 20th September

My student loan came last Friday (I'M RICH!), so I've been shopping this week with Ammi. It was so nice having her come with me, because usually I have to do this sort of shopping on my own.

I have a massive list of all the things I needed to buy for uni. The first thing I bought was my first-ever mobile phone! I got a Nokia 6310 on contract with BT Cellnet. It's such a wicked phone. It actually looks beautiful. Ufft. It's black with a gold front at the top. And being a buttons pervert, I'm so glad that the buttons are really smooth and nice to feel.

And the best thing is, no one I know has one of these! The man in the shop said it's really a phone for businesspeople. I immediately said, 'I'll have one, thank you.' Now to clock Snake II.

I looked through the Argos book with Ammi last weekend and chose some things I wanted to buy from there. I got:

- Dictation machine* (for lectures)
- Lamp and bulb

---

* I never used this once.

- Alarm clock
- Iron
- Toaster
- Kettle
- Rucksack

And from T. J. Hughes I got:

- Duvet, bedcovers, pillows, pillowcases, towel, hand towel
- Spoons, forks, knives, plates, bowl, glasses, mugs, tin-opener, frying pan, round pan and a glass bowl
- Bin

I also bought a new lota* and topi and toothbrush and tooth-paste and a Lynx set.

From one of my favourite shops, Stationery Box, I got:

- 3 big lever-arch files
- 3 divider packs
- Pack of labels
- Stapler and staples
- Blu-Tack
- Scissors
- Sellotape
- Pack of Bic biro pens

I bought a few new clothes as well, from Duffer and River Island. Oh, and three passport-size photos, for my uni card, my LUSU* card and my gym membership. This is definitely the most money I've ever spent on myself.

Then I treated Ammi to a McDonald's. It felt really nice.

---

* Lancaster University Student Union.

'I'm really proud of you, Tahir.' Wow.

'Thank you, Ammi.'

She put her Filet-O-Fish down. 'I know it hasn't been easy for you. You and Rosey have been through a lot together; a lot of other people won't understand. Especially these last two years. I'm very proud of you and I love you.'

'I love you too, Ammi.' I didn't cry as I finished my fillet.

'Behave at university. Remember your halal and haram – you're Muslim, don't forget that. And do good, okay? Make us proud.'

'Jee, Ammi.' I love her so much.

Monday 24th September

It was the football presentation for the Witton Park seven-a-side league this evening. New Bank Bulls finally got their hands on the trophy!

The presentation was at the Blues Bar at Ewood Park and, to be honest, most of it was boring. There were a lot of leagues to get through, but when it was our turn, I realised . . . I kinda messed up. Hahahaha.

Because when they called out the winner of the Under-15s League – New Bank Bulls! – I got so carried away I went up to lift the trophy with Zak, instead of our captain, Nasir.

Hahahahaha!

I didn't even realise until ages after, when we got back to the Maliks' house and Nasir goes, 'Wasn't I supposed to go up and collect the trophy?'

Me and Zak looked at each other and burst out laughing.

'OH YEAH!'

I guess, having never had a sporting achievement to speak of in my life, I got carried away and overcompensated. I'm still laughing about it now.

Nasir will be all right. I'm sure he'll win loads more trophies.

But imagine if Arsenal win the FA Cup, and Arsène Wenger pushes Tony Adams out the way and collects the trophy his self! Hahahaha.

Friday 5th October

I did the last of my uni shopping yesterday. I had to buy textbooks and stuff for my course. I went to Manchester, and even though in my imagination I was going to Diagon Alley, I ended up in a shop called Waterstone's.

Then I went to a specialist science shop to buy a lab coat that fastens at the side. Why it needs to fasten at the side will be the first question I ask when uni starts.

I don't know why, but I almost wanted to say to the shopkeepers, 'Don't worry, I'm not a terrorist, I'm not gonna make anthrax.' But I thought, well, they haven't brought it up, so it would be a weird thing to say.

It all cost a ~~bomb~~ ton, though! The books alone cost around £150! I never realised education was gonna be this expensive. Still, I'm ready for the next chapter in my life now.

Lancaster, here I come!

Saturday 6th October

BECKHAMMMMMM!!!

Oh my days! From the villain to the hero!

Ninety-third-minute free kick into the top corner to send England to the World Cup! Yes!!!

We were playing Greece at Old Trafford in our last qualifying game. We only needed a draw to go through, but crazily we were losing 2–1, until the ninety-third minute, when Beckham, who I've never ever seen play this well, smashed a trademark free kick into the top corner.

Kasam, I went proper pagal* in the living room. I was jumping on poor Pai Uneeb! Haha. I'm trying to get him into football, but he keeps saying he supports Liverpool, so on second thoughts, if he's not gonna support Rovers, maybe he shouldn't get into football?

I love this game. I hope my new friends at uni like football. It'll be something easy to talk about straight away.

I quit JJB today. Well, I handed in my notice. I have to work the next four weekends. But that's fine. I plan to come home most weekends this year anyway. I liked the people I worked with, but I'm not going to miss it at all. I doubt I'll stay in touch with anyone from there. Maybe Fidge.

One thing I've noticed about myself is that when I leave a place, I'm really bad at keeping in touch with my friends. There's a saying, out of sight, out of mind. It's not that I don't care. Also, I guess it takes two people to stay in touch, so it's not just my fault, is it?

But I look back . . .

Hickory Street and Cedar Street Infant School:
   Shazad, Atiq, Zafar, Abid, Tassadaq and Fozia.

Edmundson Street and St Barnabas:
   Sikandar, Ziarab, Anjem, Mustafa, Mujtaba, Lateef, Hadi, Addy, Jenaid, Ross, Kyle, Sheraz, Shabaz,* Mubarak, Saleem and Gyasudin (he had the best name ever).

Mosque:
   Yasser, Peggy, Farooq, Naeem, Mujtaba, Mustafa, Yahya, Sehr, Ziggy, Aqib, Omar and Faz.

*

---

* I have never ever met a Shabaz in my travels around the world, but in Blackburn I knew four different ones growing up, including the two in my family!

Witton Park:

Hassim (this breaks my heart), Haider, Zaheer, Kelloggs, Golly, Mustaqeem, Geery, Asma, Faiza, Deela, Halima, Amina, Fiona, Vicki, Karolia, Imran, Junaid, Yasin, Kalpesh, Buxy, Chucky, Jack, Steven and Christian.

I hardly even see Was these days and he's my cousin, AND I walked with him to school every day for four years.

So many friendships. Lost or forgotten. Obviously, if I see any of those lot, it'd be fine and we'd say hi/bye and have a little catch-up, but you know, we don't stay in touch properly. It does make me sad.

Right, I've got a mobile phone now, I have people's numbers, I have to keep in touch with my cousins (Shibz, Was, Shiry), Hussain, Ebrahim, Neelam and the New Bank crew: Chyna, Pats and the Maliks.

Oh, and make some new lifelong best friends at university. Please. Khuda de vaste*.

Sunday 7th October

'Have you packed everything?'

'Yeah, Baj.' We sat down on opposite settees. It's my last night before I go to uni. We were waiting for Pai Uneeb with the pizzas, and then we're gonna watch *Lagaan*.

'How are you doing?' I haven't asked her too many questions, because, well, obviously she's bound to be sad and stuff.

'I'm okay. These things are in Allah's hand, you know.'

'Yeah, but are you okay? Like health-wise and stuff?'

'Yeah. Thanks. The doctors said to rest, which I have, but yeah, thank you, I'm almost back to my old self.' She smiled at me.

'Good. I'm glad.'

'InshAllah you'll have a niece or nephew one day."* She laughed.
'InshAllah! I can't wait.' And then I said: 'Thank you.'

'For what?'

'For letting me stay this last year.'

'Don't be a daft sod. You're my brother. You'll always have a place here whenever you need it.'

We got interrupted by Pai Uneeb. We ate some delicious Goodfellas pizza and watched Amir Khan twat some goreh at cricket.

I was thinking ... Sometimes you don't always end up where you want to be, but that's okay, because actually you are exactly where you're supposed to be. The place you wanted to be: that's not meant for you.

Think about the journey you were on that brought you to the place you're actually in. Reflect on it, learn from it and remember it.

And where you are now, enjoy it, embrace it, make the most of it.

That's what I intend to do. InshAllah.

Because the next journey starts tomorrow.

Monday 8th October

Today I am exactly 18½ years old.

Today I left Blackburn to study at Lancaster University for three years.

Today I said goodbye to my old life, my room, my family, my favourite spoon (even though I'll be back next weekend, actually, so stop being a drama queen).

*

---

* Eight of them. Five are Baji Rosey's.

Before I left the house to start this exciting new chapter in my life, the news was on and it said that America has invaded Afghanistan.

Today, the 'war on terror' has started.

Today I finally understood what an oxymoron is.

Glossary of Arabic, Punjabi and Urdu Words

aakar	attitude
Alhamdulillah	praise be to God
Allah da shukr eh	thank God
Allah di kasam	I swear to God
ammi	mum
anth	chaos
apna	Desi man/boy
apne	Desi people
apnia	Desi women/girls
Asr	the later afternoon prayer
Ayatul Kursi	a special verse in the Qur'an, 2:255
baisti (baist)	disrespected/owned
baitak	a room in Pakistan houses that also has a door that leads straight outside
baji/baj	older sister
bechara	poor man/boy
bechari	poor woman/girl
Bismillah	I begin in the name of God
boojo	monkey
buddah	old man

buddeh	old people
buddie	old woman
chaat	a chickpea starter
chacha (chach)	dad's younger brother
chalo	oh well
chapra	somewhere between a large pond and a swamp
chawal	rice
cholay chawal	chickpea pilau
chooza	chicken
Dajjal	the Antichrist
dars	Islamic seminary
dholki	drum
djinn	invisible supernatural entities, made from 'smokeless fire'
doodh sawiya	vermicelli milk dessert
dua	supplication prayer
Eidi	money given to kids at Eid
elaichi	cardamom
Fajr	the early morning prayer
falooda	milk-based dessert
farz	something compulsory in Islam
gajrela	carrot-based Indian dessert
gora	white man/boy
goreh	white people
gori	white woman/girl
gosht	meat (usually beef or lamb)
gujjar	an ethnic caste of the Indian subcontinent
gunnah	sin
haar	garland
Hafiz	the title awarded to someone who memorised the entire Qur'an. An honour in Islam

halal	permissible in Islam
haram	forbidden in Islam
Hazrat Isa	the Prophet Jesus
hookah	instrument for heating, vaporising and smoking tobacco
i'tikaaf	a spiritual retreat
iftari	the meal served at the end of the day during Ramadan, to break the day's fast
inshAllah	God willing
Isha	the night-time prayer
istikhara	a special prayer to seek blessings and guidance from Allah when making a decision
izzat	honour
jaali	net curtain
jaan	loved one, darling
jamaat khana	prayer room in the mosque
jamaat	congregational prayer or religious retreat
jananza	funeral
janglees	animals, barbaric
Jannat	heaven/paradise
jugnoo	firefly
Jumma	the name for Friday and of the special Friday prayer
kacheh	underwear
kalimeh	declarations of faith
kameeneh	bastards
kasam/kasameh	I swear
khatam	a prayer gathering, often finished with a communal meal
khooh	water well
Khuda de vaste	for God's sake
Khuda Hafiz	God protect you

khusseh	fancy slippers
kofta	meatball
kuteh	dogs
lota	a receptacle Muslims fill with water to wash our bums with. Really
machar	mosquitos
madrassa	after-school mosque class
Maghrib	the evening prayer
mameh	Punjabi slang for cops
mammu	maternal uncle
manji	a traditional woven bed used in South Asia
mashAllah	God has willed. Used to express joy, praise or thankfulness
masjid	mosque
mela	Desi festival
mitai	Desi sweets
miteh	sweet
molbi	madrassa teacher
mukkay	punches
muppi	kiss
mura	a pouffe
nafs	the self. In particular the part of our self that has desires and appetite. Some people call it the ego
namaaz (or salah)	the daily prayers
nikkah	the marriage ceremony in a wedding
paandeh	crockery and tableware
pagal	stupid, crazy
pai/paijan	older brother
painchod	sister-fucker
paratah	shallow-fried roti, often stuffed with something

pateh	tall grass roughage, which is ground into food for cattle
Pathans	an Iranian ethnic group in Afghanistan and Pakistan
pind	rural area, village
puttar	son
Qari	someone who understands the Qur'an in the original Arabic
rakat	a unit of namaaz (salah). There are always either two, three or four. Never more, never less
Ramazan	Ramadan. Sometimes Rozay is used too. The ninth month of the Islamic calendar, in which Muslims fast for thirty days
ras malai	a milk based Indian dessert
rishta	marriage proposal
rishwat	bribe
roza	A fast. No eating or drinking anything during daylight hours
ruku	the bowing position with hands on knees, within namaaz (salah)
saab	an informal title of respect, like calling someone 'sir'
saag	spinach
saalan	curry
sabak	homework
salaam	peace (shorthand greeting)
salooneh chawal	pilau rice
samaan	literally means luggage, but also means a bride's dowry, which where we're from usually means furniture
sark	main road
shaabash	well done

shaadi	wedding
shalwar kameez	item of clothing commonly worn in Pakistan, bottoms (shalwar) and top (kameez)
sher	city
spaara	one of the thirty sections of the Qur'an. Plural spaareh
subhanAllah	Glory be to God
sunnah	the way of the Prophet (Muhammad, Peace Be Upon Him)
surah	a chapter of the Qur'an
tamashe	shenanigans
tarawee	additional night prayers during Ramadan
taubah	repent
tawaf	as part of the pilgrimage to Makkah, pilgrims go around the Kabaah (the most sacred site in Islam) seven times in a counterclockwise direction
thail	oil
tombi	bull race in Pakistan
topi	hat worn for prayer
ungle	getting involved unnecessarily
walaikumSalaam	may peace be upon you
walima	the party after an Islamic wedding
wudhu	ritual cleanse before prayer
yaraa	mate
Zuhr	the early afternoon prayer

Acknowledgements

I'd like to thank my brilliant and patient editor, Emily Barrett. Without her guidance and wisdom this wouldn't have been the finished product it became. She also broke her arm during one of the edits! Not because of me, mind. So she drafted in Jo Lane, who helped out with the final edit. Thanks Jo, your comments in the margins were so heart-warming. Big up Zoe for the copy-edit and big up Little, Brown for publishing me, innit.

I want to give a special and eternal thank you to my managers Polly and Geli at UTC Artist Management. Your belief and confidence in me means the world. Thank you for everything. Always.

Thank you to my wonderful and supportive family, who have been so excited throughout this entire process. Love every single one of you to death, man.

To all my friends at school, college, mosque and in ends: tussi great oh. Thank you for the good times and bad.

Thank you to everyone from all communities in Blackburn. I wouldn't swap us for the world. Well, another run in the Premier League maybe.

Finally, thank you Allah for all the blessings you've given me in my life. I am not worthy.

*

Thank you for reading. If you've enjoyed this, please recommend it to everyone you know. If you haven't, chalk it up to experience; no one else need know.

If you want to see what else I've done, or what I'll do next, visit: tezilyas.com/hello and/or follow me on my socials @tezilyas everywhere.

As-salamu alaykum x

Credits

Tez Ilyas is one of the most exciting rising stars on the comedy circuit, cemented by his nomination for Club Comedian of the Year in the 2020 Chortle Awards. He was featured on the BBC New Talent Hot List in 2017 and was a Chortle Best Breakthrough Nominee in the same year. His 2015 debut stand-up hour TEZ Talks had a sell-out run at the Soho Theatre and three hit BBC Radio 4 series based on the show followed. His 2016 show Made in Britain sold out every performance at the Edinburgh Fringe, and his third show, Teztify, achieved a sell-out nationwide tour and was released as a self-produced stand-up special in the summer of 2020, racking up over 100,000 views to date.

As well as delivering his politically astute stand-up, he is one of the stars of hit sitcom *Man Like Mobeen* (BBC Three) and has appeared on a host of panel shows, including *Mock the Week* and *The Last Leg*, as well as fronting his own critically acclaimed cult-hit satirical series *The Tez O'Clock Show* (Channel 4). His own sitcom pilot *(Blap) Bounty* for Channel 4 is approaching a million views (the most-watched in the strand's ten-year history), his TEDx Talk has over 170,000 views and his Live at the Apollo performance has been watched more than ten million times online.